Intellectual Property Rights
as Obstacles to Legitimate Trade?

IEEM AND INTERNATIONAL INTELLECTUAL PROPERTY LAW

The involvement of the Institute of European Studies of Macau (IEEM) in matters of intellectual property is based on annual conferences that take up topical issues of intellectual property from a comparative perspective with a particular focus on Asia and Europe. The first of these conferences was held back in 2000, and has meanwhile become an annual event complemented by an IP Law School and IP Master Classes. All three venues serve as a platform for academic teaching and discussion on intellectual property awareness and the proper place and function of intellectual property law in the context of society and public interest.

From the very start, the intellectual property conferences, the IP Law School and the Master Classes have enjoyed the support, assistance and commitment of Mr. Gonçalo Cabral, who is an advisor to the Government of Macau, of Ms. Maria do Céu Esteves, past president of the IEEM, and of the IEEM's current president Dr. José Luís de Sales Marques. Dr. de Sales Marques was also instrumental in setting up an IEEM chair for intellectual property law at Maastricht University in 2004, thereby further contributing to IEEM's academic commitment to the field of intellectual property law. During the five years of its existence, this chair has been held by Anselm Kamperman Sanders.

The conference papers, as revised and updated, are edited by Christopher Heath and Anselm Kamperman Sanders as an IEEM Intellectual Property Series, the volumes of which are listed at the end of this book. For this volume, Anke Moerland is also a co-editor.

Intellectual Property Rights as Obstacles to Legitimate Trade?

Edited by

Christopher Heath, Anselm Kamperman Sanders
and Anke Moerland

Published by:
Kluwer Law International B.V.
PO Box 316
2400 AH Alphen aan den Rijn
The Netherlands
E-mail: international-sales@wolterskluwer.com
Website: lrus.wolterskluwer.com

Sold and distributed in North, Central and South America by:
Wolters Kluwer Legal & Regulatory U.S.
7201 McKinney Circle
Frederick, MD 21704
United States of America
Email: customer.service@wolterskluwer.com

Sold and distributed in all other countries by:
Air Business Subscriptions
Rockwood House
Haywards Heath
West Sussex
RH16 3DH
United Kingdom
Email: international-customerservice@wolterskluwer.com

Printed on acid-free paper.

ISBN 978-94-035-0330-1

e-Book: 978-94-035-0205-2
web-PDF: 978-94-035-0234-2

© 2018 Kluwer Law International BV, The Netherlands

All rights reserved. No part of this publication may be reproduced, stored in a retrieval system, or transmitted in any form or by any means, electronic, mechanical, photocopying, recording, or otherwise, without written permission from the publisher.

Permission to use this content must be obtained from the copyright owner. More information can be found at: lrus.wolterskluwer.com/policies/permissions-reprints-and-licensing

Printed in the United Kingdom.

Summary of Contents

Part 1 – Historical Introduction

Chapter 1
Avoiding Barriers to Legitimate Trade: Objectives and Obligations 3
Matthew Kennedy, University of International Business and Economics, Beijing

This introductory chapter explains the links between GATT 1947, the WTO/TRIPS Agreement 1994 and how the notion of avoiding barriers to legitimate trade was developed in the context of determining the lawfulness of enforcement measures under GATT 1947. The chapter concludes with an analysis of how this concept should be interpreted within the framework of GATT 1994, and whether it also has significance beyond the field of enforcement.

Part 2 – Intellectual Property Rights as Obstacles to International Trade?

Chapter 2
Parallel Imports of Patented Goods 33
Christopher Heath, Boards of Appeal, EPO, Munich

This chapter looks at patent exhaustion regimes in the context of international trade. Although one might have expected that one of the major concerns of the WTO Agreement would have been to define the concept of legitimate trade for goods lawfully marketed in one country and subsequently exported to others, no definition of this core question for international trade could be agreed upon. 'Legitimate trade' thus remains a controversial concept in this area.

Summary of Contents

Chapter 3
Geoblocking and 'Legitimate Trade'   53
Marketa Trimble, University of Nevada, Las Vegas, Law School

This chapter addresses the territorial separation of digital markets with regard to copyrighted works and to what extent right owners can invoke legitimate reasons for such separation.

Chapter 4
The Registration of Descriptive Terms in International Trade   77
Anke Moerland, Maastricht University

This topic arises in the context of trade marks and geographical indications. For trade marks, it concerns the registration of foreign descriptive terms with the purpose or result of preventing competition by importation and thereby legitimate trade. For geographical indications, it concerns the protection of terms that are considered generic in certain domestic markets.

Chapter 5
The Seizure of Goods in Transit – Can EU Trade Mark Legislation Serve as a Model?   107
Martin Senftleben, Free University of Amsterdam

The issue of IP enforcement over goods in transit has been particularly controversial and also gave rise to complaints before the WTO due to conflicts with the principle of free transit enshrined in the GATT Agreement.

Part 3 – Obstacles to Domestic Trade

Chapter 6
The Green, Green Grass of Evergreening Patents   131
Roberto Reis and Claudia Chamas, Fundação Oswaldo Cruz, Rio de Janeiro

This topic concerns tensions between the limited duration of patents and attempts to extend such duration by filing, marketing or enforcement strategies, thereby creating legal uncertainty and a possibly unlawful deterrent for possible competitors. Due to the complex interplay between law and technology, it is particularly difficult to determine what should be legitimate interests of the patentee to preserve its monopolistic rights, and what should be considered abusive.

Chapter 7
Exhaustion and Second-Hand Digital Goods/Contents   159
Matthias Leistner and Lucie Antoine, University of Munich

Rules on the domestic exhaustion of copyrighted goods serve the freedom of commerce and do not allow the copyright owner to control the second-hand market in such goods. This established balance may considerably shift in favour of copyright owners should the exhaustion principle not apply to digital products. This chapter critically asks how and whether a regime of limited exhaustion for digital goods should be considered an obstacle to legitimate trade,

Chapter 8
Unjustified Threats and the Repression of Unfair Competition 181
Anselm Kamperman Sanders, University of Maastricht

Enforcement of intellectual property rights by way of warning letters sent to alleged infringers and their customers may be a cheap but problematic way of asserting rights. After all, such allegations may be unfounded where the IP right that is invoked turns out to be invalid, or not infringed. This chapter looks at threats, in which context they become barriers to legitimate trade, and how legislation should set appropriate standards of liability.

Preface

The English Statute of Monopolies of 1623 decreed that all monopolies 'shalbe utterlie void and of none effecte, and in noe wise to be putt in ure or execucion'. The Statute was regarded as a milestone of free trade.

The only exception to this general prohibition were patents, yet even these should only be granted on condition that 'soe as alsoe they be not contrary to the Lawe nor mischievous to the State, by raisinge prices of Commodities at home, or hurt of Trade, or generallie inconvenient'. In the following centuries, not only patents but also other industrial property rights, and more recently also copyright, were regarded as useful instruments of industrial and cultural policy, yet with the potential to 'hurt trade'. In international agreements such as GATT 1947 or regional agreements such as the Treaty of Rome 1957, they were thus regarded as exceptions. The European Court of Justice interpreted them narrowly by reducing them to their specific subject-matter, while the GATT panels were more concerned with potential abuses at the level of enforcement.

The WTO/TRIPS Agreement, and subsequent bilateral trade agreements, took a very different approach: free trade required a level playing field of trade-related domestic laws, including those of intellectual property. Minimum standards of protection thereby became a pre-condition for free trade rather than an obstacle thereto.

This of course prompts the question as to whether substantive levels of IP protection, or certain patterns of enforcement, can in themselves become obstacles to legitimate trade. Are there certain notions inherent in legitimate trade, in the GATT 1947 or in other international agreements that would put limits to broadly legislating or interpreting intellectual property rights and their enforcement?

It is this question that the following chapters look at in the context of different intellectual property rights, both for international and domestic trade.

Table of Contents

Summary of Contents   v
Preface   ix
Authors and Editors   xvii

PART 1 – HISTORICAL INTRODUCTION

Chapter 1
Avoiding Barriers to Legitimate Trade: Objectives and Obligations   3
Matthew Kennedy
- A. Introduction   3
- B. TRIPS Preamble   4
  - I. Punta del Este Declaration   5
  - II. Section 337 and Certain Aramid Fiber   6
  - III. Some Implications of US – Section 337 Tariff Act   9
- C. TRIPS Enforcement Obligations   11
  - I. General Obligations   11
  - II. Specific Enforcement Procedures   13
  - III. Performance Standards   16
- D. GATT 1994 and Other WTO Agreements   20
  - I. Non-discrimination   21
  - II. Freedom of Transit   22
  - III. Transparency and Procedural Fairness   23
  - IV. Quantitative Prohibitions and Restrictions   24
  - V. General Exceptions   25
  - VI. Unnecessary Obstacles to International Trade   27
  - VII. Trade in Services   29
- E. Conclusion   30

PART 2 – INTELLECTUAL PROPERTY RIGHTS AS OBSTACLES TO INTERNATIONAL TRADE?

Chapter 2
Parallel Imports of Patented Goods 33
Christopher Heath

A. Introduction 33
  I. The Legal Context 33
  II. The Factual Context 34
B. The GATT 1994 context 36
  I. Free Trade and the Protection of 'Patents, Trade Marks and Copyrights' 36
  II. The Case Law of the ECJ on Free Trade and the Protection of Patent Rights 37
  III. Free Trade and Patent Rights in the GATT Context 39
C. The Paris Convention Context 42
  I. Territoriality as a Fundamental Principle of the Paris Convention 42
  II. Territoriality and Trade 43
D. The WTO/TRIPS Context 45
E. Analysis 47
  I. Free Trade and Arbitrary Obstacles Thereto 47
  II. Obstacles to a WTO Dispute Settlement 50
  III. Result 51

Chapter 3
Geoblocking and 'Legitimate Trade' 53
Marketa Trimble

A. Introduction 53
B. Territorialisation of the Internet and the Tools of Territorialisation 54
  I. The Territorialisation Trend 54
  II. Geolocation 56
  III. Geoblocking 57
  IV. Evasion of Geolocation and Circumvention of Geoblocking 59
C. The Legality of Geoblocking 61
  I. Mandatory vs. Voluntary Territorial Restrictions 61
  II. The Legality of Geoblocking when it Implements Mandatory Territorial Restrictions 63
  III. The Legality of Geoblocking when it Implements Voluntary Territorial Restrictions 67
  IV. The Anti-Geoblocking Regulation in the European Union 71
D. Geoblocking and The Future of Trade 73
E. Conclusion 76

Chapter 4
The Registration of Descriptive Terms in International Trade 77
Anke Moerland

A. Introduction 77

Table of Contents

	I.	Rapadura	78
	II.	Feta	79
	III.	A Barrier to Legitimate Trade	80
B.		The Protection of Foreign Descriptive Terms as Trade Marks	82
	I.	Absolute Ground of Refusal Regarding Signs Designating Characteristics of the Goods or Services	83
		1. The Relevant Public Following ECJ *Matratzen Concord* [2006]	85
		2. Barrier to Legitimate Trade? Consequences for Traders	86
		3. The Way Forward: Assessing Multiple Languages	88
	II.	Absolute Ground of Refusal Regarding Registrations Made in Bad Faith	91
		1. Undue Monopolisation of a Product and Consequences for Traders	92
		2. Barrier to Legitimate Trade?	93
C.		Protection of Geographical Indications that are Considered Generic	94
	I.	Definition of Generic Terms	95
	II.	Recognition and Automatic Protection of Geographical Indications in Annexes	97
	III.	Limitations to Claiming back Prior Uses	99
	IV.	Scope of Protection of Generic Terms	100
	V.	Use of Generic Terms Defence	101
	VI.	A Barrier to Legitimate Trade? Consequences for Traders	102
D.		Conclusions	104

Chapter 5
The Seizure of Goods in Transit – Can EU Trade Mark Legislation Serve as a Model?   107
Martin Senftleben

A.	Introduction	107
B.	New Right Against Goods in Transit in the EU	109
C.	Safeguards Against Excessive Measures	112
	I. Burden of Proof	114
	II. Reference to International Freedom of Trade	116
D.	Compliance with International Guarantee of Free Transit	117
	I. Broader GATT Context	119
	II. No Circular Line of Reasoning	120
	III. Cautious Approach Required	121
	IV. Medicinal Products	121
E.	Guidelines for Other Regions	123
F.	Conclusion	126

PART 3 – OBSTACLES TO DOMESTIC TRADE

Chapter 6
The Green, Green Grass of Evergreening Patents   131
Roberto Reis and Claudia Chamas

A.	Introduction	131
B.	The Pharmaceutical Industry and Patenting Strategies	132

Table of Contents

C.	Evergreening Practices based on Chemical Modifications	136
	I. Selection Patents/'Me-too' Patents	136
	II. New Formulations/New Concentration Patents	138
	III. Polymorph Patents	138
	IV. Enantiomers	140
	V. Combination Patents	142
	VI. Hydrates and Solvates	142
	VII. Second Medical Use Patents	143
D.	Evergreening based on Legal Strategies	144
	I. Research Exemption Blockage	144
	II. Data Exclusivity	145
	III. Patent Linkage	149
	1. Patent Linkage in United States and the Paragraph IV Provision	150
	2. Patent Linkage in the European Union	150
	3. Patent Linkage in Other Relevant Countries	151
	IV. Other Strategies	152
	1. Pay-for-Delay	152
	2. Establishment of Generic Units by Innovative Companies	152
	3. 'Give away' Patents	153
E.	Developing Countries' Initiatives to Mitigate Evergreening	153
F.	Final Remarks	156

Chapter 7
Exhaustion and Second-Hand Digital Goods/Contents   159
Matthias Leistner and Lucie Antoine

A.	The Starting Point in European Law: *UsedSoft* and its Application in the Member States	159
	I. The Facts	160
	II. The Ruling	160
	1. Introduction	160
	2. Conditions of Online Exhaustion	161
	a. Appropriate Remuneration	161
	b. Unlimited Use Right	162
	c. Making Copy Unusable	162
	III. Remaining Problems and Practical Difficulties of Implementation in the Member States	163
	1. Sale	163
	2. Scope of the Second Acquirer's Rights of Use	163
	3. Making the Copy Unusable	164
	4. Unlimited Period of Time	166
	5. Maintenance Agreement	166
	6. Excluded Objects of Exhaustion	166
	a. Consequences in Practice	167
B.	Extension of the *UsedSoft* Doctrine to Other Second-Hand Digital Goods	168
	I. Legal Framework and Status Quo	168
	1. UsedSoft Judgment	168
	2. Further European Case Law	169

		a. Attempts at Generalising *Usedsoft* Beyond Software	169
		b. Nintendo: Inconsistencies in the Legal Framework for Complex Software Products	170
		3. European Primary and Secondary Law	171
		4. Member States	174
	II.	Main Problems with Regard to Other Digital Goods	174
		1. Construction of the Second Acquirer's Rights of Use	175
		2. Economic Considerations	176
	III.	Conclusion	177
C.	Future Perspective: Alternative Mechanisms in European Law to Guarantee the Free Movement of Copyright-related Goods & Services		178

Chapter 8
Unjustified Threats and the Repression of Unfair Competition 181
Anselm Kamperman Sanders

A.	Introduction		181
	I.	Information and Disparagement	181
	II.	Threats and Warning Letters (Definitions)	181
	III.	Threats and Obstacles to Legitimate Trade	183
B.	The Paris Convention		183
C.	Threatening Practices in Historical Perspective		185
	I.	A UK Case of 1881	185
	II.	Threats in Practice	186
D.	Comparison		188
	I.	The United States	188
	II.	Germany	189
	III.	France	190
	IV.	The Netherlands	191
	V.	Canada	192
	VI.	Australia	195
	VII.	The United Kingdom	196
E.	Analysis		200
F.	Conclusion		203

Authors and Editors

Lucie Antoine (1992) is Doctoral Student and Research Assistant at the Chair of Private Law and Intellectual Property Law, with Information and IT Law (German Association for the Protection of Intellectual Property (GRUR) Chair) at LMU Munich. She studied Law at LMU Munich and has completed her law studies with her First State Examination in 2017.

Claudia Chamas (1967) has dedicated her career to studying the impact of intellectual property rights on access to medicines. She is a researcher at the Centre for Technological Development in Health (CDTS) of the Oswaldo Cruz Foundation (Fiocruz). She played an active role in the creation of the Master and Doctoral Programme in Public Policies, Strategy and Development at the Institute of Economics, Federal University of Rio de Janeiro where she teaches and supervises dissertations. Claudia was the representative of the Ministry of Health at the Brazilian Interministerial Group on Intellectual Property and vice-chair of the WHO Expert Consultative Working Group on Research and Development (CEWG). Claudia co-chaired the WHO public health, innovation and intellectual property review panel.

She is the author of articles and book chapters in the fields of international intellectual property policies, health innovation and technology transfer. Claudia holds a Bachelor's degree in Chemical Engineering and a Doctoral degree in Industrial Engineering from the Federal University of Rio de Janeiro.

She can be reached by e-mail at chamas@cdts.fiocruz.br

Christopher Heath (1964) studied law at the Universities of Konstanz, Edinburgh and the LSE. He lived and worked in Japan for three years, and between 1992 and 2005 headed the Asian Department of the Max Planck Institute for Patent, Copyright and Competition Law in Munich. Christopher, who wrote his PhD thesis on Japanese unfair competition prevention law, is a Member of the Boards of Appeal at the European Patent Office in Munich and co-editor of IIC.

He can be reached by e-mail at blitzblitzblau@web.de

Authors and Editors

Anselm Kamperman Sanders (1968) is Professor of Intellectual Property Law, Director of the Advanced Masters Intellectual Property Law and Knowledge Management (IPKM LL.M/MSc), and Academic Director of the Institute for Globalization and International Regulation (IGIR) at Maastricht University, the Netherlands.

He acts as Academic Co-director of the Annual Intellectual Property Law School and IP Seminar of the Institute for European Studies of Macau (IEEM), Macau SAR, China and is Adjunct Professor at Jinan University Law School, Guangzhou, China.

Anselm holds a PhD from the Centre for Commercial Law Studies, Queen Mary University of London, where he worked as a Marie Curie Fellow before joining Maastricht University in 1995. He is a member of the European Commission expert group on development and implications of patent law in the field of biotechnology and genetic engineering.

He can be reached by e-mail at a.kampermansanders@maastrichtuniversity.nl

Matthew Kennedy (1965) is a Professor in the Faculty of Law, University of International Business and Economics, Beijing, China. He was formerly a senior lawyer in the World Trade Organization Secretariat and Secretary of the WTO Council for TRIPS. Matthew holds a PhD in Law from the University of Bern, Switzerland.

Matthias Leistner (1974) is Professor of Private Law and Intellectual Property Law, with Information and IT Law at LMU Munich. He holds a Doctoral Degree of LMU Munich, and a Master's Degree of the University of Cambridge.

Matthias Leistner was Head of the Commonwealth Unit at the Max Planck Institute, Munich, until 2007. From 2007-2016 he was Professor of Civil Law, Intellectual Property Law and Competition Law and Director of the Institute for Commercial and Economic Law at the University of Bonn. Apart from his Chair at LMU Munich, at present he is a Faculty Member of the Munich Intellectual Property Law Center (MIPLC), and a Guest Professor at the University of Xiamen, China, and at the Tongji University, Shanghai.

His specialties are Intellectual Property Law (in particular Copyright and Patents), Unfair Competition Law and Internet Law. He has published seven books and numerous articles in these fields. He was co-editor of the bi-lingual *Zeitschrift für Geistiges Eigentum/Intellectual Property Journal,* and is co-editor of a commentary on German unfair competition law (*Grosskommentar UWG,* Berlin, 2013), and the standard commentary on German copyright law (*Schricker/Loewenheim/Leistner/Ohly, Urheberrecht,* 5th edition, 2017).

Anke Moerland (1983) is Assistant Professor of Intellectual Property Law in the European and International Law Department, Maastricht University. Her research relates to the interface of intellectual property law and political science, with a focus on governance aspects of intellectual property regulation, in particular the protection of geographical indications, and the negotiation settings of IP chapters in free trade agreements. Anke holds degrees in Law (Maastricht University) and International Relations (Technical University Dresden), with a PhD in Intellectual Property Protection in EU Bilateral Trade Agreements from Maastricht University. Since 2017, she has coordinated the EIPIN Innovation Society, a 4-year Horizon 2020 grant under the Marie Skłodowska Curie Action ITN-EJD.

She can be reached by email at anke.moerland@maastrichtuniversity.nl.

Authors and Editors

Roberto Reis (1974) is an Intellectual Property and Technology Transfer expert at the Centre for Technological Development in Health, Oswaldo Cruz Foundation (Fiocruz), Brazilian Ministry of Health, and a researcher at the Brazilian National Institute of Science and Technology of Innovation on Diseases of Neglected Populations (INCT-IDPN). He is a member of the Expert Advisory Group (Tuberculosis Sub-Group) at the Medicines Patent Pool (MPP).

Roberto holds degrees in Law and Pharmacy–Biochemistry, with a PhD in Intellectual Property related to Public Policies and Development.

He can be reached by e-mail at roberto.reis@cdts.fiocruz.br

Martin Senftleben (1975) is Professor of Intellectual Property at the Centre for Law and Internet, Vrije Universiteit Amsterdam, Guest Professor at the Intellectual Property Research Institute, University of Xiamen, and Of Counsel at Bird & Bird, The Hague. His activities focus on the reconciliation of private intellectual property rights with competing public interests of a social, cultural or economic nature. Martin studied Law at the University of Heidelberg. He worked as a researcher at the Institute for Information Law of the University of Amsterdam and the Max Planck Institute for Innovation and Competition in Munich. In 2004, he was awarded a PhD by the University of Amsterdam. From 2004 to 2007, he was a legal officer in the trademarks, industrial designs and geographical indications law division of the World Intellectual Property Organization (WIPO) in Geneva. His main publications include *Copyright, Limitations and the Three-Step Test* (Kluwer Law International, 2004) and *European Trade Mark Law – A Commentary* (with Annette Kur, Oxford University Press, 2017).

He can be reached by e-mail at m.r.f.senftleben@vu.nl

Marketa Trimble (1973) is the Samuel S. Lionel Professor of Intellectual Property Law at the William S. Boyd School of Law at the University of Nevada, Las Vegas. She specialises in International Intellectual Property Law and publishes extensively on issues at the intersection of Conflict of Laws/Private International Law and Intellectual Property Law, particularly Patent Law and Copyright Law. She has authored numerous works on these subjects, including *Global Patents: Limits of Transnational Enforcement* (Oxford University Press, 2012), and is the co-author of a leading international intellectual property law casebook, *International Intellectual Property Law* (with Paul Goldstein, Foundation Press, 2012 and 2016). She has also authored several works in the area of Cyberlaw, particularly relating to the legal issues of geoblocking and its circumvention.

She can be reached by email at marketa.trimble@unlv.edu

PART 1

HISTORICAL INTRODUCTION

CHAPTER 1
Avoiding Barriers to Legitimate Trade: Objectives and Obligations

Matthew Kennedy

A. INTRODUCTION

The avoidance of barriers to legitimate trade appears among the objectives and obligations of the world's most comprehensive multilateral treaty on intellectual property, the Agreement on Trade-Related Aspects of Intellectual Property Rights ('TRIPS'),[1] administered by the World Trade Organization ('WTO'). This is unusual in an intellectual property treaty. Older intellectual property conventions in WIPO largely defer to national legislation on matters of enforcement against infringement[2] and do not address the impact of enforcement procedures on legitimate trade. Even more recent intellectual property treaties that provide for effective enforcement and expeditious remedies omit any provision for the avoidance of barriers to legitimate trade.[3] Meanwhile, the multilateral trading system has pursued the substantial reduction of barriers to trade as an express goal since the signature of the General

---

1. Agreement on Trade-Related Aspects of Intellectual Property Rights, Annex 1C to the WTO Agreement (*infra* n. 5).
2. Paris Convention for the Protection of Industrial Property of 20 March 1883, last revised at Stockholm on 14 July 1967, 828 U.N.T.S. 305, and as amended on 28 September 1979, Arts. 9, 10, 10*bis* and 10*ter*; Berne Convention for the Protection of Literary and Artistic Works of 9 September, 1886, last revised at Paris on 24 July 1971, 1161 U.N.T.S. 3 and as amended on 28 September 1979, Art. 16; noted in Panel report, *China – Intellectual Property Rights*, WT/DS362/R, para. 7.241. See Heath and Cotter, 'Comparative Overview and the TRIPS Enforcement Provisions', in C. *Heath*, Patent Enforcement Worldwide, Writings in Honour of Dieter Stauder. Hart Publishing, Oxford and Portland Oregon, 2005, 3–53 at p. 6.
3. WIPO Copyright Treaty of 20 December 1996, 2186 U.N.T.S. 121, Art. 14(2); WIPO Performances and Phonograms Treaty of 20 December 1996, 2186 U.N.T.S. 203, Art. 23(2). See also the International Convention for the Protection of New Varieties of Plants (UPOV) of

3

Agreement on Tariffs and Trade ('GATT') in 1947.[4] That goal is now part of the overarching object and purpose of the WTO, which subsumed GATT in 1994.[5] TRIPS is a product of these mixed origins.

The avoidance of barriers to legitimate trade in intellectual property enforcement was first raised in the GATT framework in relation to work on measures to discourage the importation of counterfeit goods.[6] Later, it became a focus of the new TRIPS disciplines on enforcement. Various WTO disputes in recent years have highlighted that GATT 1994 continues to play a role in addressing barriers to legitimate trade in intellectual property protection and enforcement. TRIPS and GATT 1994 are both covered by the WTO's integrated dispute settlement mechanism and can be invoked together, or separately, in a given case.[7]

This chapter begins by recalling the circumstances that led to the inclusion of an objective to avoid barriers to legitimate trade in the TRIPS preamble. The second section examines the operational significance of this language today in enforcement obligations in Part III of TRIPS and considers whether it creates an obligation to avoid over-enforcement of intellectual property rights. The third section considers how obligations aimed at reducing non-tariff barriers to trade under GATT 1994 and other WTO agreements apply to intellectual property laws and regulations to prohibit discriminatory and unduly trade-restrictive protection and enforcement.

B.   TRIPS PREAMBLE

The first recital of the TRIPS preamble provides for 'effective' intellectual property protection while, at the same time, providing that intellectual property enforcement measures and procedures shall not themselves become barriers to legitimate trade.[8] This combination of objectives reflects the fact that the agreement builds on the foundation of the pre-existing intellectual property conventions in WIPO but was negotiated as part of the Uruguay Round of multilateral trade negotiations under the auspices of GATT. Barriers to legitimate trade due to intellectual property enforcement were a contemporary concern within GATT at the time of the launch of the Uruguay Round, which was later addressed in a dispute settlement process that ran in parallel with the TRIPS negotiations.

---

2 December 1961, as revised at Geneva on 10 November 1972 and on 23 October 1978, 1861 U.N.T.S 281, and as revised at Geneva on 19 March 1991, Art. 30(1)(i).

4. General Agreement on Tariffs and Trade. 1994, Annex 1A to the WTO Agreement (*infra* n. 5) (hereinafter GATT 1994), preamble, 2nd recital.
5. Agreement Establishing the World Trade Organization, done at Marrakesh on 15 April 1994, 1867 U.N.T.S. 154 (hereinafter WTO Agreement), preamble, 3rd recital.
6. See notes 16 and 17 *infra*.
7. Understanding on Rules and Procedures Governing the Settlement of Disputes, Annex 2 to the WTO Agreement (*supra* n. 5) (hereinafter Dispute Settlement Understanding), Art. 1.1.
8. TRIPS preamble, 1st recital.

I. Punta del Este Declaration

The first recital of the TRIPS preamble restates the initial negotiating mandate for TRIPS agreed by trade ministers at Punta del Este in September 1986 when they launched the Uruguay Round.[9] The first recital of the TRIPS preamble reads as follows:

> 'Desiring to reduce distortions and impediments to international trade, and taking into account the need to promote effective and adequate protection of intellectual property rights, and to ensure that measures and procedures to enforce intellectual property rights do not themselves become barriers to legitimate trade'[10]

At the time, the suitability of GATT as a forum for intellectual property negotiations was hotly contested and some justification was required to begin work there rather than in WIPO, the organisation specialised in this field.[11] The first recital begins by recalling the justification offered during preparations for the launch of the Uruguay Round, where intellectual property was presented in terms of 'distortions and impediments to international trade'. These were familiar terms in GATT from the Tokyo Round of multilateral trade negotiations.[12] It had been recognised that subsidies could unfairly displace or impede imports or exports of like products into a subsidising country or from third countries.[13] As regards TRIPS, the premise was that *inadequate* standards of intellectual property protection distorted and impeded international trade by reducing market share for IP-protected goods in the non-protecting country and third countries.[14] This justification for conducting the TRIPS negotiations in the GATT framework was not elaborated further in the text. The first recital of the TRIPS preamble continues by noting the proponents' aspiration to establish comprehensive minimum standards of 'effective and adequate' intellectual property protection, rather than merely a customs procedure to discourage the importation of counterfeit

---

9. Ministerial Declaration on the Uruguay Round, GATT doc. MIN.DEC, 20 September 1986 ('Punta del Este Declaration').
10. *Ibid.*, p. 9.
11. GATT Preparatory Committee, Record of Discussions of 8–31 July 1986, GATT doc. PREP. COM(86)SR/9, (26 August 1986), paras. 33–41.
12. Declaration of Ministers agreed at Tokyo on 14 September 1973, GATT doc. MIN(73)/1, para. 4, regarding 'tariffs, non-tariff barriers and other measures which impede or distort international trade'.
13. See Agreement on Interpretation and Application of Articles VI, XVI and XXIII of the General Agreement on Tariffs and Trade of 12 April 1979 ('Subsidies Code') preamble 1st recital, and Art. 8.4.
14. GATT Preparatory Committee, 'Trade and Intellectual Property Rights', Communication from the United States, PREP.COM(86)W/46, (8 July 1986); discussed in the GATT Preparatory Committee (*supra* n. 11). See *Gervais*, The TRIPS Agreement: Drafting History and Analysis, London 2012, para. 2.09. See also Uruguay Round, Negotiating Group on Trade-Related Aspects of Intellectual Property Rights, including Trade in Counterfeit Goods, Meeting of 25 March 1987, Note by the Secretariat, MTN.GNG/NG11/1 (10 April 1987), para. 4; and Suggestion by the United States for achieving the negotiating objective, 20 October 1987, MTN.GNG/NG11/W/14, p. 2

goods. That aspiration led to the outline of a comprehensive agreement in 1989[15] which now appears in the second recital of the TRIPS preamble and tracks the body of the final text.

Amid this debate, the Punta del Este Declaration included an objective similar to work already undertaken in GATT, which was to ensure that intellectual property enforcement measures and procedures did not themselves become barriers to legitimate trade (quoted in italics above). Provisions to ensure that procedures avoided the creation of non-tariff barriers to legitimate trade had been proposed in successive drafts of an agreement to discourage the importation of counterfeit goods, circulated near the end of the Tokyo Round in 1979 and later, in 1982.[16] Comparable language had also been considered in a GATT expert group on trade in counterfeit goods in 1985.[17] That work had not led to any final agreement.

However, the objective as established in the Punta del Este Declaration regarding the avoidance of barriers to legitimate trade responded to other concerns besides trade in counterfeit goods. The Declaration broadened the language to cover 'measures and procedures to enforce intellectual property rights' in general and addressed the future framework on international trade in counterfeit goods in a separate paragraph, as does the TRIPS preamble.[18] Tellingly, this particular objective was not part of the original US proposal for intellectual property negotiations in the Uruguay Round.[19] Rather, it can be traced to concerns about particular US patent enforcement measures and procedures that were also being raised in GATT during the same period.

II. Section 337 and Certain Aramid Fiber

The Punta del Este Declaration was drafted at the time of a looming GATT dispute between the European Economic Community ('EEC') and the United States regarding intellectual property enforcement measures and procedures under section 337 of the US Tariff Act of 1930 ('section 337').[20] These procedures, which are administered by the US International Trade Commission ('USITC'), apply in

---

15. Uruguay Round Trade Negotiations Committee, 'Meeting at Level of High Officials, Geneva, 5–8 April 1989', GATT doc. MTN.TNC/9 (11 April 1989) ('Mid-Term Review Decision'), pp. 9–10.
16. Proposal for an 'Agreement on the Sanctions to be Imposed upon the Importation of Counterfeit Merchandise', submitted by the United States, GATT doc. MFN/NTM/W/225 (9 March 1979), Art. II:6; revised as a proposal for an 'Agreement on Measures to Discourage the Importation of Counterfeit Goods', submitted by the United States and the EEC, GATT doc. L/4817 (31 July 1979), Art. II:6; further revised as 'Draft Agreement to Discourage the Importation of Counterfeit Goods', proposed by the United States, the European Community, Japan and Canada, GATT doc. L/5382 (18 October 1982), Art. 2.5 and Note.
17. 'Report of the Group of Experts on Trade in Counterfeit Goods', GATT doc. L/5878 (9 October 1985), para. 11: 'In this regard, the Group noted that what was under consideration was possible joint action aimed at curbing the trade disruptive and inhibiting effects of commercial counterfeiting, *while safeguarding against obstacles to trade in genuine goods*' (emphasis added).
18. TRIPS preamble, 3rd recital.
19. *Supra* n. 11.
20. 19 U.S. Code § 1337 – Unfair practices in import trade.

cases of violation of all forms of intellectual property rights involving imported products.[21] An investigation under section 337 can lead to an 'exclusion order' that prohibits infringing products from entering the United States. The procedures are frequently used in cases of patent infringement but also as regards infringement of copyright and trade marks, false designations of origin and misappropriation of trade secrets. Section 337 was a long-standing source of trade friction between the United States and its major trading partners by the time of the Punta del Este meeting.[22] Canada unsuccessfully challenged section 337 before a GATT panel in *US – Spring Assemblies* in 1981.[23] The EEC notified section 337 in the GATT inventory of non-tariff measures in 1982.[24] The number of USITC investigations only increased, with over 100 new cases under section 337 in the three-year period 1983–85 that targeted products from many different countries.[25]

The GATT dispute filed by the EEC was triggered by an exclusion order issued by the USITC in the *Certain Aramid Fiber* case in November 1985. A US patentee, DuPont, had complained to the USITC that certain products produced in Europe by a Dutch company, Akzo, and its affiliates, were manufactured by a process covered by DuPont's US patent and that importation would have the tendency to substantially injure US industry.[26] The EEC complained of 'abuse of intellectual property legislation for protectionist purposes' under the section 337 procedures in December 1985,[27] launched a trade defence investigation of section 337 in February 1986[28] and decided to initiate a GATT dispute settlement proceeding in *US – Section 337 Tariff Act* in March 1987.[29] The mandate to launch TRIPS negotiations in the Punta del Este

---

21. As of 31 December, 2016, there were 101 active exclusion orders under section 337. Source: USITC.
22. Recourse to section 337 became more frequent after amendments in the Trade Act of 1974 authorised the USITC to make determinations and provide remedies.
23. See GATT panel report, *United States – Imports of Certain Automotive Spring Assemblies* GATT doc. L/5333, adopted on 26 May 1983.
24. GATT, Inventory of Non-Tariff Measures (Industrial Products), Addendum (1 September 1982), NTM/INV/I-V/Add.1, Item V.F.4; re-circulated in the TRIPS negotiating group (9 May 1987), MTN.GNG/NG11/W/8.
25. See list of cases instituted prior to October 2008 available at https://pubapps2.usitc.gov/337external/ (accessed 14 May 2018).
26. Order issued 25 November 1985: see 'In the Matter of Certain Aramid Fiber, Inv. No. 337-TA-194', USITC Publication 1824 (1986).
27. 'E.C. Hands Trade-Barriers List to U.S.', European Community News, No. 42/1985 (18 December 1985) 4.
28. Notice of initiation of an examination procedure concerning illicit commercial practices within the meaning of Regulation (EEC) No. 2641/1984 (OJ C 25/02 of 5 February 1986).
29. Commission Decision of 12 March 1987 on the initiation of an international consultation and disputes settlement procedure, 87/251/EEC (OJ L 117/18 of 5 May 1987); Request for consultations, United States – Section 337 of the Tariff Act of 1930, Recourse by the European Communities to Article XXIII:1, GATT doc. L/6160 (29 April 1987); Request for establishment of a panel, GATT doc. L/6198 (3 July 1987).

Declaration was debated contemporaneously[30] and adopted in September 1986.[31]

When the Punta del Este mandate was first discussed in the TRIPS negotiating group in March 1987, USITC exclusion orders and section 337 of the US Tariff Act of 1930 were evidently identified by some participants as enforcement measures and procedures that had become barriers to legitimate trade. While many issues were raised in relation to the need to promote effective and adequate protection of intellectual property rights, the sole concern expressed in connection with the objective 'to ensure that measures and procedures to enforce intellectual property rights do not themselves become barriers to legitimate trade' was the following:

> '[R]eference was made to procedures in some contracting parties which were said to entail not only a separate treatment of imported goods, but outright discrimination, for example, by imposing substantial procedural disadvantages.'[32]

That is a concise summary of the claims filed by the EEC regarding section 337 the following month in its formal request to initiate the GATT dispute in *US – Section 337 Tariff Act*.[33]

Later discussion of this objective in the TRIPS negotiating group in 1987–88 elaborated on the alleged procedural disadvantages affecting imported goods under section 337, although that provision was not named in the records of discussions. These alleged disadvantages included shorter time-limits for investigations than in patent litigation involving domestic goods, an absence of remedies for damage caused by erroneous measures taken against non-infringing goods, continuation of investigations under border control procedures while patents were under re-examination, a failure to lift exclusion orders promptly after an infringement had ceased, non-admissibility of counterclaims, general exclusion orders that covered products of parties other than the respondent and the possibility of double proceedings.[34] Most of these arguments were being presented at the same time to the GATT panel in *US – Section 337 Tariff Act* by the EEC, Canada, Japan, Korea and Switzerland[35] and bilaterally by Canada in relation to another complaint regarding section 337 filed in 1987.[36]

---

30. See GATT Preparatory Committee, Discussions of 8–31 July 1986 (*supra* n. 11). The language appears in GATT Preparatory Committee, 'Draft ministerial declaration', Communication from Colombia and Switzerland, PREP.COM(86)W/47 (18 July 1986), p. 6, which was preceded by a draft declaration circulated informally by nine countries. See generally Gervais, (*supra* n. 14), para. 1.14.
31. See Punta del Este Declaration (*supra* n. 9).
32. See Meeting of 25 March 1987, Note by the Secretariat (*supra* n. 11), para. 5.
33. See Request for consultations (*supra* n. 28).
34. Uruguay Round, 'Trade in Counterfeit Goods: Compilation of Written Submissions and Oral Statements', Prepared by the Secretariat, GATT doc. MTN.GNG/NG11/W/23 (26 April 1988), paras. 18 to 20.
35. The panel was established in October 1987 and met the parties in March and May 1988: see GATT panel report, *United States – Section 337 of the US Tariff Act of 1930*, GATT doc. L/6439, adopted on 7 November 1989, paras. 1.1 and 1.5. See parties' and third parties' arguments in Sections III and IV of that report.
36. 'United States – Section 337 of the Tariff Act of 1930, Recourse by Canada to Article XXIII:1', GATT doc. L/6213 (15 September 1987) arising from *Cellular Mobile Telephones*

Interestingly, the USITC expressly took account of the need to avoid 'a disruption of legitimate trade' in the *Certain Aramid Fiber* case when determining the scope of the exclusion order. This was a difficult issue because the product obtained by the patented process at issue had such a diverse range of applications. Aramid fibre is a synthetic product (marketed as 'Kevlar') that is five times stronger than steel and does not melt. DuPont requested an exclusion order covering many finished products that incorporated aramid fibre such as protective clothing, ropes, cables, tyres, boat and aircraft parts, brake blocks and clutches, hose, power transmission and conveyor-belts, tires, printed wiring boards, and fabric. However, a majority of commissioners decided that such a wide order would be burdensome on 'legitimate' trade in finished products and difficult to enforce. Therefore, they limited the product coverage of the exclusion order to basic forms of aramid fibre such as chopped fibre, yarn, fabric, felt and paper[37] even though many downstream products containing the infringing fibre were also infringing.[38] A dissenting opinion favoured a wider order but even then accepted that the exclusion of all infringing goods could impose an unjustifiable burden on trade, such as where an infringing component represented a small share of the total value of a product, or where it was difficult to separate an infringing component from the finished product.[39]

The *Certain Aramid Fiber* case was later settled by DuPont and Akzo but the GATT panel proceeding continued between the EEC and the United States regarding section 337 'as such', that is, regarding its general and prospective application.

III. Some Implications of US – Section 337 Tariff Act

The 1989 GATT panel report on *US – Section 337 Tariff Act* demonstrates that GATT itself can avoid the creation of barriers to trade in intellectual property enforcement and provides an interpretative framework for intellectual property laws and regulations within GATT. The report was circulated in January 1989 during the Mid-Term Review of the Uruguay Round, when the scope of ongoing TRIPS negotiations was decided. The report also has implications for the concurrent application of GATT 1994 and TRIPS.

The GATT panel examined the procedures and orders used to enforce patents under Section 337 for their conformity with GATT, not TRIPS, but it addressed some of the concerns that had also been raised in the TRIPS negotiating group at the same time. The panel found that section 337 discriminated against imported products in several respects, as compared to the procedures and remedies available in patent infringement actions in federal district courts against domestic products. The panel concluded that section 337 was inconsistent in these respects with the GATT

---

and Subassemblies and Components Parts Thereof, Inv. 337-TA-273, initiated 12 August 1987, 52 F.R. 29901.
37. Even the patentee did not request an order to cover high-value items such as aircraft and cars that contained relatively minor components of aramid fibre.
38. See the explanation in GATT panel report, *US – Section 337 Tariff Act* (*supra* n. 35), para. 3.52.
39. See Additional and Dissenting Views of Vice Chairman Susan W. Liebeler, 'In the Matter of Certain Aramid Fiber' (*supra* n. 26).

national treatment obligation in Art. III:4 and that these could not be fully justified under the general exception in Art. XX(d).[40] The panel's conclusions demonstrate that GATT obligations can contribute to the objective of ensuring that intellectual property enforcement measures and procedures do not themselves become barriers to legitimate trade.

The panel did not treat intellectual property as a barrier to trade that required justification by a general exception. Even though the case concerned orders excluding the importation of patent-infringing goods, the panel never applied the prohibition on quantitative import restrictions in Art. XI:1 of GATT. It was only because section 337 treated imported and domestic products differently, in violation of Art. III:4, that the panel examined whether the general exception in Art. XX(d) provided a justification. The panel viewed intellectual property laws and enforcement procedures as part of a country's internal regulation affecting the sale of goods, which could be enforced against imported goods at the border as long as the procedures were non-discriminatory.[41] If section 337 had not favoured domestic industry, it could have been quite compatible with GATT.

Moreover, the panel recognised that GATT does not create any obligation to adopt a substantive patent law or to enforce patent rights to any particular degree.[42] TRIPS, on the other hand, prescribes minimum standards of protection and sets out general obligations that refer to the degree of enforcement.[43] Consequently, TRIPS can complement GATT obligations, as they were clarified by the panel in *US – Section 337 Tariff Act*.

Certain TRIPS disciplines address concerns regarding section 337 that GATT was inadequate to resolve. Given that the United States could bring itself into compliance with the GATT national treatment obligation by *extending* the availability of section 337 on a non-discriminatory basis, the GATT panel report alone could not solve all problems experienced with section 337 and might actually make them worse.[44] The new TRIPS disciplines address some of those problems directly.[45] Art. 41.2 provides that enforcement procedures shall not be 'unnecessarily complicated' or 'costly' or entail 'unreasonable time-limits'. These recall concerns regarding section 337 regarding double proceedings against imported products in the USITC and a federal district court, the costs of preparing a good defence to a section 337 complaint, and fixed time-limits for proceedings under section 337.[46] Further, Art. 41.1 provides that

---

40. GATT panel report, *US – Section 337 Tariff Act* (*supra* n. 35), paras. 5.20, 5.35 and 6.3.
41. *Ibid.*, para. 5.10.
42. *Ibid.*, paras. 5.26 and 6.1. However, the degree to which enforcement restricts trade may be relevant to the general exception in Art. XX(d), discussed *infra*.
43. This depends on the nature of the general obligations in Art. 41.1 of TRIPS as obligations of purpose or of result, and is without prejudice to the responsibility of private right holders to initiate enforcement procedures.
44. Uruguay Round, 'Trade in Counterfeit Goods: Compilation of Written Submissions and Oral Statements', Prepared by the Secretariat (*supra* n. 34), para. 18.
45. The TRIPS non-discrimination obligations in Arts. 3.1 and 4 cover intellectual property enforcement. Unlike Arts. I:1 and III:4 of GATT 1994, they apply in terms of the nationality of persons, rather than the country of origin of goods.
46. GATT Inventory of Non-Tariff Measures (*supra* n. 24); GATT panel report, *US – Section 337 Tariff Act* (*supra* n. 35), para. 3.12. Section 337 was amended in 1994 to provide for

enforcement procedures shall be applied in such a manner as to avoid the creation of barriers to legitimate trade. This recalls a concern regarding section 337 that general exclusion orders are applied to imported products from all sources and not just from the respondent.[47] These TRIPS obligations cannot be satisfied merely by ensuring that procedures are non-discriminatory.[48]

The TRIPS preamble refers to the need to ensure that intellectual property enforcement measures and procedures do not themselves become barriers to legitimate trade, not only in relation to border measures against counterfeit goods but also due to contemporary concerns regarding section 337 of the US Tariff Act of 1930 at the time of the launch of the Uruguay Round in 1986. The subsequent GATT panel report on *US – Section 337 Tariff Act* illustrated how GATT 1947 (now GATT 1994) pursues the objective of avoiding barriers to legitimate trade, in a way that has been complemented by TRIPS.

C. TRIPS ENFORCEMENT OBLIGATIONS

The avoidance of 'barriers to legitimate trade' in intellectual property enforcement also appears among the obligations in Part III of TRIPS. Where Part II of TRIPS provides minimum standards of protection of rights, Part III specifies the enforcement procedures and remedies that must be available when rights are infringed. The inclusion of Part III was 'one of the major accomplishments' of TRIPS because the pre-existing intellectual property conventions contained little on the subject of enforcement against infringement beyond national treatment and certain optional provisions.[49] The objective of avoiding barriers to legitimate trade is reflected throughout Part III of TRIPS but, as a general obligation, it may also discipline the application of the specific enforcement procedures in practice, thereby preventing over-enforcement, depending on how it is interpreted.

I. General Obligations

The avoidance of 'barriers to legitimate trade' appears in the first section of Part III, on general obligations. The first paragraph of Art. 41 provides as follows:

---

stays of district court proceedings and to replace the fixed time-limits with target dates: see WTO Council for TRIPS, 'Review of Legislation on Enforcement – United States', IP/Q4/USA/1, p. 17.
47. Ibid.
48. European Community filed a follow-up complaint in 2000 that raised claims under both GATT 1994 and the new disciplines in Art. 41 of TRIPS: see Request for consultations, *US – Section 337 of the Tariff Act of 1930 and amendments thereto*, (18 January 2000), WT/DS186/1. That complaint did not proceed beyond the consultations stage.
49. Panel report, *China – Intellectual Property Rights*, WT/DS362/R, para. 7.241, citing Panel report, *US – Section 211 Appropriations Act*, WT/DS176/R, para. 8.97; despite the approach to the enforcement obligation at issue in that same dispute: cf. Appellate Body report, WT/DS176/AB/R, Section VIII. See also *Kirk*, WIPO Asian Regional Round Table on Implementation of [TRIPS], WIPO doc. WIPO/IP/SIN/97/2 (1 December 1997) cited in *Watal*, 'US-China Intellectual Property Dispute – A Comment on the Interpretation of the TRIPS Enforcement Provisions', 13 The Journal of World Intellectual Property 605 [2010].

> 'Members shall ensure that enforcement procedures as specified in this Part are available under their law so as to permit effective action against any act of infringement of intellectual property rights covered by this Agreement, including expeditious remedies to prevent infringements and remedies which constitute a deterrent to further infringements. These procedures shall be applied in such a manner as to avoid the creation of barriers to legitimate trade and to provide for safeguards against their abuse.' [Emphasis added]

The scope of these obligations covers enforcement procedures only. The first sentence is limited to 'enforcement procedures as specified in this Part' and the second sentence refers to the same procedures. These are the specific procedures prescribed by Arts. 42 to 61 of TRIPS. These procedures do not define what constitutes an infringement, which rather depends on the substantive standards of protection in a Member's law.[50] By its own terms, the second sentence of Art. 41.1 does not apply to substantive standards of protection.

The core of Art. 41.1 of TRIPS consists of twin obligations to provide procedures that permit 'effective' action against infringement, in the first sentence, while ensuring that those same procedures are not applied in a manner that creates 'barriers to legitimate trade', in the second sentence. The interpolated clause regarding remedies is illustrative of the first sentence and not an exhaustive description of all remedies specified in Part III.[51] These twin obligations pursue different and potentially opposing purposes.[52] 'Effective' action against infringement, including remedies that are 'expeditious' and that constitute a 'deterrent', promotes better, faster and stricter enforcement, respectively. The avoidance of barriers to legitimate trade requires more targeted enforcement. Better enforcement can entail choices as to how to execute procedures and which remedies to order. Faster enforcement disrupts legitimate trade for less time. Yet stricter enforcement may deliver a negligible increase in effectiveness and entail a disproportionate trade impact.

These twin obligations are subject to the general freedom of each Member to determine the appropriate method of implementation within its 'own legal system and practice', guaranteed by Art. 1.1 of TRIPS. Differences between national legal systems are particularly apparent in the field of enforcement, as highlighted in the TRIPS preamble.[53] However, as the 2009 panel report in *China – Intellectual Property Rights* confirmed, that is not a freedom to derogate from the obligations in Part III.[54]

---

50. For example, footnote 13 to TRIPS confirms that there is no obligation to apply the special border procedures to parallel imports or goods in transit, which follows from the lack of any substantive obligation to treat these goods as infringing.
51. This clause begins with the word 'including', indicating that it does not apply to all specified procedures in Part III. It refers to 'expeditious remedies to prevent infringements', such as injunctions, and 'remedies which constitute a deterrent', such as fines and imprisonment. The use of the word 'remedies', which is used interchangeably with 'penalties' in Art. 61, does not imply that civil remedies must constitute a deterrent.
52. See generally Seuba, The Global Regime for the Enforcement of Intellectual Property Rights, Cambridge University Press, 2017, p. 8.
53. TRIPS preamble, 2nd recital, paragraph (c) *in fine*. See Correa, Trade Related Aspects of Intellectual Property Rights, A Commentary on the TRIPS Agreement, Oxford University Press 2007, p. 409.
54. Panel report, *China – Intellectual Property Rights*, WT/DS362/R, para. 7.513.

Further, all enforcement obligations are subject to the guarantee in Art. 41.5 that there is no obligation to create a dedicated judicial system for intellectual property enforcement.

The twin obligations in Art. 41.1 reflect the mixed origins of TRIPS, like the combined objectives in the first recital of the TRIPS preamble (discussed above). The *first* sentence of Art. 41.1 provides for enforcement of the minimum standards of protection in Parts I and II of TRIPS, which build on those in the pre-existing intellectual property conventions in WIPO. Meanwhile, the *second* sentence reflects the trade liberalisation objectives of GATT, within which framework TRIPS was negotiated and concluded. The two sentences are examples of the differing approaches of international intellectual property law and international trade law insofar as the former generally prescribes treatment that governments *must* provide (so-called 'positive integration')[55] while the latter prohibits treatment that governments *must not* provide (so-called 'negative integration').[56] Consequently, trade law can place limits on national intellectual property measures, as illustrated by the GATT panel report in *US – Section 337 Tariff Act*.

The question arises as to whether the inclusion of a GATT-inspired obligation in Art. 41.1 of TRIPS also places a limit on national intellectual property systems, even though it is part of a minimum standards agreement. This would not be unique as the basic principles in Part I of TRIPS are also inspired by GATT and they also provide disciplines for intellectual property measures. Yet the obligation to avoid the creation of barriers to legitimate trade is already reflected in many specific enforcement obligations throughout Part III, as discussed in the next section.

II. Specific Enforcement Procedures

Part III of TRIPS contains many specific procedures that reflect the policy objective behind the general obligation to apply enforcement procedures in such a manner as to avoid the creation of barriers to legitimate trade.[57] However, the object and purpose of Part III of TRIPS is to prescribe procedures and remedies for domestic legal frameworks within which decisions on individual cases are taken and few features of the specified procedures are mandatory in any given instance.

The specific procedures in Part III of TRIPS comprise the civil judicial enforcement procedures (including provisional measures) in sections 2 and 3, which apply to infringements of all intellectual property rights covered by TRIPS, as well as the

---

55. International intellectual property law also provides for certain substantive maxima: see *Kur and Grosse Ruse-Khan*, Enough Is Enough: The Notion of Binding Ceilings in International Intellectual Property Regulation, Max Planck Institute for Intellectual Property, Competition and Tax Law Research Paper Series No. 09-01, 2009.
56. *Hoekman and Kostecki*, The Political Economy of the World Trading System: WTO and Beyond, Oxford University Press, 2001, 274; *Petersmann*, 'From Negative to Positive Integration in the WTO: The TRIPs Agreement and the WTO Constitution', in *Cottier and Mavroidis* (eds.), Intellectual Property: Trade, Competition, and Sustainable Development the World Trade Forum, University of Michigan Press, 2003, pp. 21–52 at 21–23.
57. *Bronckers, Verkade and McNelis*, TRIPs Agreement: Enforcement of Intellectual Property Rights, vol. 836, Office for Official Publications of the European Communities, Luxembourg 2000, p. 51.

special border procedures in section 4 and the criminal procedures in section 5, which apply as a minimum only to more egregious forms of infringement.[58] The specific procedures also include administrative procedures that lead to any civil remedy, where available, such as USITC procedures under section 337 of the US Tariff Act of 1930.[59]

Many features of the specific procedures in Part III of TRIPS, particularly those in sections 3 and 4, are intended to avoid the creation of barriers to legitimate trade or to provide for safeguards against abuse in particular enforcement procedures and remedies, or both.[60] For example, requirements that applicants provide adequate evidence of a *prima facie* case of infringement[61] are designed to avoid enforcement actions against non-infringing goods and services. Requirements that applicants put up security[62] and the prospect of paying compensation for injury due to wrongful enforcement[63] can discourage abuse of procedures. Requirements to enable faster identification of suspected infringing goods during execution of measures[64] and the provision of information on production and distribution chains[65] can facilitate more targeted enforcement actions that avoid or reduce their impact on trade in other goods and services. Time-limits on provisional and border measures reduce delays to trade in goods where further proceedings are not promptly initiated.[66] Further, the right holder has the primary responsibility to initiate most of the specific procedures[67] which can reduce the frequency of interventions by customs and courts. These features of the specific procedures were all raised during the TRIPS negotiations in connection with the avoidance of barriers to legitimate trade[68] as were certain general obligations in Art. 41.[69]

---

58. Section 4 applies as a minimum to suspected counterfeit trademark goods and pirated copyright goods presented for importation: see TRIPS, Art. 51 and footnote 14. Section 5 applies as a minimum to wilful trademark counterfeiting or copyright piracy on a commercial scale: see TRIPS, Art. 61. This latter phrase was interpreted in Panel report, *China – Intellectual Property Rights,* WT/DS362/R, para. 7.516 ff.
59. TRIPS, Arts. 49 and 50.8.
60. Provisions regarding security and compensation refer expressly to the prevention of abuse but these are not the only specific safeguards provided in the text: *Micara,* 'TRIPS-plus Border Measures and Access to Medicines', 15 The Journal of World Intellectual Property, 73–101 [2012] p. 81.
61. TRIPS, Arts. 50.3 and 52. For an illustration of the potential impact on trade of the burden of proof, see *Senftleben,* 'Wolf in Sheep's Clothing? Trade Mark Rights Against Goods in Transit and the End of Traditional Territorial Limits', 47 International Review of Intellectual Property and Competition Law (IIC) 941–59 [2016] pp. 948–950.
62. TRIPS, Arts. 50.3 and 53.1.
63. TRIPS, Arts. 48, 50.7 and 56. See further *Heath and Cotter* (*supra* n. 2) at p. 11.
64. TRIPS, Arts. 50.5 and 52.
65. TRIPS, Arts. 47 and 57.
66. TRIPS, Arts. 50.6 and 55; see also Art. 53.2.
67. See Panel report, *China – Intellectual Property Rights,* WT/DS362/R, para. 7.247.
68. Uruguay Round, 'Compilation of Written Submissions and Oral Statements', Prepared by the Secretariat, (*supra* n. 34) paras. 37–38; Information from other international organizations, Communication from the Customs Co-operation Council, Addendum, (15 January 1988), MTN.GNG/NG11/W/5/Add.5, pp. 2–3.
69. General obligations in Art. 41.2 to 41.4 were also raised during the TRIPS negotiations in connection with the avoidance of barriers to legitimate trade: see Uruguay Round,

Only a few of these features of the specific procedures are mandatory in any given case. Art. 50.6 provides that after a certain period, provisional measures 'shall be revoked or otherwise cease to have effect', while Art. 55 provides that within a certain period after customs suspension of goods at the border, 'the goods shall be released', if certain conditions are met. Further, Art. 52 provides that any right holder initiating the special border procedures 'shall be required' to provide adequate evidence of a *prima facie* case of infringement.[70] These requirements are mandatory in every relevant case, which is rare in Part III of TRIPS.

Some features of the specific procedures are entirely optional. For example, Art. 50.5 only provides that applicants *may* be required to supply information necessary for identification of goods subject to provisional measures while Arts. 47 and 57 provide that Members *may* provide authority to order the infringer or customs authorities to provide information on production and distribution chains. Members have no obligation to make these procedures available at all.

Most features of the specific procedures in Part III are discretionary or otherwise subject to domestic law in any given case. Part III of TRIPS sets out many obligations that judicial and other competent authorities 'shall have the authority' to make certain orders, but the decision as to whether and how that authority should be exercised is left up to those domestic authorities. The panel report in *China – Intellectual Property Rights* clarified this point as follows:

> '[…] The obligation is to "have" authority not an obligation to "exercise" authority. The phrase "shall have the authority" is used throughout the enforcement obligations in Sections 2, 3 and 4 of Part III of the TRIPS Agreement, specifically, in Articles 43.1, 44.1, 45.1, 45.2, 46, 48.1, 50.1, 50.2, 50.3, 50.7, 53.1, 56 and 57. It can be contrasted with terminology used in the minimum standards of protection in Part II of the TRIPS Agreement, such as "Members shall provide" protection, or that certain material "shall be" protected. [Footnotes omitted]

> […] Therefore, the obligation that competent authorities "shall have the authority" to make certain orders is not an obligation that competent authorities shall exercise that authority in a particular way, unless otherwise specified.'[71]

The availability of specific procedures with all the features prescribed by TRIPS allows domestic tribunals to refuse enforcement in given cases. This may discourage over-enforcement of intellectual property rights although it does not prohibit abuse of the procedures outright.[72] Parties can argue before courts and government agencies as to which remedies, if any, are warranted and defendants can refer to the general obligation in Art. 41.1 of TRIPS regarding the avoidance of barriers to legitimate trade. However, with rare exceptions, the specific procedures do not create mandatory requirements that prevent over-enforcement.

'Compilation of Written Submissions and Oral Statements', Prepared by the Secretariat, (*supra* n. 23), paras. 37–38. See also 1979 US proposal (*supra* n. 16).
70. Cf. Art. 58 which allows *ex officio* action to initiate the special border procedures.
71. Panel report, *China – Intellectual Property Rights*, WT/DS362/R, paras. 7.236 and 7.238.
72. 'USTR official predicts difficulty in forcing compliance with TRIPS', Inside US Trade, (16 July 1999) cited in *Watal* (*supra* n. 49), p. 607.

Outside Part III, Art. 69 of TRIPS promotes targeted enforcement through international cooperation to eliminate trade in infringing goods, particularly through the exchange of information between customs services regarding trade in counterfeit and pirate goods.[73] Information such as country of origin, the routing of consignments, the declared value of goods and patterns of infringement can be used in risk analysis to identify those consignments most likely to contain infringing goods.

Other means are available to prevent intellectual property protection and enforcement from creating barriers to legitimate trade. In particular, Arts. 8.2 and 40 of TRIPS recognise the potential need for competition laws to prevent abuses of intellectual property rights, including in licensing practices. However, they do not create any obligation to adopt a competition law or to apply it in any particular circumstances.

Many features of the specific enforcement procedures in Part III of TRIPS are designed to avoid the creation of barriers to legitimate trade. However, they do not provide disciplines to ensure that domestic enforcement systems are effective and not overly trade-restrictive in practice. Such disciplines may be found elsewhere including, potentially, the general obligations in Art. 41 of TRIPS.

III. Performance Standards

The general obligation to avoid barriers to legitimate trade in Art. 41.1 of TRIPS is potentially important because many of the specific obligations in Part III only require WTO Members to grant discretionary authority without disciplining the ways in which courts and government agencies exercise their discretion in practice. However, the prospects for the general obligation to provide a basis for claims under TRIPS against over-enforcement of intellectual property rights depend on the nature of the obligation, the meanings of 'legitimate' and 'trade' according to the customary rules of treaty interpretation, and the types of measures that can be challenged regarding the manner in which procedures are 'applied'.

The general obligations in Art. 41.1 may be read either as obligations of purpose or result, but only the latter reading would discipline the exercise of discretionary authority in enforcement. Art. 41.1 expresses the purposes behind the specific procedures that follow in Arts. 42 to 61 but it is worded as two obligations.[74] If they were mere expressions of purpose, implementation of all the specific procedures in a domestic legal framework would satisfy the general obligations in Art. 41.1, even though the system might be ineffective or overly trade-restrictive in practice. Alternatively, the general obligations may provide performance standards for the operation of the specific procedures.[75] For example, the specific obligation in Art.

---

73. Contact points in Members' administrations are circulated in the IP/N/3/* document series.
74. Appellate Body report, *US – Section 211 Appropriations Act*, WT/DS176/AB/R, para. 206.
75. See *Seuba* (*supra* n. 52), p. 105, citing *Bronckers* et al. (*supra* n. 57), at p. 15. A sweeping remark that WTO Members are free to determine the level of enforcement of their laws and regulations was made in relation to Art. XX(d) of GATT 1994 without consideration of TRIPS: see Appellate Body report, *Korea – Various Measures on Beef*, WT/DS161/AB/R, para. 176.

50.1 requires preliminary injunctions to be available (that is, it addresses what the courts *can* order) but the general obligations in Art. 41.1 could discipline the manner in which that remedy is granted (that is, what the courts *do* order), in particular, the factors taken into account when considering applications for preliminary injunctions (that is, *when* the courts make orders and *why*).[76] If the general obligations in Art. 41.1 are read as performance standards, they would provide a basis for claims under TRIPS and the Dispute Settlement Understanding.

Dispute settlement has provided no clarification of the terms used in Art. 41.1.[77] The words 'effective', 'expeditious' and 'deterrent' in the first sentence have broad meanings. Although an early claim under Art. 41 was successful in alleging that Greece did not provide or enforce 'effective' remedies against broadcasting piracy, no interpretation of the term 'effective' was ever provided. The respondent adopted new legislation and took actual enforcement action, including the closure of four television stations, but the dispute never reached the panel stage.[78] The claims under Art. 41.1 in *China – Intellectual Property Rights* concerned the unavailability of the specific procedures with respect to certain acts of infringement rather than their effectiveness or value as a deterrent.[79] The claims in *EU and the Netherlands – Seizures of Generic Drugs in Transit* in 2010 included an allegation that patent enforcement measures against goods in transit created 'barriers to legitimate trade' but that dispute has not proceeded to the panel stage.[80]

The word 'trade' in the WTO context refers to international trade. The multilateral trading system administered by the WTO – of which TRIPS forms an integral part – regulates international commerce, which includes the treatment of foreign goods, services and service suppliers in domestic markets. TRIPS obligations concern the treatment accorded to foreign nationals[81] but the second sentence of Art. 41.1 is unusual in that agreement insofar as it appears to reflect the GATT focus on the treatment of foreign goods, particularly in the context of the TRIPS special border procedures and provisional measures to prevent entry of imported goods. Other TRIPS enforcement procedures apply to both infringing goods and infringing services[82] and

---

76. See, for example, WTO Council for TRIPS, 'Review of Legislation on Enforcement – United States', IP/Q4/USA/1, p. 29. See also mutually agreed solution, *Argentina – Certain measures on the protection of patents and test data*, 20 June 2002, WT/DS171/3 & WT/DS196/4, point 6. See generally *Heath and Cotter* (*supra* n. 2), pp. 19-24; *Seuba* (*supra* n. 52), p. 413.
77. Regarding difficulties of enforcing the enforcement provisions, see *Reichman and Lange*, 'Bargaining Around the TRIPS Agreement: The Case for Ongoing Public-Private Initiatives to Facilitate Worldwide Intellectual Property Transactions', 9 Duke Journal of Comparative and International Law, 11 [1998] 34-39. In practice, most US free trade agreements omit the general obligations in Art. 41.1 of TRIPS.
78. Requests for consultations, *EC/Greece – Enforcement of intellectual property rights for motion pictures and television programs*, WT/DS124/1, WT/DS125/1. Cf. Mutually agreed solution WT/DS124/2, WT/DS125/2.
79. See Panel report, *China – Intellectual Property Rights*, WT/DS362/R, paras. 7.161-7.181, 7.676-7.680.
80. Request for consultations by India, *EU and the Netherlands – Seizures of Generic Drugs in Transit*, WT/DS408/1. See also request by Brazil, WT/DS409/1.
81. TRIPS, Art. 1.3. This includes persons assimilated to foreign nationals.
82. TRIPS, Art. 47.

the second sentence of Art. 41.1 may be interpreted to include the GATS focus on the treatment of foreign services and service suppliers as well.

The concept of 'legitimate trade' is more elastic.[83] As a minimum, it would include goods and services that are not within the scope of a given enforcement procedure, which varies. For example, goods and services infringing any intellectual property right can be targeted by provisional measures but those that are not suspected to be either counterfeit trademark goods or pirated copyright goods need not be targeted by the special border measures.[84] These infringing goods could benefit from the general obligation to avoid barriers to 'legitimate trade' under the special border measures, but not necessarily under the provisional measures.

More importantly, the word 'legitimate' can have a broader meaning than 'legal', more synonymous with 'justifiable', which involves a wider range of factors than infringement and can include consideration of the public interest. 'Legitimate' is frequently used in TRIPS with the word 'interests' in a broader sense than legal rights.[85] In the context of enforcement, a flexible interpretation of 'legitimate trade' is illustrated by USITC practice under section 337 of the US Tariff Act of 1930. Following cases such as *Certain Aramid Fiber*,[86] which led to the inclusion of language on barriers to legitimate trade in TRIPS, the USITC established a list of nine non-exhaustive factors in 1989 that it consistently considered when issuing limited exclusion orders in cases involving downstream products incorporating infringing components, in order to avoid disruption to legitimate trade.[87] These so-called *EPROMs* factors were 1) the value of the infringing articles (say, memory chips) compared to the value of the downstream products in which they are incorporated (say, computers, telecommunications equipment and cars); 2) the identity of the manufacturer of the downstream products (i.e., are the downstream products manufactured by the party found to have committed the unfair act, or by third parties); 3) the incremental value to complainant of the exclusion of downstream products; 4) the incremental detriment to respondents of such exclusion; 5) the burdens imposed on third parties resulting from exclusion of downstream products; 6) the availability of alternative

---

83. 'Legitimate trade' has been contrasted with smuggling and under-invoicing in the context of a defence under Art. XX(d) of GATT 1994: see Panel report, *Colombia – Ports of Entry*, WT/DS366/R, paras.7.590–7.602.
84. TRIPS, Art. 51 and *supra* n. 14.
85. See Arts. 13, 17, 26.2, 30 and 31(g) and also Arts. 34.3 and 63.4. In this context, see Panel report, *Canada – Pharmaceutical Patents*, WT/DS114/R, paras. 7.68–7.73; Panel report, *US – Section 110(5) Copyright Act*, WT/DS160/R, paras. 6.223–6.224; Panel reports, *EC – Trademarks and Geographical Indications*, WT/DS174/R and WT/DS290/R, paras. 7.662–7.663. Art. 7 of TRIPS, on the objectives of intellectual property protection and enforcement, also provides relevant context.
86. *Supra* n. 26. See also the presidential disapproval of the USITC Determination in *Certain Dynamic Random Access Memories*, 52 Fed. Reg. 46,011 (3 December 1987).
87. Additionally, general exclusion orders are not the default remedy due to their inherent potential to disrupt legitimate trade. These orders apply regardless of source and do not allow the US customs service to target suspect imports without undue delays in the movement of other merchandise covered by the relevant tariff classification: see *Certain Airless Spray Pumps*, Inv. 337-TA-90, USITC Pub. No. 1199 (November 1981) 18. See generally Hnath, 'General Exclusion Orders under Section 337', 25 Northwestern Journal of International Law & Business [2005] p. 356.

downstream products which do not contain the infringing articles; 7) the likelihood that imported downstream products actually contain the infringing articles and are thereby subject to exclusion; 8) the opportunity for evasion of an exclusion order which does not include downstream products; and 9) the enforceability of an order by Customs, etc.[88] The *EPROMs* factors entailed a 'careful and common-sense balancing' of the complainant's interest in obtaining complete protection from all infringing imports against the potential of the order to disrupt legitimate trade in downstream products and other relevant factors.[89]

On this view, the scope of 'legitimate trade' can include some infringing goods and services. Part III of TRIPS is not solely concerned with the effectiveness of enforcement. Art. 41.1 can prohibit enforcement where the added effectiveness of a measure in given circumstances is outweighed by the barrier that measure would create for legitimate trade. The fact that the affected products are infringing according to a Member's substantive standard of protection is not necessarily a justification to apply an enforcement measure in particular circumstances.

Lastly, the obligation to avoid barriers to legitimate trade in the second sentence of Art. 41.1 is also unusual in TRIPS because it concerns the manner in which measures are 'applied'.[90] This is another reflection of its trade law origins. Challenges under trade law obligations may address the application of measures in individual instances as well as measures 'as such', that is, in terms of their general and prospective application.[91] In contrast, TRIPS generally concerns only measures 'as such', providing for a domestic legal framework and leaving decisions on how to apply those measures in individual instances to domestic authorities.[92]

The inclusion of an obligation regarding the manner in which enforcement procedures are applied raises the question whether enforcement measures in individual instances can be challenged through the WTO dispute settlement mechanism. The issue arose in *EU and the Netherlands – Seizures of Generic Drugs in Transit*, where Brazil and India challenged patent enforcement measures both 'as such' and 'as applied' to individual consignments of drugs.[93] The claims did not specify whether

---

88. *Certain Erasable Programmable Read-Only Memories*, Inv. 337-TA-276, USITC Pub. No. 2196 (May 1989) 125. This approach was upheld on appeal in *Hyundai Electronics Industries Co. Ltd v. USITC*, 899 F.2d 1204 (Fed. Cir. 1990) but cf. *Kyocera Wireless Corp. v. USITC*, 545 F.3d 1340, 1356 (Fed. Cir. 2008). See *Busey*, 'Downstream Remedy at the ITC: The Continuing Applicability of the *EPROMs* Analysis', Federal Circuit Bar Association Newsletter (October 2016).
89. *Hyundai Electronics Industries Co. Ltd v. USITC* (*supra* n. 88).
90. Another such provision is Art. 3.2 of TRIPS. Different considerations arise in Art. 61 of TRIPS.
91. See Appellate Body report, *US – Oil Country Tubular Goods Sunset Reviews*, WT/DS268/AB/R, para. 172. This has important implications where the measure, on its face, can be applied in different ways: see GATT panel report, *US – Superfund*, GATT doc. L/6175, adopted on 17 June 1987, paras. 5.2.9–10.
92. Decisions in individual instances may nevertheless serve as evidence of the meaning and operation of the domestic law in a WTO dispute settlement proceeding regarding consistency with TRIPS. See, for example, Panel report, *China – Intellectual Property Rights*, WT/DS362/R, paras. 7.51, 7.232, 7.297, 7.306 and 7.350.
93. WT/DS408/1; WT/DS409/1.

the challenges to measures 'as applied' related to GATT 1994 only or also to TRIPS and the dispute has not proceeded to the panel stage.

It is unclear whether the second sentence of Art. 41.1 allows challenges to enforcement measures 'as applied'. Read in the context of the rest of that sentence (which refers to what Members 'provide')[94] and in light of the object and purpose of TRIPS as a whole (which prescribes a legal framework for decisions in individual instances at the domestic level), the sentence would cover, at most, general practices in the exercise of enforcement authority.[95] On the other hand, reading the term used in the second sentence (which refers to 'trade' rather than rights, protection or treatment) and in the context of the WTO as a whole (which includes many trade agreements that discipline the application of trade policy measures in individual instances), the second sentence might apply to measures as applied in individual instances.

The general obligation to avoid barriers to legitimate trade in Art. 41.1 of TRIPS may establish performance standards for the application of the specific procedures in Part III of TRIPS and thereby prohibit over-enforcement. The obligation only concerns the avoidance of barriers to international trade but appears to have a broader scope than trade in non-infringing goods. The obligation concerns the manner in which procedures are applied, which could allow challenges to general practices in the exercise of enforcement authority or, on one view, the application of enforcement procedures in individual instances.

D.   GATT 1994 AND OTHER WTO AGREEMENTS

WTO agreements besides TRIPS apply to intellectual property measures and to trade in IP-protected goods and services. The 1989 GATT panel report in *US – Section 337 Tariff Act* confirmed that GATT 1947 applied to an intellectual property enforcement procedure but it did not treat intellectual property as a barrier to trade. The first recital in the TRIPS preamble indicates that TRIPS is intended to complement GATT 1994 rather than to exclude its application. The 2005 panel reports in *EC – Trademarks and Geographical Indications* confirmed that TRIPS applies cumulatively with other WTO agreements, in particular, GATT 1994 and the Agreement on Technical Barriers to Trade ('TBT Agreement').[96] These trade liberalisation agreements can place limits on intellectual property protection and enforcement measures.

TRIPS and other WTO agreements are integral parts of the single Marrakesh Agreement Establishing the WTO,[97] hence they should be interpreted in a coherent and consistent manner, giving meaning to all applicable provisions harmoniously.[98] There

---

94. It reads as follows: '[t]hese procedures shall be *applied* in such a manner as [...] to *provide* for safeguards against their abuse' (emphasis added).
95. For example, in *EU and the Netherlands – Seizures of Generic Drugs in Transit*, India challenged *inter alia* 'the reiterated conduct and practice' of seizing generic drugs in transit: see WT/DS408/1.
96. Panel report, *EC – Trademarks and Geographical Indications (US)*, WT/DS174/R, paras. 7.208 and 7.227; Panel report, *EC – Trademarks and Geographical Indications (Australia)*, WT/DS290/R, paras. 7.244 and 7.263.
97. WTO Agreement, Art. II:2.
98. Appellate Body report, *US – Upland Cotton*, WT/DS267/AB/R, para. 549; Appellate Body report, *US – Anti-Dumping and Countervailing Duties (China)*, WT/DS379/AB/R, para. 570.

is no precedence clause between TRIPS and the WTO agreements on trade in goods and services. Although TRIPS is a minimum standards agreement that authorises higher levels of protection,[99] that authorisation does not extend to measures that violate provisions of other WTO agreements. While TRIPS and other WTO agreements may apply to the same measures in different ways, potential conflicts between them should be avoided to the extent possible through treaty interpretation.

This section considers several provisions of GATT 1994 that have a bearing on intellectual property measures as regards non-discrimination, freedom of transit, transparency and quantitative restrictions as well as the general exception for intellectual property enforcement measures. It then considers provisions of the TBT Agreement on unnecessary obstacles to trade and, finally, those in GATS on trade in services.

I. Non-discrimination

The national treatment obligation in Art. III:4 of GATT 1994 prohibits barriers to trade arising from protectionist domestic regulation, which includes intellectual property protection and enforcement measures. Art. III:4 applies to all laws, regulations and requirements affecting the domestic 'sale, offering for sale, purchase, transportation, distribution or use' of imported products, which intellectual property rights clearly affect. Governments remain free to choose their own level of regulation but must ensure that it does not discriminate in favour of domestic products.[100]

Claims regarding intellectual property measures have been upheld under Art. III:4 of GATT 1994 before and after the conclusion of TRIPS. The 1989 GATT panel in *US – Section 337 Tariff Act* found that an administrative procedure to enforce patents against imported products denied national treatment under GATT 1994 because it accorded less favourable treatment than US federal district court procedure, which was the only means available to enforce patents against US domestic products. The discriminatory treatment arose from the choice of forum, the possibility of simultaneous proceedings, the time-limits, the nature of the remedy, the automatic enforcement of the remedy and the inadmissibility of counterclaims.[101] The 2005 WTO panels in *EC – Trademarks and Geographical Indications* found that an EU regulation on geographical indications denied national treatment under GATT 1994 (and under TRIPS) because protection of geographical indications for imported products was conditional upon reciprocal and equivalent protection in the country of origin, and because government participation was required in the application procedure and product inspection structures.[102]

No absolute minimum standard of intellectual property protection or enforcement is prescribed by GATT 1994; the benchmark is relative and depends on the

---

99. TRIPS, Art. 1.3.
100. For example, this prohibits the enforcement of intellectual property rights in such a manner as to favour domestic products.
101. GATT panel report, *US – Section 337 Tariff Act* (*supra* n. 35), para. 5.20. Note that certain aspects were found justified under Art. XX(d): *ibid.*, para. 5.35.
102. Panel report, *EC – Trademarks and Geographical Indications (US)*, WT/DS174, para. 8.1(h); Panel report, *EC – Trademarks and Geographical Indications (Australia)*, WT/DS290/R, para. 8.1(i).

treatment accorded to like domestic products. The measures in the above cases were not found inconsistent with the national treatment obligation because they accorded ineffective or excessive intellectual property protection or enforcement. The panel in *EC – Trademarks and Geographical Indications* actually found no *prima facie* case regarding an allegedly prescriptive requirement of product inspections in the geographical indication regulation. While GATT 1994 does contain an obligation in Art. IX:6 regarding the use of geographically misleading trade names, it only requires consultation and sympathetic consideration.[103]

Measures subject to the national treatment obligation in Art. III:4 of GATT 1994 are also subject to the most-favoured-nation ('MFN') treatment obligation in Art. I:1. This obligation does not prescribe an absolute level of protection or degree of enforcement of intellectual property rights either, but in this case the relative benchmark depends on the treatment accorded to imported products from other countries of origin rather than domestic products. Unlike intellectual property conventions and TRIPS, the non-discrimination obligations in GATT 1994 apply as between products from different countries rather than between persons of different nationalities.

II.   Freedom of Transit

Freedom for goods to transit through the territory of other WTO Members is provided for in Art. V of GATT 1994.[104] Among other obligations, para. 3 prohibits 'any unnecessary delays or restrictions' to traffic in transit while para. 4 requires that regulations imposed on traffic in transit be 'reasonable'. Art. V does not define the circumstances in which intellectual property enforcement against goods in transit might be considered 'unnecessary' or 'reasonable'. Presumably, the risk of diversion of goods from transit into free circulation would be one relevant factor. The claims in *EU and the Netherlands – Seizures of Generic Drugs in Transit* alleged that enforcement of patent rights against traffic in transit (carried out on the basis that the goods infringed patents protected in the country of transit) violated these obligations as well as various TRIPS obligations but that dispute has not proceeded to the panel stage.[105]

The interpretation of the terms in Art. V of GATT 1994 needs to take account of TRIPS. While TRIPS does not prohibit intellectual property enforcement against goods in transit, it appears to imply that Members may apply its special border procedures to such goods, at least in some circumstances.[106] Therefore, as long as

---

103. See GATT panel report, *Japan – Alcoholic Beverages I*, GATT doc. L/6216, adopted 10 November 1987.
104. Para. 1 defines 'traffic in transit'. See further Panel report, *Colombia – Ports of Entry*, WT/DS366/R.
105. WT/DS408/1, WT/DS409/1. See further Grosse Ruse-Khan and Jaeger, 'Policing Patents Worldwide? – EC Border Measures against Transiting Generic Drugs under EC and WTO Intellectual Property Regimes', 40 International Review of Intellectual Property and Competition Law (IIC) 502 [2009]; Senftleben (*supra* n. 61) and M. Senftleben, 'The Seizure of Goods in Transit', chapter 5 of this book; Seuba (*supra* n. 52), chapter 11.
106. TRIPS, footnote 13 provides, relevantly: '[i]t is understood that there shall be no obligation to apply such procedures [...] to goods in transit'. See also Art. 9(4) of the Paris Convention (1967), as incorporated by Art. 2.1 of TRIPS.

intellectual property enforcement against goods in transit is considered necessary and reasonable in at least some circumstances for the purposes of Art. V of GATT 1994 (or justified by a general exception), a harmonious interpretation can give meaning to the provisions of both GATT 1994 and TRIPS with regards to goods in transit.

The Trade Facilitation Agreement ('TFA') may also provide relevant context. This new agreement has been inserted into the WTO Agreement to clarify and improve relevant aspects of Art. V and other articles of GATT 1994 with a view to further expediting the movement, release and clearance of goods, including goods in transit. It entered into force on 22 February 2017 for those WTO Members that had accepted it.[107] Among other things, Art. 11.7 of the TFA provides that goods under a transit procedure will not be subject to 'unnecessary delays or restrictions' until they conclude their transit and Art. 11.8 specifically prohibits the application of technical regulations or conformity assessment procedures to goods in transit. However, the TFA does *not* prohibit the application of intellectual property enforcement procedures to goods in transit, unlike these other types of measures.

III. Transparency and Procedural Fairness

Transparency and procedural fairness in the administration of trade regulation are provided for in Art. X of GATT 1994.[108] Para. 1 provides for publication of trade regulations, para. 2 provides for publication prior to enforcement and para. 3 provides for administration of these regulations in a 'uniform, impartial and reasonable manner', including tribunals and procedures for independent review of administrative action relating to customs matters.[109] These obligations deal with the publication and administration of measures rather than their substantive content.[110]

'Trade regulation' for the purposes of Art. X:1 includes intellectual property measures affecting the sale, distribution, exhibition and use of goods, and import and export restrictions, among other things. Abuses of intellectual property measures by government agencies could breach the obligation to administer trade regulations in a reasonable manner. Art. X overlaps with the procedural fairness and transparency obligations in Arts. 41, 62 and 63 of TRIPS. The claims in *EU and the Netherlands – Seizures of Generic Drugs in Transit* alleged violations of Art. X:3 of GATT 1994 as well as certain of these TRIPS obligations but the dispute has not proceeded to the panel stage.[111]

---

107. WTO, Protocol Amending the Marrakesh Agreement Establishing the World Trade Organization done at Geneva on 27 November 2014, Agreement on Trade Facilitation, Notification of entry into force, WT/Let/1241.
108. Appellate Body report, *US – Shrimp*, WT/DS58/AB/R, para. 182-3.
109. See, for example, Panel report, *Dominican Republic – Import and Sale of Cigarettes*, WT/DS302/R, paras. 7.383-7.388; Panel report, *Thailand – Cigarettes (Philippines)*, WT/DS371/R, para. 7.969; Panel report, *US – Certain Country of Origin Labelling Requirements*, WT/DS384/R, paras. 7.850-7.864.
110. Appellate Body report, *EC – Poultry*, WT/DS69/AB/R, para. 115.
111. See *supra* n. 105.

IV. Quantitative Prohibitions and Restrictions

The obligation in Art. XI:1 of GATT 1994 provides for the general elimination of quantitative prohibitions and restrictions on imports and exports. This obligation applies to any type of measure (besides duties, taxes and other charges[112]) that has a limiting effect on the quantity or amount of a product being imported or exported.[113] For example, the 1984 GATT panel report in *US – Manufacturing Clause* considered a provision in the US Copyright Act that banned the importation of printed material in which US authors owned the copyright, unless the materials were printed in the United States or Canada. There was no dispute that the ban was a quantitative prohibition inconsistent with Art. XI:1.[114]

The obligation in Art. XI:1 need not apply to border enforcement of intellectual property rights against imports. Enforcement of domestic regulation against imported products at the time or point of importation is subject to the national treatment obligation in Art. III, which allows border enforcement but prohibits discrimination between like domestic and imported products.[115] The position is the same regardless of whether the imported products are counterfeit, pirated or parallel imports under a national or regional exhaustion regime. The same analysis can also apply to the enforcement of exclusive importation rights, if they are considered part of a bundle of exclusive rights affecting domestic regulation of IP-protected products. If intellectual property enforcement at the time or point of importation is subject to Art. III, there is no need for Art. XI:1 to apply.[116]

However, the obligation to eliminate quantitative prohibitions and restrictions must apply to exclusive *exportation* rights. Border enforcement against exports is not part of domestic regulation and is not subject to Art. III. Therefore, border measures to enforce intellectual property rights against infringing goods at the point of exportation, allowed by Art. 51 of TRIPS, are inconsistent with Art. XI:1 of GATT 1994 (but they can nevertheless be justified under a general exception, considered below). Unlike TRIPS, the 1991 Act of UPOV provides for exclusive exportation rights for plant breeders and it also provides that these rights revive after national exhaustion, which prevents exportation of otherwise non-infringing material to countries where further propagation would be lawful.[117] These rights are also inconsistent with Art. XI:1 of GATT 1994.[118]

Further, compulsory licensing conditions that prohibit the export of products produced without the authorisation of the right holder are also inconsistent with Art. XI:1 of GATT 1994. A requirement of this kind is obligatory for copies of

---

112. However, the obligation does not apply to a closed list of measures in Art. XI:2.
113. Appellate Body report, *China – Raw Materials*, WT/DS431/AB/R, para. 320.
114. GATT panel report, *US – Manufacturing Clause*, GATT doc. L/5609, adopted 15 May 1984.
115. GATT 1994, *Ad* Note to Art. III. See GATT panel report, *US – Section 337 Tariff Act* (*supra* n. 41).
116. GATT panel report, *Canada – FIRA*, GATT doc. L/5504, adopted 7 February 1984, para. 5.14. See also panel report, *EC – Asbestos*, WT/DS135/R, paras. 8.86–8.100; Panel report, *India- Autos*, WT/DS146, paras. 7.255–7.261.
117. UPOV (1991), Arts. 14(1)(a)(v) and 16(1)(ii).
118. *Kennedy*, Export Restrictions in Plant Breeder's Rights, 20 Journal of International Economic Law 883 [2017].

translations or reproductions of copyright works produced in accordance with the Berne Appendix, as incorporated by Art. 9.1 of TRIPS.[119] A similar requirement applies to the predominant part of production under patent compulsory licences in accordance with Art. 31(f) of TRIPS.

Balance-of-payments import restrictions are not permitted where they would prevent compliance with 'patent, trade mark, copyright, or similar procedures'.[120] These would ensure imports of goods sufficient to satisfy patent working, trademark use and copyright translation requirements.

V. General Exceptions

The general exception in Art. XX(d) of GATT 1994 can justify inconsistencies between certain intellectual property enforcement measures and GATT obligations. However, no general exception is necessarily required for border enforcement of intellectual property laws and regulations against imports because, under GATT 1994, that is subject to the non-discrimination obligation in Art. III:4 and may therefore not be subject to the prohibition on quantitative restrictions in Art. XI:1 at all.[121] For example, the GATT panel report in *US – Section 337 Tariff Act* only considered the general exception in Art. XX(d) because it found border enforcement under section 337 to be discriminatory, not because it excluded imports.[122] General exceptions only serve a purpose where a GATT obligation is applicable to a given measure and the measure is inconsistent with that obligation.

The introductory clause to Art. XX and para. (d) read as follows:

> 'Subject to the requirement that such measures are not applied in a manner which would constitute a means of arbitrary or unjustifiable discrimination between countries where the same conditions prevail, or a disguised restriction on international trade, nothing in this Agreement shall be construed to prevent the adoption or enforcement by any contracting party of measures: [...]
>
> (d) necessary to secure compliance with laws or regulations which are not inconsistent with the provisions of this Agreement, including those relating to customs enforcement, the enforcement of monopolies operated under paragraph 4 of Article II and Article XVII, the protection of patents, trade marks and copyrights, and the prevention of deceptive practices;'

The general exceptions apply to all obligations in GATT 1994, as indicated by the words 'nothing in this Agreement' in the introductory clause. The general exceptions can justify measures inconsistent with any obligation set out above, not just quantitative restrictions. In practice, Art. XX(d) is raised in WTO disputes more often than not in relation to measures that are inconsistent with non-discrimination obligations in Art. III.[123]

---

119. Berne Appendix, Art. IV(4), as incorporated by TRIPS, Art. 9.1.
120. GATT 1994, Arts. XII:3(c)(iii) and XVIII:10.
121. *Supra* n. 115.
122. *Supra* n. 40.
123. For example, *Argentina – Hides and Leather*, WT/DS155; *Korea – Various Measures on Beef*, WT/DS161; *Canada – Wheat Exports and Grain Imports*, WT/DS276; *Dominican*

Art. XX(d) only applies to 'measures [...] to secure compliance', that is, enforcement measures. It does not apply to substantive standards of protection in intellectual property laws and regulations (the 'primary' laws and regulations).[124] Moreover, the primary laws and regulations themselves must not be inconsistent with GATT 1994.[125] Thus, Art. 51 of TRIPS can allow special border procedures against infringing goods at the point of exportation to secure compliance with exclusive rights that are consistent with GATT 1994. However, UPOV (1991) cannot provide for enforcement of exclusive exportation rights against otherwise non-infringing goods because that right in the primary law constitutes a quantitative restriction in breach of Art. XI:1.[126] Art. XX(d) is not an exception for GATT-*inconsistent* intellectual property laws and regulations but only for the enforcement of GATT-*consistent* intellectual property laws and regulations.

Art. XX(d) requires that the enforcement measures must be 'necessary' to secure compliance. In WTO jurisprudence, the assessment of necessity involves weighing and balancing a series of factors. The factors are the contribution made by the compliance measure to the enforcement of the law or regulation at issue, the relative importance of the interests protected by that law or regulation, and the impact on international trade of the law or regulation.[127] A comparison is also made with any reasonably available alternative that is GATT-consistent, or less GATT-inconsistent.[128] The express reference to patent, trademark and copyright laws in Art. XX(d), and the conclusion of TRIPS itself, are indicative of the importance of intellectual property protection and enforcement but nothing in either GATT 1994 or TRIPS calls for a blanket exception from GATT obligations for intellectual property rights. On the contrary, Art. XX(d) of GATT 1994 is heavily qualified and Art. 41.1 of TRIPS confirms that its enforcement procedures shall be applied in such a manner as to avoid the creation of barriers to legitimate trade.

Additional conditions in the introductory clause of Art. XX must also be satisfied to benefit from a general exception. These additional conditions, set out above, focus

---

Republic – Import and Sale of Cigarettes, WT/DS302; Mexico – Taxes on Soft Drinks, WT/DS308; Thailand – Cigarettes (Philippines) WT/DS371. Cf. Brazil – Retreaded Tyres, WT/DS332; US – Shrimp (Thailand) WT/DS343; Colombia – Ports of Entry, WT/DS366.

124. Patent, trademark and copyright laws are three examples of primary laws but the list is not exhaustive. Measures to secure compliance with laws and regulations regarding other intellectual property rights (including at least all of those provided for in TRIPS) can be covered.

125. For example, primary laws or regulations failed this condition in GATT panel report, *Japan – Agricultural Products I*, GATT doc. L/6253, adopted 2 February 1988, para. 5.2.2.3; Panel report, *Brazil – Retreaded Tyres*, WT/DS332, paras. 7.387–7.388; Panel report, *Thailand – Cigarettes (Philippines)*, WT/DS371, para. 7.758.

126. See *Kennedy* (supra n. 118) regarding plant variety protection laws that implement UPOV (1991).

127. Appellate Body report, *Korea – Various Measures on Beef*, WT/DS161/AB/R, paras. 162–164; Appellate Body report, *Dominican Republic – Import and Sale of Cigarettes*, WT/DS302/AB/R, paras. 65–66.

128. Appellate Body report, *Korea – Various Measures on Beef*, WT/DS161/AB/R, paras. 165–166, citing GATT panel report, *US – Section 337 Tariff Act*, para. 5.26; Appellate Body report, *Dominican Republic – Import and Sale of Cigarettes*, WT/DS302/AB/R, paras. 67–70.

on the manner in which a measure is applied in practice and are designed to prevent abuse of the general exceptions.[129]

Art. XX(d) was used to justify two discriminatory aspects of section 337 by the GATT panel in *US – Section 337 Tariff Act*. In contrast, the WTO panels in *EC – Trademarks and Geographical Indications* did not find any aspect of an EU geographical indications regulation justified by Art. XX(d). Art. XX(d) can also justify the application of TRIPS' special border procedures to infringing goods at the point of *exportation* provided that they are 'necessary' to secure compliance and the primary intellectual property laws are GATT-consistent.

There are significant differences between the context, terms and interpretation of Art. XX(d) of GATT 1994 and a similar provision in Art. 36 of the Treaty on the Functioning of the European Union ('TFEU').[130] The justification of quantitative restrictions is the sole function of Art. 36 TFEU, unlike Art. XX(d) of GATT 1994. The enforcement of intellectual property rights to restrain imports (in intra-EU trade) is *a priori* inconsistent with the prohibition on quantitative restrictions in Art. 34 TFEU, but not Art. XI:1 of GATT 1994. There is no condition that intellectual property measures must be consistent with the TFEU in Art. 36 because the purpose of the exception is to justify those that are not. EU jurisprudence has developed a concept of the specific subject-matter of an intellectual property right to reconcile border enforcement with free trade obligations[131] but GATT/WTO jurisprudence looks at the 'necessity' of a measure to secure compliance.[132]

Other general exceptions in Art. XX may also apply to intellectual property measures, if those measures satisfy the relevant conditions. For example, the general exception in Art. XX(b) for measures necessary to protect human, animal or plant life or health may justify restrictions on re-export of pharmaceuticals produced under compulsory licence for export to countries without manufacturing capacity in accordance with Art. 31*bis* of TRIPS.

VI.   Unnecessary Obstacles to International Trade

The TBT Agreement furthers the objectives of GATT 1994 as regards technical regulations, voluntary standards and procedures to assess conformity with them. The TBT Agreement not only includes national treatment and MFN treatment obligations in

---

129. Appellate Body report, *US – Gasoline*, WT/DS2/AB/R, p. 22; Appellate Body report, *Brazil – Retreaded Tyres*, WT/DS332/AB/R, para. 215.
130. Art. 36 TFEU provides, relevantly, as follows:
    'The provisions of Articles 34 and 35 shall not preclude prohibitions or restrictions on imports, exports or goods in transit justified on grounds of [...] the protection of industrial and commercial property. Such prohibitions or restrictions shall not, however, constitute a means of arbitrary discrimination or a disguised restriction on trade between Member States.'
131. See *Christopher Heath*, 'Parallel Imports, Exhaustion and International Trade', chapter 2 of this book.
132. On the contrary, a WTO panel rejected the notion of an essential right or hierarchy among exclusive rights, albeit in a different context regarding 'limited' exceptions to patent rights for the purposes of Art. 30 of TRIPS: see Panel report, *Canada – Pharmaceutical Patents*, WT/DS114/R, para. 7.33.

Arts. 2.1 and 5.1.1 but it also contains obligations that prohibit unnecessary obstacles to international trade in Arts. 2.2 and 5.1.2, while recognising WTO Members' right to implement measures to achieve legitimate policy objectives. Among other things, legitimate objectives include the prevention of deceptive practices, which is interpreted widely to cover preventing consumers from being misled.[133]

Certain systems for the protection of geographical indications operate like technical regulations and may therefore be subject to the obligations of the TBT Agreement, as well as TRIPS. A 'technical regulation' is defined as a document that lays down 'product characteristics' with which compliance is 'mandatory'.[134] The EU schemes for geographical indications specify requirements for the use of protected terms on a label, which is a 'product characteristic'.[135] The labelling requirements may be considered 'mandatory' because the product specifications are binding and enforceable, even though there is no legal obligation to use a protected term. Two claims in EC – Trademarks and Geographical Indications (Australia) challenged labelling and product inspection requirements in a geographical indication regulation under the TBT Agreement.[136] Other WTO dispute settlement reports have found labelling requirements for the use of trade descriptions 'mandatory' even though products could legally be marketed without them.[137] If the conditions of use of geographical indications on labels are 'technical regulations', the inspection structures that ensure conformity with the conditions of use would constitute conformity assessment procedures, and both would be subject to the obligations in the TBT Agreement. Aspects of geographical indication protection that implement TRIPS obligations would benefit from a presumption that TRIPS and the TBT Agreement do not conflict, but that is not an authorisation to implement TRIPS obligations in the most trade-restrictive manner.

Labelling requirements in related quality schemes to protect traditional terms for wines – which are not required by TRIPS – may also constitute technical regulations. These schemes regulate the use of certain particulars on wine labels: both those indicating that a wine has a geographical indication (such as *Appellation d'origine contrôlée*) and descriptive terms for product characteristics (such as *Auslese, château, reserva* and *vino dulce natural*).[138] The scheme protects many dictionary terms but restricts their use and registration as trademarks to wines that have certain geographical indications and conform to certain product specifications. This creates a barrier

---

133. Panel report, *US – Tuna II (Mexico)*, WT/DS381/R, para. 7.437.
134. TBT Agreement, Annex 1.1.
135. Regulation (EU) No. 1308/2013, establishing a common organisation of the markets for agricultural products, (OJ L 347/671 of 20 December 2013), Art. 103 (regarding geographical indications for wines); Regulation (EU) No. 1151/2012 on quality schemes for agricultural products and foodstuffs (OJ L 343/1 of 14 December 2012), Art. 13.
136. The claim of discrimination failed due to lack of evidence of differential treatment. The claim of an unnecessary obstacle to trade failed because it was filed under the wrong provision of that agreement: see Panel report, *EC – Trademarks and Geographical Indications (Australia)*, WT/DS290/R, Sections VII:B.5 and C.
137. Appellate Body report, *EC – Sardines*, WT/DS231/AB/R, para. 195 re 'preserved sardines'; Appellate Body report, *US – Tuna II (Mexico)*, WT/DS381/AB/R, paras. 178–199, re 'dolphin-safe' tuna.
138. Regulation (EU) No. 1308/2013 (*supra* n. 135), Arts. 112 to 116.

to trade in wines from countries with different definitions of the same terms that are not recognised in the country of importation, while the variety of definitions of particular terms recognised for use with domestic wines may not prevent consumer confusion. The scheme may be inconsistent with obligations in the TBT Agreement on non-discrimination and unnecessary obstacles to international trade.[139]

Product marking and labelling requirements – including those that apply to goods produced under compulsory licence – are 'technical regulations' covered by the TBT Agreement. Certain requirements of this kind are obligatory for copyright works produced under compulsory licence in accordance with the Berne Appendix, as incorporated by Art. 9.1 of TRIPS,[140] and for patented products produced under compulsory licence in accordance with the 2003 Waiver[141] or Art. 31*bis* of TRIPS and the TRIPS Annex. Measures implementing these requirements also need to respect TBT obligations.

The claims in *Australia – Tobacco plain packaging* are made under the TBT Agreement, as well as TRIPS and GATT 1994. The measures at issue regulate the use of trademarks on tobacco packaging to discourage smoking. The complainants allege, among other things, that the measures discriminate against imported products and are more trade-restrictive than necessary to fulfil a legitimate objective, inconsistently with Arts. 2.1 and 2.2 of the TBT Agreement.[142] The panel reports are expected in 2018.

VII. Trade in Services

The General Agreement on Trade in Services[143] ('GATS') is modelled on GATT 1994 and applies to measures affecting trade in services even if they also affect trade in goods. The scope of trade in services includes not only cross-border supply (where the supplier and consumer are in different countries, as in many online transactions) but also services consumed abroad and services supplied domestically by foreign companies through commercial establishment or staff. GATS provides for MFN treatment, subject to a list of exemptions, while important obligations on market access and national treatment only apply where a WTO Member has made a specific commitment in terms of the relevant service sub-sector and mode of delivery. For example, Members may make commitments on, say, cross-border supply of telecommunications services which may have implications for the blocking of access to Internet content based on the determined location of a networked device or 'geoblocking'.[144]

Intellectual property enforcement can affect trade in services and therefore be subject to GATS disciplines and commitments. Enforcement measures can affect

---

139. See *Kennedy*, Sober reflection on traditional terms for wines, 8 Queen Mary Journal of Intellectual Property 114 [2018].
140. Berne Appendix, Arts. IV(3) and IV(5), as incorporated by TRIPS, Art. 9.1.
141. Decision of the General Council of 30 August 2003, Implementation of paragraph 6 of the Doha Declaration on the TRIPS Agreement and Public Health, WT/L/540 and Corr.1 (1 September 2003).
142. Requests for the establishment of a panel, *Australia – Tobacco Plain Packaging*, WT/DS435/16; WT/DS441/15; WT/DS458/14; WT/DS467/15.
143. General Agreement on Trade in Services, Annex 1B to the WTO Agreement (*supra* n. 5).
144. See *Marketa Trimble*, 'Geoblocking and "Legitimate Trade"', chapter 3 of this book.

the delivery of infringing services (such as audiovisual) or services associated with infringing goods (such as retailing). Many exclusive rights conferred by intellectual property protection (such as broadcasting, selling and manufacturing) are services while trademarks can themselves be protected in respect of services. Section 2 of Part III of TRIPS refers expressly to enforcement against infringing services.[145] A 2008 claim was filed under TRIPS alleging a failure to protect confidential information in a case involving trade in financial information services.[146] Free trade agreement provisions on limitations on civil liability for copyright infringement by online service providers also illustrate the potential for intellectual property enforcement to create barriers to trade in services.[147]

In summary, TRIPS is not the only WTO agreement that applies to intellectual property protection and enforcement. Certain recent WTO disputes have focused attention on the fact that GATT 1994 and the TBT Agreement can also prevent intellectual property measures from creating barriers to legitimate trade.

E. CONCLUSION

The need to ensure that intellectual property enforcement measures and procedures do not themselves become barriers to legitimate trade is part of the object and purpose of TRIPS. Although it applies in relation to border measures against the importation of counterfeit goods, it was also motivated by concerns regarding section 337 of the US Tariff Act of 1930 at the time of the launch of the Uruguay Round in 1986. The subsequent GATT panel report on *US – Section 337 Tariff Act* clarified that GATT 1947 applied to intellectual property laws and regulations. Today, GATT 1994 and TRIPS can operate in a complementary manner to avoid barriers to legitimate trade.

Part III of TRIPS establishes a general obligation to apply its specific intellectual property enforcement procedures in such a manner as to avoid the creation of barriers to legitimate trade. This is reflected in numerous aspects of the specific enforcement procedures and remedies provided for in Part III, few of which are mandatory in any given instance. However, the general obligation may also create a performance standard regarding the way in which competent authorities apply those specific procedures in practice, notably as regards the manner in which they exercise their discretionary authority to grant, deny or limit particular remedies.

Other WTO agreements can discipline intellectual property protection and enforcement measures. GATT 1994 contains obligations on non-discrimination, freedom of transit of goods, the elimination of quantitative restrictions and transparency while the TBT Agreement also contains obligations on non-discrimination and unnecessary obstacles to international trade. As highlighted in recent intellectual property disputes, these obligations can prevent intellectual property measures from creating barriers to legitimate trade, including in circumstances where TRIPS itself does not.

---

145. TRIPS, Art. 47.
146. Request for consultations, *China – Measures Affecting Financial Information Services and Foreign Information Service Suppliers,* WT/DS372/1. The matter later settled: see WT/DS372/4.
147. See, for example, United States-Australia free trade agreement (2004), Art. 17.11.29; United States-Peru Trade Promotion Agreement (2006), Art. 16.11.29.

PART 2

INTELLECTUAL PROPERTY RIGHTS AS OBSTACLES TO INTERNATIONAL TRADE?

CHAPTER 2
Parallel Imports of Patented Goods

Christopher Heath

'It is astonishing that the WTO Agreement should still consider it compatible with fair world trade for consumers in different countries to be played off against each other'[1]

A. INTRODUCTION

I. The Legal Context

In the context of international trade, the territorial nature of intellectual property rights may be perceived as an obstacle. This indeed is the position taken by the **General Agreement on Tariffs and Trade 1947/1994** (hereinafter GATT 1994)[2] and the **Treaty establishing the European Economic Community** (hereinafter EC Treaty).[3] Particularly in the context of the latter, the ECJ identified under which circumstances these obstacles were legitimate, thereby also defining what it perceived as legitimate trade.[4]

The **Paris Convention**[5] from 1883, on the other hand, makes the principle of territoriality and independence of industrial property rights one of its cornerstones

---

1. *Ullrich*, 'Technology Protection according to TRIPs', in *Beier/Schricker* (eds.), From GATT to TRIPS, Weinheim 1996, 357, 385.
2. In fact, the provisions of the GATT Agreement referred to are those of 1947, yet formally incorporated in the GATT 1994. See General Agreement on Tariffs and Trade 1994, Annex 1A to the Marrakesh Agreement Establishing the World Trade Organization, signed on 15 April 1994, entered into force on 1 January 1995, 33 I.L.M. 1167 (1994).
3. Treaty establishing the European Economic Community as signed on 25 March 1957, 298 U.N.T.S. 3. This treaty was amended by the Treaty on European Union, signed on 7 February 1992, 31 I.L.M. 253.
4. See also chapter 4 for a discussion of the case-law regarding the relationship between the free movement of goods and the application of IP rules as barriers to trade.
5. Paris Convention for the Protection of Industrial Property, adopted in Paris on 20 March 1883, entered into force on 7 July 1884; last revised at the Stockholm Revision Conference,

that Member States ('*ressortissants*') have to respect. This may also have – albeit different – repercussions on what should be considered as legitimate obstacles to trade.

The Agreement on Trade-related Aspects of Intellectual Property Rights[6] (hereinafter TRIPS), concluded in 1994 within the World Trade Organization framework, embraces both of the above rather contradictory concepts by starting from a different paradigm: that the protection of intellectual property rights is a precondition to free trade in providing a level playing field.[7] This again may require a re-definition of legitimate trade and thereby legitimate obstacles to trade by balancing both of the above concepts, or giving precedence to one, or developing an entirely new solution.

II. The Factual Context

'**Parallel importation**' refers to goods lawfully produced in the country of origin and subsequently imported into another country by a person who is not the original manufacturer or licensee.[8] Where such goods fall within the scope of a patent in the country of importation, the act of importation (and, of course, subsequent sale) already fall under to the exclusive scope of the patent granted to the domestic patentee, and the latter could prevent such importation without consent unless the patentee is barred from exercising his rights. In that sense, the domestic patent becomes an import restriction and thereby an obstacle to trade. Whether the importation of such goods in the above-described circumstances is legitimate will be the subject of the following analysis.

For the importation of patented products, the following scenarios can be envisaged:

(a) The patentee in the country of importation has marketed the goods abroad either himself or they have been marketed with his consent. In the country of exportation, one of the following conditions applied:
 (i) there was a corresponding patent in force;
 (ii) there was no patent protection because the patentee never sought patent protection;
 (iii) there was no patent in force at the time of marketing because the patent has expired;
 (iv) there was no patent protection because the patent application was rejected for not meeting the criteria of patentability; or

---

adopted in Stockholm on 14 July 1967 and entered into force 26 April 1970, 828 U.N.T.S. 305 (hereinafter Paris Convention).
6. Agreement on Trade-Related Aspects of Intellectual Property Rights, Annex 1C of the Marrakesh Agreement Establishing the World Trade Organization, signed on 15 April 1994, 33 I.L.M. 1197 (1994).
7. 'The notion of the free trade in goods is replaced by the idea of a qualified trade in technologies and in goods embodying or including technologies' (Ullrich, *supra* n. 1, 377). This is also clear from Art. 7 TRIPS, which states the objective of TRIPS as promotion of technological innovation. Note that Matthew Kennedy in chapter 1 of this book takes a different view and regards the approach to intellectual property rights in GATT and TRIPS as consistent.
8. Also referred to as 'grey' goods. Yet, as these are goods produced and sold legally, there is nothing 'grey' about them, as the English Patents Court in a decision of 9 October 1995 correctly pointed out: *Roussel Uclaf v. Hockley Int'l*, [1996] R.P.C. 441.

(iv) there was no patent protection because the invention was not considered patentable subject matter.
(b) The goods have not been marketed in the country of exportation by the patentee or with his consent, but these goods were lawfully marketed there by a third party:
  (i) in the absence of any patent protection;
  (ii) under a compulsory licence; or
  (iii) having obtained the patent from the patentee of the country of importation.

The consequences of a patentee's ability to prevent parallel importation and thereby to interfere with international commerce have been forcefully described in a decision of the Commercial Court Zurich (note that Switzerland is a small, land-locked country that particularly depends on free commerce):

> 'As the Judicial Commission of the High Court Lucerne in its decision of 11 December 1987 has stated, [a patentee's right to prevent parallel imports] would lead to untenable consequences. 'An international businessman could, e.g., use a patented writing tool in the course of his business only in the country where it was bought'. The example is harmless. Indeed, international trade would collapse. E.g., every foreign merchant travelling to Switzerland on business would not be allowed to use his technical appliances (if patented here and there) and would thus be unable to work. If, to take an example based on the subject matter of this case, an English commercial photographer bought the Kodak films in question in England, he would not be allowed to use them for shooting in Switzerland. In order not to commit a patent infringement, he would have to buy the films here. Then, however, he would not be allowed to export them for development to England, as he would have to do this here. The same for further copies. He could only sell the negatives in the country where the film was bought. And if one further imagines that such photographer was following, e.g., the Tour de France that for one etappe comes to Switzerland and that all patented products (helmets, glasses, gloves, tools, wireless devices, film and photo cameras, medicinal products, doping products, etc.) that were not purchased in Switzerland and do not come under Art. 5ter(2) Paris Convention would have to be left at the border and purchased again in Switzerland to be used, it becomes clear that such a scenario is not in conformity with the purposes of patent law. Patent law should serve promotion of the economy, not its paralysis. Also in industrial production where products in the course of their manufacture are transported from one country to another, it would hardly be thinkable that the patentee having sold a patented device in country A to be built into a product that is further processed in country B and finalised in country C, in order to be sold in countries D and E, would claim licensing fees for countries B and C and seizure of the infringing products in countries D and E. Obviously, the interests of the patentee have to give way in favour of those of commerce and consumers interested in the free circulation of products once sold by the entitled person [...] In addition, there is no public interest, let alone an overwhelming public interest in preventing parallel imports.'[9]

---

9. Zurich Commercial Court, decision of 23 October 1998, GRUR Int. 1999, 555 (*Kodak*) (overturned by the Swiss Federal Supreme Court).

At first glance, one would thus assume that international trade agreements were meant to facilitate international trade and reduce barriers thereto.

B. THE GATT 1994 CONTEXT

I. Free Trade and the Protection of 'Patents, Trade Marks and Copyrights'

The case of GATT 1994 and parallel imports is relatively straightforward: according to Art. XI GATT 1994[10,11] importation of products is permitted unless specifically mentioned in this provision, or under the general exceptions of Art. XX. As invoking intellectual property rights to prevent importation is not covered by Art. XI, it is necessary to interpret the exception specified in Art. XX(d) GATT 1994, which reads:

> *Article XX: General Exceptions*
>
> Subject to the requirement that such measures are not applied in a manner which would constitute a means of arbitrary or unjustifiable discrimination between countries where the same conditions prevail, or a disguised restriction on international trade, nothing in this Agreement shall be construed to prevent the adoption or enforcement by any contracting party of measures: [...]
>
> (d) necessary to secure compliance with laws or regulations which are not inconsistent with the provisions of this Agreement, including those relating to customs enforcement, the enforcement of monopolies operated under paragraph 4 of Article II and Article XVII, the protection of patents, trade marks and copyrights, and the prevention of deceptive practices.

While the exception mentions patents, such exception in itself must not be interpreted as an arbitrary or unjustifiable discrimination or a disguised restriction on international trade. In addition, as an exception (and in the framework of GATT, an obstacle to international trade) it must as such be interpreted narrowly. The scope of the patent right invoked against the importation of goods must thus be interpreted in conformity with the general purposes of GATT to facilitate international trade. It is

---

10. Article XI GATT: 'General Elimination of Quantitative Restrictions 1. No prohibitions or restrictions other than duties, taxes or other charges, whether made effective through quotas, import or export licences or other measures, shall be instituted or maintained by any contracting party on the importation of any product of the territory of any other contracting party or on the exportation or sale for export of any product destined for the territory of any other contracting party.'
11. Note that Art. XI is a more appropriate provision than Art. III. Art. III from its wording covers goods after they have been imported: 'should be applied to imported products'. But see also GATT panel report, *US – Section 337 Tariff Act*, paras. 5.7 and 5.10 that applies Art. III (and the corresponding note to Art. III that applies Art. III to border enforcement measures). The latter is not at issue here, because the case of parallel imports does not concern the enforcement of a law, but its substantive interpretation. If importation of products put into commerce abroad by the domestic patentee is not deemed infringing, there is nothing to enforce when such goods are imported. If they are deemed infringing, border enforcement measures apply. In other words, the problem concerning the importation of goods without the consent of the right owner is not one of border measures or border enforcement, but of the interpretation of the substantive laws at issue (patent, trade marks, copyrights).

based on this premise that the jurisprudence of the ECJ to balance intra-Community free trade with the protection of intellectual property rights can be a useful guidance in balancing both interests. After all, the provisions of Arts. 28, 30 EC Treaty (now Arts. 34, 36 Treaty on the Functioning of the European Union, TFEU) are worded in exactly the same way as Arts. XI, XX(d) GATT 1994.[12]

II. The Case Law of the ECJ on Free Trade and the Protection of Patent Rights

Until Art. 29 of the Agreement on a Unified Patent Court enters into force, substantive patent law and thus also the corresponding exhaustion rules remain a domestic affair of the respective EU Member States. Still, national exhaustion rules may be superseded by the principles of intra-Community free trade according to Arts. 28 and 30 of the EC Treaty (as they then were in Treaty of Nice; now Arts. 33, 36 TFEU). According to European case law, intra-Community parallel imports of patented products can only be objected to where the 'specific object'[13] of patent law would so require. Or, worded differently, the patent existing in the country of importation can only be invoked against parallel imports from other Member States in situations that would merit a derogation from the principle of free intra-Community trade. This is the case where the specific object of the patent is concerned. The latter is defined as:

> 'Inter alia to ensure to the holder, so as to recompense the creative effort of the inventor, the exclusive right to utilise an invention with a view to the manufacture and first putting into circulation of industrial products, either directly or by the grant of licences to third parties as well as the right to oppose any infringement.'[14]

The specific object thus seemed to refer to two conditions: compensation and consent. It was thus uncontroversial that the patentee could object to the parallel importation of patented products in cases where these had been produced in another Member State under a compulsory licence:[15] the patentee had not consented, nor could it be said that he had obtained an equitable reward under market conditions. The issue was far more controversial in cases of parallel imports from Community countries where no patent protection (at least for this type of invention) was available. The first case concerned the parallel importation of pharmaceuticals from Italy to the Netherlands. The products had been manufactured in Italy by the Dutch patentee who, however, was unable to obtain an Italian patent for these, as patent protection for pharmaceuticals did not exist in Italy at that time. The court decided that *consent* was enough and held that:

---

12. Note that the exception in Art. XX(d) GATT already refers back to the common principles by requiring exceptions not to be 'inconsistent with the provisions of this agreement', in other words requiring the provisions of e.g. patent law to be measured against the freedoms of GATT rather than to give a blanket exception. The test developed by the European Court of Justice for the TFEU is thereby already explicitly mandated by Art. XX GATT.
13. ECJ, *Deutsche Grammophon GmbH v. Metro-SB-Grossmarkte GmbH & Co, KG*, case C-78/70, [1971] ECR. 487, para. 11.
14. ECJ, *Centrafarm v. Sterling Drug*, 31 October 1974, case C-15/74, [1974] ECR 1147.
15. ECJ, *Pharmon v. Hoechst*, 9 July 1985, case C-19/84, [1985] ECR 2281.

'It is for the proprietor of the patent to decide, in the light of all the circumstances, under what conditions he will market his product, including the possibility of marketing it in a member state where the law does not provide patent protection for the product in question. If he decides to do so he must then accept the consequences of his choice as regards the free movement of the product within the common market, which is a fundamental principle forming part of the legal and economic circumstances which must be taken into account by the proprietor of the patent in determining the manner in which his exclusive right will be exercised.'[16]

This approach of course disregards the function of securing the patentee a market-based reward for every product sold *under the monopolistic conditions of a patent*. After all, a product sold in the absence of a patent can never give the producer a reward under monopolistic conditions, and thus never trigger exhaustion:

'The doctrine of exhaustion was hardly appropriate to the *Merck* case: there was no Italian right to be exhausted by Merck selling a drug in Italy. The result was that to some extent Merck was deprived of any benefit from their patent rights in Holland. The parallel imported drugs were free of royalty [...] I think these matters are a good reason for referring the question to the court.'[17]

The subsequent case referred to the ECJ by the English High Court concerned the parallel importation of pharmaceutical products from Spain and Portugal into the United Kingdom. While the products had been placed on the market in those countries by the patentee or with his consent, no pharmaceutical patent protection could have been obtained in these countries at that time. The Advocate General was in favour of overturning *Merck v. Stephar*:

'The strongest argument in favour of the pharmaceutical companies' interpretation of *Centrafarm v. Sterling Drug* is that, since the specific subject matter consists of the exclusive right of first marketing the patented product, a rule permitting parallel imports of such products marketed by the patentee in a member state where no patent protection exists and where, consequently, the patentee was subject to potential competition at the first marketing stage, would empty that exclusive right of much of its significance, i.e. the patentee must at least have had the opportunity of obtaining monopoly profits in the exporting member state before its national rights in the importing member state can be said to have been exhausted.'[18]

Also some academics, including this author, took the view that consent to marketing was insufficient to describe the specific object of a patent.[19]

---

16. ECJ, *Merck v. Stephar*, 14 July 1981, case C-187/80, [1981] ECR 2063.
17. English High Court, *Merck v. Primecrown*, (1995) F.S.R. 909, 913, 914.
18. Opinion of AC Fennelly for joined cases *Merck v. Primecrown*, C-267/95, and *Beecham v. Europharm*, case C-268/95, decided 5 December 1996, [1996] ECR I-6285.
19. *Demaret*, 'Industrial Property Rights, Compulsory Licenses and the Free Movement of Goods Under Community Law', 18 International Review of Intellectual Property and Competition Law (IIC) 161, 176 (1987); *Heath*, 'Zur Paralleleinfuhr patentierter Erzeugnisse', 1997 Recht der Internationalen Wirtschaft (RIW) 541, 544. But see, *Beier*, 'Gewerblicher Rechtsschutz und freier Warenverkehr im europäischen Binnenmarkt und im Verkehr mit Drittstaaten',

The ECJ remained unconvinced and affirmed the principle of *Merck v. Stephar*:

> 'The court held, finally, in paragraphs 11 and 13 of *Merck* that it was for the holder of the patent to decide, in the light of all the circumstances, under what conditions he would market his product, including the possibility of marketing it in a member state where the law did not provide patent protection for the product in question. If he decides to do so, he must then accept the consequences of his choice as regards free movement of the product within the common market. This being a fundamental principle forming part of the legal and economic circumstances which the holder of the patent must take into account in determining how to exercise his exclusive right. Under those conditions, to permit an inventor to invoke a patent held by him in one member state in order to prevent the importation of the product freely marketed by him in another member state where the product was not patentable would cause a partitioning of national markets contrary to the aims of the treaty.'[20]

Based on the above case law, patentees would thus be unable to prevent the parallel importation of products from newly acceding Member States even where patent protection was not available in the country of exportation.

The ECJ's approach of consented marketing has also been adopted by a number of other countries that permit *international* exhaustion on such a condition, for example Thailand,[21] Argentina,[22] South Africa[23] and the United States.[24]

III. Free Trade and Patent Rights in the GATT Context

As mentioned above, also in the GATT context, the exception under Art. XX(d) must be interpreted in a way that does not negate or supersede the rule of free importation

---

 1989 Gewerblicher Rechtsschutz und Urheberrecht (GRUR) Int. 603, 613. Only as an aside, such interpretation would have made superfluous the introduction of a so-called 'specific mechanism' in order to prevent the parallel importation of patented products from East European EU Member States.
20. ECJ, *Merck v. Primecrown*, 5 December 1996, joined cases C-267/95, and ECJ, *Beecham v. Europharm*, case C-2668/95, both decided 5 December 1996, [1996] ECR I-6285.
21. Sec. 36(3)(vii) Thai Patent Act as of 27 March 1999.
22. According to Sec. 36 Argentinean Patent Act, 'The right granted by any patent shall not have effect against: [...] (c) any person that acquires, uses, imports or commercialises in any way the product patented or obtained by the patented process, *once such product has been lawfully marketed in any country*.' (Emphasis added.) This provision, of course, goes way beyond the above consent rule, as it basically obliges any patentee to obtain patents in all countries of the world to obtain proper protection. In the author's opinion, this is difficult to justify within the framework of TRIPS.
23. The relevant provision cannot be found in South Africa's Patent Act, but in Sec. 15C(a) of the Medicines and Related Substances Control Act of 1965, as amended in 1997. The amendment at first did come into force due to lawsuits by several pharmaceutical companies. As these lawsuits were withdrawn in 2002, the amendment could be enacted. For details, see *Kongolo*, 'Towards a new fashion of protecting pharmaceutical patents in Africa', 33 IIC 185, 194 (2002).
24. US Supreme Court, *Impression Products v. Lexmark International*, 30 May 2017, 581 US.___ (2017).

stipulated in Art. XI, as otherwise the exception would be 'inconsistent with the provisions of this agreement'. This indicates that patent rights cannot be invoked against any importation of products covered by a patent in the country of importation, but only against the importation of goods that do not conform to 'legitimate trade'. In this respect, the European Court of Justice has defined legitimate trade in patented goods as the trade in such goods that have been marketed abroad by the patentee (that is, the owner of the patent in the country of importation), or with his consent. As mentioned above, also other definitions are possible, namely a definition that examines whether the patentee could receive a monopolistic reward in the country of first marketing.[25]

It appears that the ECJ (and the jurisdictions listed above) would permit parallel importation under any of scenarios as listed under A.II above (a), but under none of scenarios (b).[26] Advocate General Fennelly opined that parallel importation should be allowed under scenario (a) (i), but not under scenario (a) (iv). There is a general agreement that parallel importation should not be allowed under scenarios (b) (i) and (ii), as the patentee has neither given consent nor received a reward. Goods marketed under these scenarios could still qualify as legitimate trade, namely within the country of first marketing, or for the purposes of transit, but not for the purposes of importation. This author has taken the view that where the core of a patent right is the reward to be obtained from the first marketing of patented products under monopolistic conditions, only scenarios (a) (i) and (b) (iii) are compliant therewith.[27] Whichever conditions one regards as the most appropriate to define 'legitimate trade', it would appear that categorically excluding parallel imports of patented products from third countries is not compliant with the GATT regime,[28] first as an arbitrary discrimination, and second as an interpretation of patent rights which goes beyond what a patent should confer and is thus 'inconsistent with the provisions of this agreement'.[29]

---

25. The question to be asked under patent law is whether and under what conditions a patent right for a specific product can no longer be exercised (is 'exhausted') – after the first domestic commercial marketing (which is generally held to be so), or also under the first marketing abroad. The Tokyo High Court (decision of 23 March 1995, 27 IIC 550 (1996) (*BBS Car Wheels II*)) saw it this way: 'There is no difference to the case of national exhaustion where the patent holder puts goods into circulation abroad and can determine the prices for the patented products of his own free will as a remuneration for the disclosure of his invention. This means, the opportunity of the patent holder to receive compensation for the disclosure of his invention is limited to one opportunity. Under the material aspect of the above-cited doctrine of national exhaustion in accordance with economic development, it does not make any particular difference whether the putting into circulation takes place within this country or abroad.'
26. See *supra* section A.II.
27. *Heath*, 'Parallel Imports and International Trade', 28 IIC 623 (1997).
28. This is true both for 'national exhaustion' that only distinguishes between domestic and imported products, and for 'regional exhaustion' where parallel imports from certain countries are considered lawful, while from others not (as is the case for the EU).
29. As is argued by *Freytag*, Parallelimporte nach EG- und WTO-Recht, 2001, 282 (based on Arts. XI and XX of GATT); *Kraus*, Les Importations Parallèles de Produits Brevetés, 2004, 178 (based on Art. XI of GATT); also *Drexl*, 'EU Competition Law and Trade in Pharmaceuticals: Lessons to be Learnt from WTO/TRIPS?', in *Rosen* (ed.), Intellectual Property at the Crossroads of Trade, Elgar 2011, 1, 17.

2. Parallel Imports of Patented Goods

One should add that apart from the 'patent-related' solutions developed by the ECJ, a trade-related approach to the question of parallel importation with a particular emphasis on unimpeded trade has also been developed in the context of the British Empire.

Under English common law,

> 'it is open to the patentee, by virtue of his statutory monopoly, to make a sale sub modo, or accompanied by restrictive conditions which would not apply in the case of ordinary chattels; [...] the imposition of these conditions in the case of a sale is not presumed, but, on the contrary, a sale having occurred, the presumption is that the full right of ownership was meant to be vested in the purchaser while [...] the owner's rights in a patented chattel would be limited, if there is brought home to him the knowledge of conditions imposed, by the patentee or those representing the patentee, upon him at the time of sale.'[30]

In other words, the patentee is allowed to impose limited conditions upon selling his goods, while an ordinary vendor of goods may not. This rule applies both to domestic sales and sales abroad. Parallel importation of goods produced abroad is permissible if these goods were produced with the consent of the domestic patent owner and subsequently sold without any clear notice of restriction. This rule applies regardless of the existence of any patent rights in the exporting country.[31]

The emphasis of this solution is on the visibility of restrictions. While the patentee can impose import restrictions on the goods, these are only valid if the purchaser bought the goods 'with the knowledge brought home to him of the limitation of his rights'. This position was then reiterated in the 1995 *Roussel Uclaf* case:

> '[The plaintiff] does say that the product as supplied from France was in drums bearing the label "For use in PRC only – re-export forbidden." The defendants answered that by an express challenge concerning the labelling of the drums. They had bought a drum which did not bear that legend [...] and I must take it that some drums were so marked but others were not so marked. I could well understand how somebody receiving two kinds of drums might think that they were entirely free positively to export those which are not so labelled, even in a joint venture company. So it is not established that it was brought home to the Chinese joint venture company by the labels on the drums that there should be no export whatever of deltamethrin technical grade.'[32]

This trade-related solution has also been embraced by the Japanese Supreme Court:[33]

> 'If the patented products were marketed abroad, then it can be naturally expected that such goods may be imported into Japan if the patentee puts such goods into circulation abroad without any reservations at the time of transfer. The transferee or any other subsequent purchaser is understood to have purchased the product without any restrictions that might apply to such products in Japan.'

---

30. UK Privy Council, *National Photograph Company of Australia Ltd. v. Menck* [1911] 28 R.P.C. 229, 248.
31. UK Court of Appeal, *Betts v. Willmott* [1871] LR 6 Ch. App. 239.
32. UK High Court, *Roussel Uclaf S.A. v. Hockley Int'l Ltd.*, [1996] R.P.C 441 (P.C.) 444.
33. Japanese Supreme Court, 1 July 1997, 29 IIC 331 (1998) (*BBS Car Wheels III*).

The above solution has the benefit of simplicity and may go some way to addressing the above-mentioned concerns of the Zurich Commercial Court regarding impediments to trade.

C. THE PARIS CONVENTION CONTEXT

I. Territoriality as a Fundamental Principle of the Paris Convention

The above result (banning parallel imports of patented products per se as non-compliant with GATT 1994) may not stand up to scrutiny if WTO Members are bound by prior agreements to give an interpretation to patent rights that would require them to ban parallel imports of patented products in all of the above-mentioned circumstances. This case has been argued for the principle of territoriality enshrined in the Paris Convention. Put differently, the exceptions for patents under Art. XX(d) GATT 1994 would have to be interpreted more broadly if the Paris Convention (as an accepted international standard of industrial property rights) required such interpretation.

The principle of territoriality (or independence of rights) for patents is enshrined in Art. 4*bis* Paris Convention, which reads:

> '(1) Patents applied for in the various countries of the Union by nationals of countries of the Union shall be independent of patents obtained for the same invention in other countries whether members of the Union or not.
>
> (2) The foregoing provision is to be understood in an unrestricted sense, in particular, in the sense that patents applied for during the period of priority are independent, both as regards the grounds of nullity and forfeiture, and as regards their normal duration.'

Historically, some countries – particularly France – made the existence of a national patent right obtained under the priority of a foreign patent right dependent upon the existence of the latter.[34] Other countries refused to grant a subsequently filed patent a longer term of protection than that of the original one (Brazil, France, US, Belgium, Italy, and Spain). This principle of dependence of patents, also applied to trade marks under the Madrid Agreement,[35] was found undesirable and indeed to contravene the original spirit of the Paris Convention. For this reason, Art. 4*bis* of the Paris Convention was inserted at the Brussels Conference in 1901, and subsequently clarified at the Washington Conference in 1911.[36] The present wording makes clear that the independence of patents concerns 'grounds for invalidation and forfeiture and as regards their normal duration.'

---

34. *Ladas*, Patents Trade Marks and Related Rights, 1975, 505.
35. Madrid Agreement concerning the International Registration of Marks, signed 14 April 1891, as revised in 1967, 828 U.N.T.S. 389 (hereinafter Madrid Agreement).
36. Actes de la Conference de Bruxelles 311 (1901); Actes de la Conference de Washington 22, 249 (1911).

II. Territoriality and Trade

The argument that is made against any kind of parallel imports of patented products is this: Due to the independence of patent rights, the exercise of the patent right in the country of importation may not in any way be influenced by acts that occur outside the scope of the domestic patent. While patent law may very well stipulate that the first commercial marketing of a patented product *on the domestic market* does not allow the domestic patentee to exercise any further patent rights over this product ('exhaustion'), it would be unlawful to stipulate the same rule for patented products first put on the market beyond the territorial scope of the domestic patent, because this would make the domestic patent dependent upon acts that occurred outside its scope.[37] In other words, a patent in Japan (country of importation) could not become exhausted because patented products were marketed by the Japanese patentee in Germany (country of first marketing of such products), which is outside the scope of the Japanese patent right. Such an argumentation, however, misinterprets the intention and wording of Art. 4*bis* of the Paris Convention in a number of ways.[38]

When looking at the wording of the provision, it is concerned with the *existence* of a domestic patent right, while the exhaustion doctrine is concerned with acts that 'exhaust' further economic exploitation with regard to specific goods marketed under a patent, and thereby with the *exercise* of the patent right in respect of certain products.

The provision is further concerned with the relationship between different national patents for the same invention. A case where the principle of territoriality could apply would thus be scenario as listed under A.II above (a) (i) or (b) (iii) (the patentee holds a patent both in the country of exportation and importation, or has sold the former to a third party), but not in any other of scenarios (a) (ii)–(iv).

Even if one were to extend the principle of territoriality to the exercise of rights, there is nothing in the provision to suggest that developments abroad cannot influence domestic patent rights at all. It is now standard practice that patents are only granted on condition of absolute novelty. Absolute novelty (as well as the examination of an inventive step), however, requires taking into account the worldwide state of the art, not only the national one. This of course has a profound influence on the existence of a patent right (that due to such foreign state of the art may either not be granted, or be subsequently revoked). In a similar fashion, national patent law may decree that foreign acts of marketing may have an effect on the exercise of the patent right with regard to particular goods marketed abroad.

The main, or perhaps the only, remaining proponent of the thesis that a regime of international exhaustion (at least for patents) would contravene the Paris Convention is *Nuno Pires de Carvalho*. He writes in this respect: 'The fact that patent rights are

---

37. This has been held by the German Federal Supreme Court *Tylosin*, 3 June 1976, 8 IIC 64 [1977]. Also the minority opinion in the US Supreme Court decision *Impression Products v. Lexmark International*, 30 May 2017, 581 U.S.___ (2017) took this view in citing the Paris Convention: 'Because a sale abroad operates independently of the U.S. patent system, it makes little sense to say that such a sale exhausts an inventor's U.S. patent rights. U.S. patent protection accompanies none of a U.S. patentee's sales abroad – a competitor could sell the same patented product abroad with no U.S.-patent-law consequence. Accordingly, the foreign sale should not diminish the protections of U.S. law in the United States.'
38. *Beier*, 'Territoriality and International Trade', 1 IIC 70 (1970).

exhausted in the territory of one country should have no impact whatsoever on the patent rights valid in the territory of another country, given that those rights are entirely independent.'[39]

This view is entirely correct. It only has nothing to do with the question of exhaustion and parallel imports. Rather, it is a misunderstanding of the nature of the principle of independence. Stripped of all disguises, independence guarantees sovereignty. Sovereignty does not allow for any legal mechanisms to tie the fate of a domestic patent to the fate of a foreign one. In other words, it would not be permissible for a domestic court to be constrained to accept exhaustion of a patent right merely because there was exhaustion in the country of exportation. The US case *Graeff v. Boesch* decided by the US Supreme Court in 1890,[40] is a good example in this respect. Here, the US importer bought products that were lawfully put on the market in Germany by a manufacturer who enjoyed a prior user right. The goods were not put into circulation in Germany by the US patentee or with his consent:

> 'Letters-patent had been granted to the original patentees for the invention by the government of Germany in 1879 and 1880. A portion of the burners in question were purchased in Germany from one Hecht, who had the right to make and sell them there [...]
>
> It appears that appellants received two invoices from Germany, the burners in one of which were not purchased from Hecht, but, in the view which we take of the case, that circumstance becomes immaterial. The exact question presented is whether a dealer residing in the United States can purchase in another country articles patented there, from a person authorized to sell them, and import them to and sell them in the United States, without the license or consent of the owners of the United States patent [...]
>
> The right which Hecht had to make and sell the burners in Germany was allowed him under the laws of that country, and purchasers from him could not be thereby authorized to sell the articles in the United States in defiance of the rights of patentees under a United States patent. A prior foreign patent operates under our law to limit the duration of the subsequent patent here, but that is all. The sale of articles in the United States under a United States patent cannot be controlled by foreign laws. This disposes of the second error relied on.'

The last sentence is the relevant one in this context: 'A United States patent cannot be controlled by foreign laws', and summarises the gist of the principle of independence:

A patent cannot be revoked for the simple fact that it has been revoked in the country of first filing. But that does not mean that a domestic patent cannot be revoked on the same grounds for which the patent in the country of first filing was revoked, e.g. a prior public use or a novelty-destroying document. It is of course permissible to take foreign circumstances into account when determining the validity and scope of a domestic patent. A European patent may be revoked because of a prior public use in India; a US patent may be revoked because the invention was first put into practice in Indonesia by an inventor there.

---

39. *Pires de Carvalho*, The TRIPS Regime of Patent Rights, 115 (3d ed. 2005).
40. US Supreme Court, *Boesch v. Graeff*, 133 U.S. 787 (1890).

For the exercise of a patent right, a domestic court *may* hold that the patentee has received a sufficient reward for a certain patented item by marketing such item abroad, or the court *may* hold that this condition as such is not sufficient, but a court due to the principle of independence *must not* be constrained to allow importation simply because such product has been lawfully marketed abroad. If this were different (e.g. in cases as listed under A.II above (b) (i) and (ii)), foreign law could determine how domestic law should determine the case, and this would be contrary to the principle of independence or territoriality. Territoriality is at stake when certain consequences that have occurred in another jurisdiction must be adopted *telle quelle*. But this is not the solution that is argued here, nor is it the solution of those who advocate the lawfulness of parallel importation due to first voluntary marketing or those who favour the doctrine of implied licence.

Seen this way, the Paris Convention does not mandate an interpretation of patent law that requires the exclusion of parallel imports. Rather, it is silent on this issue and leaves it to national legislation or jurisprudence.

So, in effect, Carvalho (and, preceding him, Josef Kohler[41]) does not argue against parallel importation, but against the view that products lawfully marketed in country A must also be regarded as lawful in country B. This would be a position contrary to the principle of independence, while the correct question should be whether the principles of domestic patent law applicable to exhaustion (namely the first marketing by the patentee or with his consent) also apply to sales that have been made abroad. This is a question to be determined purely under domestic law.

As a result, the Paris Convention with its principle of independence of rights does not require an interpretation of 'patents' in Art. XX(d) GATT that would oblige Member States to categorically prevent the parallel importation of patented products.

D. THE WTO/TRIPS CONTEXT

As mentioned in the introductory part, TRIPS was concluded in 1994 within the framework of the GATT/WTO Agreement. It shifts the perspective on intellectual property rights in the context of international trade. While under GATT 1994, these were regarded as obstacles[42] (hence the exception provision in Art. XX(d)), TRIPS makes them a precondition of legitimate trade by requiring a (minimum) level playing field of protection. Still, and given the consequences that excluding parallel imports from international trade can have, one would have expected from a treaty covering all aspects of intellectual property rights that the matter of parallel importation be regulated in some manner so as to address the above scenarios as listed under A.II above. In fact, any definition of legitimate trade would have to address this point. Yet although it was recognised that parallel importation would indeed fit nicely within

---

41. *Kohler*, Handbuch des deutschen Patentrechts, 1900, 455.
42. Just as monopolies in general are regarded as a hindrance to free trade, a position re-iterated in the UK Statute of Monopolies 1623. It is well-noted that the GATT panel report in *US – Section 337 Tariff Act* did not regard the *enforcement* of intellectual property rights as obstacles (see chapter 1), but on the assumption that IP rights were a given.

the objective of international free trade under the GATT (see above),[43] agreement could not be reached to generally allow the parallel importation of goods protected by intellectual property rights in certain circumstances (e.g. in a situation where they were marketed abroad by the IP owner with his consent).

As a consequence thereof, Art. 6 TRIPS now provides that

> 'for the purposes of dispute settlement under this Agreement, [...] nothing [...] shall be used to address the issue of exhaustion of intellectual property rights.'

The dispute settlement mechanism in general allows every WTO Member to bring an action against another WTO Member if there is insufficient compliance with the principles of the GATT 1994 or any of the other agreements under the auspices of the WTO, see Art. 64 TRIPS and the WTO Agreement on Dispute Settlement. Yet, whatever national stance is taken on the matter of exhaustion, no complaint can be heard in this respect. While this certainly means that no TRIPS case can be brought to the WTO dispute settlement system based on a country's choice of its exhaustion regime, it does not necessarily mean that TRIPS as such would not favour a certain type of exhaustion regime.[44]

In particular, the obligation of WTO Members to grant patentees a specific right of importation along with other exclusive rights such as for production and sale may be an indication that any sort of importation without the consent of the patentee may be regarded as infringing and that consequently 'legitimate trade' is only an importation with the consent of the patentee In this respect, Art. 28 states:

> '1. A patent shall confer on its owner the following exclusive rights:
>
> (a) where the subject matter of a patent is a product, to prevent third parties not having the owner's consent from the acts of: making, using, offering for sale, selling, or importing for these purposes that product;'

Yet there is a caveat on the right of importation that reads:

> 'This right, like all other rights conferred under this Agreement in respect of the use, sale, importation or other distribution of goods, is subject to the provisions of Article 6.'

This first of all means that the issue of exhaustion may not be addressed under the cloak of a violation of the right of importation, which again is a procedural matter.

But also in substance, a right of importation has no bearing on the issue of exhaustion or parallel importation. An importation right is certainly useful once it comes to preventing products entering the country that infringe a patent right. Without an importation right, the patentee would have to wait until the infringing products are put on the market in order to obtain relief. This is certainly undesirable

---

43. *Cottier*, 'The Prospect for Intellectual Property in GATT', 28 Common Market Law Review 383, 401 [1991].
44. *Bronckers*, 'The Impact of TRIPS: Intellectual Property Protection in Developing Countries', 31 Common Market L. Rev. 1245 [1994]; *Straus*, 'Implications of the TRIPS Agreement in the Field of Patent Law', in *Beier and Schricker* (eds.), From GATT to TRIPS 191 (Weinheim 1996).

and inadequate. However, it is difficult to argue that the right of importation should follow different rules from the rights of production and sale.

The importation right concerns an aspect of economic exploitation just as much as production and sale. If, under the classical doctrine of exhaustion, further rights in commercial exploitation are exhausted upon the first sale of a patented article, and if such exhaustion is also assumed when such patented article is marketed abroad, then the exhaustion relates to all aspects of commercial exploitation of this product including importation. This becomes particularly obvious in the case of re-imports. If a patented article is put on the market in, say, Japan, by the patentee or with his consent, then further acts of economic exploitation are 'exhausted'. If the patentee therefore would not be able to prevent further acts of sale and distribution, then it is difficult to see how and why the patentee should be able to exert any influence over this article once it has been exported to another country and subsequently re-imported to Japan. If a patentee is granted a bundle of rights under his patent, such as production, sale and importation, then upon the act of first sale, the whole bundle becomes 'exhausted' for this specific product. In other words, if a patentee cannot prevent a parallel importer from the acts of marketing and selling the product in the country of importation (because, for example, the article was put in commerce abroad by the patentee), then the patentee cannot equally prevent the article's importation, because the importation right belongs to the same bundle of economic rights for a given product that are exhausted upon the first sale. Consequently, no importation right can be invoked later on for the very article that has already been marketed previously to the extent that national law of the country of importation deems this first sale to exhaust the patentee's control of further rights of commercial use. In other words, the scope of the right of importation follows the rules of exhaustion, and not vice versa: The importation right is limited by the exhaustion rule, not the exhaustion rule by the right of importation.[45]

The Doha Declaration on the TRIPS Agreement and Public Health of 14 November 2001 (WT/MIN(01)/DEC/2) under item 5(d) made clear that 'the effect of the provisions in the TRIPS Agreement that are relevant to the exhaustion of intellectual property rights is to leave each member free to establish its own regime for such exhaustion without challenge, subject to the MFN and national treatment provisions of Articles 3 and 4.'

This leads to the conclusion that under the TRIPS regime, each Member State is free to determine its own regime of exhaustion and thus to give a meaning to the term 'legitimate trade' in the context of parallel imports.

E.   ANALYSIS

I.   Free Trade and Arbitrary Obstacles Thereto

Even if there is significant leeway in the definition of 'legitimate trade' when it comes to the parallel importation of patented products, in order to comply with the

---

45. On the negotiating history, see *UNCTAD-ICTSD*, Resource Book on TRIPS and Development [2005] at 97–104.

notion of free trade under GATT 1994, countries should at least be required not to create arbitrary obstacles merely based on political considerations rather than law. One should thus take a closer look at the arguments for justifying the impediments to the parallel imports of patented products.

a) One of the legal arguments against the parallel importation of patented products, namely the principle of territoriality, has already been dealt with under C. II. above in the context of the Paris Convention and was found not convincing.

b) A further argument advanced by the minority opinion in a US Supreme Court case relates to the different scope of patent protection in different countries:

> 'Copyright protections, unlike patent protections, are harmonized across countries. Under the Berne Convention, which 174 countries have joined,* members "agree to treat authors from other member countries as well as they treat their own." *Golan v. Holder*, 565 U. S. 302, 308 (2012) (citing Berne Convention for the Protection of Literary and Artistic Works, Sept. 9, 1886, as re- vised at Stockholm on July 14, 1967, Arts. 1, 5(1), 828 U. N. T. S. 225, 231–233). The copyright protections one receives abroad are thus likely to be similar to those received at home, even if provided under each country's separate copyright regime.'[46]

The irony in this argument is the fact that the TRIPS Agreement itself acted as such a harmonising factor in introducing minimum requirements of production and thereby a level playing field of protection. In other words, TRIPS was introduced in order to address this concern. It further remains unclear from the above passage why copyright protection amongst the WTO Member States should be less diverse in scope than patent protection. For copyright law, one could mention the issue of moral rights, the protection of applied art or the exception of fair dealing that have not been uniformly addressed. Yet it is difficult to see what consequence it should have that certain differences exist for certain countries, and which differences would justify a blocking of parallel imports. One could for example argue that a patentee could block parallel imports from those countries where he could not obtain patent protection (above scenario (a) iv). But a mere reference to alleged differences in the level of protection appears an arbitrary argument in itself and not suited to explain why this should lead to a patentee's right to block importation of parallel imports from all countries in all circumstances.

c) Further, a number of court decisions against the parallel importation of patent products held that international exhaustion needed an explicit provision in the law and could not be affirmed without such basis.[47] While these decisions are certainly correct in pointing out that a clear provision in the law would help the interpretation of the exhaustion question, the verdicts reached raise two questions. First, why the lack of any clear provision in the law should not lead to the assumption that parallel imports are *permitted* rather than prohibited. Only such an interpretation would be

---

46. Minority opinion in the US Supreme Court decision *Impression Products v. Lexmark International*, 30 May 2017, 581 U.S.___ (2017).
47. Swiss Supreme Court, decision of 7 December 1999, GRUR Int. 2000, 639 – *Kodak II*; Paris Appeal Court, 29 May 1999 – *Phyteron*; German Federal Supreme Court, 14 December 1999, GRUR Int. 2000, 635 – *Karate*.

in accordance with the principle that intellectual property rights as exceptions to the rules of free competition cannot be interpreted beyond the scope granted by law. In the absence of any provision to the contrary, and in the absence of any result that can be deduced from the rationale of patent law as such, the rules of free competition should be applied at least for the importation of products that, if first put on the domestic market, would be deemed exhausted (namely because they were marketed by the patentee or with the patentee's consent).

d) When push comes to shove, the remaining argument for allowing patentees to prevent the parallel importation of patented products in any circumstances appears to be a patentee's possibility of (or possibly right to) market separation in order to maximise profit.[48] In other words, the patentee should be able to extract the maximum profit from each domestic market. One answer to this argument has been given by the US Supreme Court:

> 'Exhaustion is a separate limit on the patent grant, and does not depend on the patentee receiving some undefined premium for selling the right to access the American market. A purchaser buys an item, not patent rights. And exhaustion is triggered by the patentee's decision to give that item up and receive whatever fee it decides is appropriate. [...] The patentee may not be able to whatever fee it decides is appropriate for the article and the invention which it embodies command the same amount for its products abroad as it does in the United States. But the Patent Act does not guarantee a particular price, much less the price from selling to American consumers. Instead, the right to exclude just ensures that the patentee receives one reward – of whatever amount the patentee deems to be "satisfactory compensation," for every item that passes outside the scope of the patent monopoly.'

One could add that the reward society confers on the patentee is justified by the inventor's contribution to society, that is, the invention for which a patent is granted. This contribution remains the same no matter in how many countries patent protection is sought. The patentee is thus not deprived of his reward if the act of marketing a patented product abroad (under a corresponding patent) also exhausts the patent in the country of importation, given that the patentee's contribution is the same in both countries and has been rewarded already.

e) It is one of the major flaws in the discussion on the lawfulness of parallel imports of patented products that the legal arguments[49] against such importation appear

---

48. Clearly spelt out by *Beier*, Zur Zulässigkeit von Parallelimporten patentierter Erzeugnisse, GRUR Int. 1996, 1.
49. Which does not necessarily mean that parallel imports necessarily benefit society at large for all types of products, or for all countries. There are studies that indicate that the parallel importation of pharmaceuticals may either lead to an unsustainable drop in revenues by patentees, or (as a reaction) a refusal to supply pharmaceutical to lower priced countries: *Redwood*, 'Advantages and Risks of Differential pricing for Prescription Drugs' Presentation at World Health Organisation- World Trade Organisation Workshop, Høsbjør, Norway – 9 April 2001, available at https://www.wto.org/english/tratop_e/trips_e/hosbjor_presentations_e/14redwood_e.pdf (accessed 22 May 2018). Yet this case is first of all based on economic rather than legal considerations, and has also not been

rather weak and either based on assumptions ('the patentee should have the right to separate markets' – but why?), or on purportedly catastrophic consequences were such imports to be allowed:

> '[A]part from the description of the 'horrors' caused by parallel trade, OSK does not indicate any positive aspect resulting from its restriction of supplies of medicinal products to the wholesalers, except that its profit margins recover, which is irrelevant for the purposes of classifying the conduct as an abuse, or for the purposes of justifying it.'[50]

II.   Obstacles to a WTO Dispute Settlement

While the blanket exclusion of parallel imports of patented products may very well make an arguable case under the rules of GATT, it is unlikely that a dispute settlement case will be brought in the context of the WTO. The reasons are essentially threefold:

a) First, in the WTO context, no country is forced to implement a certain exhaustion regime, see above. A country could thus at the most argue that the (restrictive) exhaustion regime of another Member State creates an undue obstacle to legitimate trade. Such a case would only be brought where domestic traders from a given country due to another country's exhaustion regime suffer economic losses at such scale that the country of exportation decides to start a dispute settlement. In other words, the diversity of economic players and the difficulty in allocating losses to traders in a given country make a case unlikely. In the case of the United States, the exhaustion decision for copyright law was triggered by a student wanting to import teaching material, and the exhaustion decision for patents by domestic traders who wanted to import second-hand cameras.

b) Neither would a WTO case be straightforward in terms of legal argumentation. Leaving aside the TRIPS angle that due to Art. 6 could not be argued in the first place, a case would have to define the substance of a specific intellectual property right in the context of a specific right under GATT. In other words, the case for the parallel importation of patented products is quite different from the case of parallel importation of trade marked products, or the transit of patented products: patents aim at a commercial monopoly for a given market that is certainly affected by imports, but not necessarily by transit (a scenario that is argued in chapter 3 of this book). Trade marks do not confer a commercial monopoly, but are meant to avoid confusion in trade, and the arguments for or against parallel importation in such cases may require a different argumentation.

---

conclusively made. It assumes that there is price discrimination of pharmaceuticals between developed and developing countries, which does not appear a given considering that prices of pharmaceuticals in, e.g. Brazil and South Africa, seem to be higher than in certain developed countries: T. Kongolo, Towards a new fashion of protecting pharmaceutical patents in Africa, 33 IIC 185 (2002). In addition, the scenario does not consider to what extent pharmaceutical companies can and do use other means of market separation, namely regulatory approval procedures and marketing authorisations.
50. AG Ruiz-Jarabo Colomer in his opinion of joined cases C-468/06 to C-478/06 *Sot. Lelos kai Sia* [2008] ECR I-7139.

c) Finally, in some cases countries are no longer autonomous in determining the exhaustion regime, but rather bound by bilateral free trade agreements that tend to further restrict parallel importation. The US government mentions in an amicus curiae for the Supreme Court decision *Lexmark* two free trade agreements that require a domestic exhaustion regime for patents (that the US is now unable to honour).[51] Countries bound by such agreements are unlikely to initiate any dispute settlement regarding a third-country exhaustion regime, and a country's commitment to a given exhaustion regime could give rise to issues under the most-favoured nation treatment obligation that are almost intractable from a legal point of view.

III.   Result

Summing up, a blanket ban on the parallel importation of patented products based on a regime of domestic exhaustion is consistent with the Paris Convention, consistent with TRIPS, yet inconsistent with the obligations under Art. XI GATT and thus an undue obstacle to legitimate trade. It is unlikely, however, that a dispute on this matter will ever be brought before the WTO.

---

51. *Abbott*, 'Comment on the US Supreme Court decision *Lexmark*', 48 IIC 2017.

Chapter 3
Geoblocking and 'Legitimate Trade'

Marketa Trimble

A. INTRODUCTION

The internet could have become a potent vehicle for free trade. When the internet left behind its modest beginnings and became a mass medium of many uses,[1] its borderless nature beckoned the free flow of information, digital goods, and services. With no borders hindering a free flow of trade, and without countries erecting trade barriers at any borders, the internet could have become the ultimate free trade zone. But it has not.

The reason the internet has not become a free trade zone is that it remained free of neither government nor private intervention. In response to the expectations of industries, governments, and internet users, the internet has evolved to enable the linking of internet activities to physical geography.[2] The geographically aware internet now enables internet actors to erect territorial limits on the internet that correspond to existing physical borders, and also to define access to information, goods, and services on the internet on a territory-based and extremely granular basis.

This chapter discusses the use of tools that facilitate the linking of the internet to physical geography and the obstacles that the use poses for free trade. Using examples of goods and services ('content') protected by intellectual property (IP) rights, the chapter reviews whether and how trade law rules, including the concept of 'legitimate trade' and the rules of competition law, apply to the use of the tools.

---

1. *Rustad and D'Angelo*, 'The Path of Internet Law: An Annotated Guide to Legal Landmarks', 1 Duke Law & Tech. Rev. 1 [2011], p. 6.
2. *Goldsmith and Wu*, Who Controls the Internet? Illusions of a Borderless World, New York 2006, pp. 58-63.

The chapter begins by introducing the current trend of linking the internet to physical geography (the 'territorialisation' trend),[3] and the geolocation and geoblocking tools that make territorialisation possible. The chapter then evaluates from the trade law and competition law perspectives the legality of using geoblocking to partition markets, and it presents recent developments in the European Union that concern the legality of geoblocking. The chapter contemplates the characteristics of geoblocking that might justify treating geoblocking differently from other methods of market partitioning.

B. TERRITORIALISATION OF THE INTERNET AND THE TOOLS OF TERRITORIALISATION

I. The Territorialisation Trend

The internet has not developed to be the borderless medium that some once hoped it would be. To the dismay of the original internet enthusiasts, some of whom wanted the internet to remain a space detached from existing jurisdictions, the internet has become subject to regulation and enforcement by existing physical jurisdictions.[4] Internet technology has undergone a process of territorialisation through the use of tools that determine the physical location of internet actors and internet activities.[5] The ability to establish links between internet actors, internet activities, and physical geography enables the erection of virtual borders on the internet that may either coincide with existing physical borders or draw on other geographical criteria, and opens possibilities for delivering content to precisely determined geographic locations or territories.

It is unclear when the process of territorialisation of the internet started; today's college students have difficulty remembering the internet when it was not geographically aware – when it did not recognise the physical location of devices connected to the internet. Some commentators have placed the rise of internet territorialisation in the mid- to late-2000s, concurrent with the release of the Google Maps API (2005) and the iOS and Android location-aware smartphone applications (2009).[6] Although these releases certainly propelled the widespread use of location-based services[7] and other

---

3. 'Territorialisation' is the action of territorialising, i.e. 'mak[ing] (something) territorial; to organize on a territorial basis; to associate with or restrict to a particular territory or district'. Oxford English Dictionary, 3rd ed., 2011.
4. Geist, 'Cyberlaw 2.0', 44 B.C.L. Rev. 323 [2003], p. 332.
5. Trimble, 'Territorialization of the Internet Domain Name System', 45 Pepperdine L. Rev. (forthcoming 2018).
6. Kitchen, Lauriault and Wilson, 'Understanding Spatial Media', in Kitchen/Lauriault/Wilson, Understanding Spatial Media, 2017, 1–21, p. 3.
7. The term 'location-based services (LBS) generally refers to all the information services that exploit the ability of technology to know where objects or people are located, and to modify the information it presents accordingly.' Sui, 'Understanding Location-Based Services: Core Technologies, Key Applications and Major Concerns', in Barney Warf (ed.), Handbook on Geographies of Technology, 2017, 85–95, p. 85.

geographically aware applications, territorialisation actually began earlier – with the delivery of localised advertisements and other content based on internet user location.

The trend of internet territorialisation is fuelled by governments' reactions to the borderless nature of the internet. For governments, territorialisation restrains the otherwise territorially unlimited power that jurisdictions attempt to exercise on the internet. Without effective technological means to limit their prescriptive and adjudicatory jurisdiction on the internet, countries have been legislating, and courts and agencies have been deciding, on matters on the internet with no territorial limits. While practical constraints have often curbed such territorial expansions (for example, a court's refusal to recognise and enforce a foreign judgment that it deemed inappropriately extraterritorial),[8] any country having enforcement power over an actor (such as a court in the country of the actor's domicile) has the ability to impose its laws and regulations against the actor globally on the internet. For example, if a court of the country of an actor's domicile orders the actor to remove copyright-infringing material from a website, the removal may have global effects because the court is able to compel the party's compliance with its order.[9]

Territorialisation makes it possible for countries to replicate on the internet their physical world framework for prescriptive, adjudicatory, and enforcement jurisdiction, confirm their sovereign 'territory' in cyberspace, and carve out their own virtual territory for the purposes of regulation and enforcement. Although global regulation might initially seem appealing, countries might still engage in territorial self-restraint in the interest of comity and expectations that other countries will reciprocate. Territorialisation also assists internet actors in delimiting their actions and protecting themselves from the laws and decisions of jurisdictions where they do not operate and have no plans to operate.

However, internet territorialisation is definitely not driven only by reactions to the possibility that countries will exercise territorially unlimited power on the internet; the popularity among users of location-based services and other geographically aware applications suggests that territorialisation of the internet resonates positively with many, or even most, internet actors and users. Tailoring content to user location makes the vast volume of content on the internet manageable and accessible and allows internet actors to develop and users to take advantage of a wide array of user-friendly services.

Whatever might be the generally positive user attitude toward some aspects of internet territorialisation, users' positive feedback should not overshadow the significant concerns of some critics about certain aspects of territorialisation, namely

---

8. E.g., *Yahoo! Inc. v. La Ligue Contre Le Racisme et L'Antisemitisme*, 433 F.3d 1199 (9th Cir. 2006); *Google LLC v. Equustek Solutions Inc.*, U.S. District Court for the Northern District of California, Order, 2017 WL 5000834, 2 November 2017.
9. Absent an international agreement that defines the territorial scope of countries' legislative and adjudicatory powers on the internet, only a country's legislative and judicial self-restraint and the lack of enforcement by other countries of that country's decisions will limit that country's extraterritorial expansion. Self-restraint has been the issue in, for example, *In re a Warrant to Search a Certain E–Mail Account Controlled & Maintained by Microsoft Corp.*, 829 F.3d 197 (2d Cir. 2016), reh'g en banc denied, 855 F.3d 53 (2d Cir. 2017), and *In re Search Warrant No. 16-960-M-1 to Google*, U.S. District Court for the Eastern District of Pennsylvania, 2017 WL 3535037, 17 August 2017.

the invasion of privacy and the potential role that territorialisation can play in facilitating censorship and discrimination.[10] Knowledge of a user's location, particularly in combination with other data that might be available about that user, may supply crucial information about the user and even result in undesirable identification of the user. Location data can be used to discriminate among users, including in the content that they receive, and the ability to carve out territory in cyberspace enables governments to impose restrictions that might limit their residents' access to information.

II. Geolocation

One of the tools of internet territorialisation is geolocation, which is a means of identifying the physical location of an internet-connected device.[11] The location of the device may correspond to the location of the user who is using the device, but the location may also be of a device that is operating without a user's physical presence; particularly in the world of the internet of things,[12] internet-connected devices may be located outside the presence of their users. Even if a device is in the presence of its user, geolocation does not necessarily reveal the identity of the user of the device because internet-connected devices may be accessible to and used by multiple users.

Geolocation tools can utilise various input data to localise internet-connected devices. In its early days, geolocation relied solely on internet protocol addresses and the fact that groups of internet protocol addresses were assigned to particular geographical areas.[13] Gradually, and particularly with the increased use of mobile devices, geolocation began to use other, more precise data points, including GPS, wifi signals, radio frequency signals, and response delays to identify the location of a device.[14] Geolocation does not require that users opt in, or not opt out of, any

---

10. E.g., Redesigning IP Geolocation: Privacy by Design and Online Targeted Advertising, Information and Privacy Commissioner, Ontario, Canada, October 2010, available at https://www.ipc.on.ca/wp-content/uploads/Resources/pbd-ip-geo.pdf (accessed 26 April 2018); *King*, 'Personal Jurisdiction, Internet Commerce, and Privacy: The Pervasive Legal Consequences of Modern Geolocation Technologies', 21 Alb. L.J. Sci. & Tech. 61 [2011], 115.
11. Other tools of territorialisation are, for example, geographical top-level domains and geo-tagged internet protocol packets.
12. The term 'internet of things', as commonly used today, refers to the internet in which 'everyday objects [...] connect to the Internet and [...] send and receive data'. Internet of Things, FTC Staff Report, January 2015, available at https://www.ftc.gov/system/files/documents/reports/federal-trade-commission-staff-report-november-2013-workshop-entitled-internet-things-privacy/150127iotrpt.pdf (accessed 26 April 2018). On the probable origin of the term see Ashton, That 'Internet of Things' Thing, RFID Journal, 22 June 2009, available at http://www.rfidjournal.com/articles/view?4986 (accessed 26 April 2018).
13. On internet protocol addresses see, e.g., *Trimble*, 'Future of Cybertravel: Legal Implications of the Evasion of Geolocation', 22 Fordham Intell. Prop. Media & Ent. L.J. 567 [2012].
14. E.g., *Muir and Oorschot*, 'Internet Geolocation: Evasion and Counterevasion', 42(1) ACM Computing Surveys, 2009, Article No. 4.

services on their devices; current geolocation tools can function without a user's consent or knowledge.[15]

Geolocation tools have become more sophisticated and now offer improved accuracy; with the accuracy the tools are capable of increased precision in identifying the location of a device. A few years ago geolocation enabled localisation only at a country, region, or city level, but today, for example, a magazine can use geolocation to tailor the delivery of its articles to certain readers based on the company at which those readers work;[16] a hospital can use geolocation to alert its systems when known patients enter the hospital emergency department;[17] and an employer can use geolocation to target with employment advertisements prospective job candidates from among the employees of its competitors.[18] Geolocation providers can now localise a mobile device 'within a few meters of accuracy',[19] allowing, for example, a vacation resort to provide different online experiences in different sections of its resort, according to a visitor's real-time location.

III. Geoblocking

Geoblocking (sometimes called 'geo-fencing') goes a step further than geolocation. Geolocation localises a device and enables the tailoring of content according to the location of the device (also referred to as 'geotargeting'). Once a device is geolocated, geoblocking can be used to block access to content based on the determined location of the device.[20] Geolocation, when implemented without geoblocking, permits a user

---

15. Mobile IP Targeting Myths and Facts: Dispelling Marketplace Misperceptions, Digital Element, available at https://www.digitalelement.com/wp-content/uploads/2016/06/mobile-myths.pdf (accessed 11 December 2017).
16. *Goodfellow*, 'Forbes Introduces Geolocation Targeting to BrandVoice Content', The Drum, 23 February 2017, available at http://www.thedrum.com/news/2017/02/23/forbes-introduces-geolocation-targeting-brandvoice-content (accessed 11 December 2017).
17. *Comstock*, Boston Children's Pilots Geolocation Technology to Help Babies with Weak Hearts, mobihealthnews, 1 May 2017, available at http://www.mobihealthnews.com/content/boston-childrens-pilots-geolocation-technology-help-babies-weak-hearts (accessed 11 December 2017).
18. *Noguchi*, Recruiters Use 'Geofencing' to Target Potential Hires Where They Live and Work, National Public Radio, 7 July 2017, available at https://www.npr.org/sections/alltechconsidered/2017/07/07/535981386/recruiters-use-geofencing-to-target-potential-hires-where-they-live-and-work (accessed 11 December 2017).
19. PinPoint, GeoComply, available at https://www.geocomply.com/solutions/pinpoint/ (accessed 11 December 2017).
20. New technology might enable the geotagging of individual internet protocol packets; internet protocol packets are the carriers of information on the internet. Such geotagged packets may then be routed only through a permitted territory, for example only within a particular country. U.S. patent 9,762,683, issued on 12 September 2017 ('Use of packet header extension for geolocation/geotargeting'); U.S. patent application 14/502682, filed on 30 September 2014 ('Applications of processing packets which contain geographic location information of the packet sender'). A group of researchers has presented internet protocol packet geotagging as an alternative to geoblocking; geotagging could also be understood to be another form of geolocation. *Dasu/Kanza/Srivastava*, Geotagging IP Packets for Location-Aware Software-Defined Networking in the Presence of Virtual

to opt out of geographically targeted delivery and view content that is not localised at all, or is localised for a different location. For example, an airline website may display content that is localised for the country of the user's current location, but it may also allow the user to select, view, and use a different country version of the website. Geoblocking, on the other hand, aims to prevent the user from accessing blocked content. For example, a television station website might notify a user that certain video content is not available in the user's location because of rights limitations, and the website might provide no tool to enable the user to de-localise the content delivery and view the geolocked content. A user might be able to access geoblocked content, but only if the user uses some extraordinary measures (as described in section B.IV below).

Website operators employ geoblocking for a number of different reasons. Some uses of geoblocking arise out of a need to comply with territorially defined laws, agency or court decisions, or contractual obligations. For example, the regulations of some jurisdictions mandate that online gambling providers utilise geoblocking to ensure that their games are offered to users only in the jurisdictions in which the providers are licensed to offer the games.[21] In the absence of such regulations, courts or agencies may order geoblocking to be implemented to comply with territorially defined laws or regulations on online gambling.[22] Holders of territorially limited copyright licences may be obligated under their licences to geoblock to ensure that only users who are connecting from the territory for which the holders hold the licences may access the licensed content.[23]

In addition to its function in legal compliance – whether that compliance be based on a jurisdiction's laws or decisions, or on a party's contractual obligations – geoblocking is also used for a variety of purposes where its use is not mandated by law. Internet actors may geoblock to limit the reach of their activities territorially for jurisdictional purposes, which is helpful when the law is unclear or unsettled about how courts and agencies should assess the reach of prescriptive and adjudicatory jurisdiction on the internet. For example, since the rules on personal jurisdiction on the internet are evolving,[24] some internet actors might geoblock to prove that they are not targeting or availing themselves of certain jurisdictions. Courts do not require,

---

Network Functions, available at http://www.cccblog.org/wp-content/uploads/2017/12/ACM_SIGSPATIAL_2017_paper_44.pdf (accessed 13 January 2018).

21. E.g., IP Geolocation Can Ensure Compliance with UIGEA Regulations, Neustar, available at https://www.neustar.biz/resources/whitepapers/ip-geolocation-ensuring-compliance-with-online-gambling-regulations (accessed 26 April 2018).
22. E.g., Court of Appeals of Kentucky, *Jazette Enterprises Ltd. v. Commonwealth of Kentucky*, 2014 WL 689044, 21 February 2014, 2.
23. It is unclear whether or not geoblocking is required when a territorially limited licence is silent on the matter. In the United States, the case of *Spanski Enterprises v. TV Polska* might shed light on this issue (*Spanski Enterprises, Inc. v. Telewizja Polska S.A.*, 222 F.Supp.3d 95 (D.DC. 2016)). For a further discussion of contractually imposed territorial limitations see section C.III *infra*.
24. See in general *Svantesson*, Private International Law and the Internet, Wolters Kluwer, Alphen aan den Rijn, 4th ed., 2016.

for now, that geoblocking be used to avoid personal jurisdiction in their forum,[25] but it is unclear what courts' positions might be in the future. The use of geoblocking might be considered the clearest evidence that an internet actor has made a best efforts attempt to avoid activities in a geoblocked jurisdiction.

Other uses of geoblocking may be completely divorced from legal rights or obligations or concerns about legal compliance. For example, geoblocking may be used to support security measures for internet banking; after a user attempts to sign into an online account from a location other than the location from which the user customarily connects, the user may be denied access or asked for second-step verification. As for any means for delimiting activities territorially, geoblocking is also used to partition markets for purposes such as the introduction of differential pricing or staggered release of content, as discussed further in section C.III below.

IV.   Evasion of Geolocation and Circumvention of Geoblocking

Geoblocking creates no impermeable barrier, but it does impose a cost on permeating the barrier that it creates. Geolocation, when employed without geoblocking, is usually simple to bypass – for example, by changing a website setting through the selection of a different country from a drop-down menu provided on the website, or by using a different top level domain version of the same website. Geoblocking is designed to prevent users from changing their location settings and accessing blocked content, but users may still be able to circumvent the geoblocking.

Tools have been developed to evade geolocation and circumvent geoblocking; the tools enable users to change their internet protocol address to appear as if they are connected to the internet from a different internet protocol address (and hence from another geographical location). The more sophisticated tools that now exist can also change other data points that might be used to geolocate a user (as explained in section B.II above). Once a user is geolocated in a different location from where the user actually is, the user may be able to access content that was geoblocked for the user's true physical location. With geoblocking becoming more prevalent, user interest in geoblocking circumvention has increased, and because tool providers are now making circumvention tools easier to use, even technically unsophisticated users can circumvent geoblocking.

Users who circumvent geoblocking may be violating national laws. What specific laws users might violate will depend on the particular context in which users circumvent geoblocking. Acts that circumvention enables, namely the accessing and use of particular content, might violate laws that concern access to or use of content;[26] laws that require a user to be truthful about his physical location would also be violated when geolocation is bypassed. Acts of circumvention themselves

---

25. U.S. District Court for the District of Columbia, Case No. 1:16-cv-00159-RDM, *Triple Up Limited v. Youku Tudou Inc.*, memorandum opinion, docket document 15, 24 January 2017.
26. For example, the circumvention of geoblocking may result in a user accessing a BBC program without paying the required television licensing fee. The Licence Fee, Inside the BBC, available at http://www.bbc.co.uk/corporate2/insidethebbc/whoweare/licencefee (accessed 13 January 2018).

might also breach laws and legal obligations; for example, acts of circumvention might violate contractual provisions if the provider of the geoblocked content includes anti-circumvention provisions in its contract with its users.[27] It is also possible that in some countries, and under certain circumstances, acts of circumvention could violate provisions on circumvention of copyright protection systems[28] or provisions against computer hacking.[29]

Notwithstanding the rise in user interest in geoblocking, enforcement actions against users who circumvent geoblocking and against providers who supply geoblocking tools appear to be infrequent. The low incidence of enforcement actions is perhaps not surprising, given that the incentives for internet actors to implement effective geoblocking may be marginal. For example, a content provider who is not itself a copyright holder to the content that the provider provides might have little incentive to act against circumvention of geoblocking if its business model relies on attracting the largest possible number of users to its website. Similarly, an online gambling provider is unlikely to be motivated to act against geoblocking circumvention if effective geoblocking will limit the number of users accessing the provider's website and the gambling revenue that the provider derives from the volume of bets placed on its website.

IP rights owners who themselves geoblock to partition markets have an incentive to make their geoblocking effective but might be unwilling to undergo the increased public scrutiny that accompanies acts of rights enforcement against individual users; the owners could lose more from public relations harm than they would gain from enforcing their rights against individual users. Rather, targeting the providers of geoblocking circumvention tools could be more cost effective and have a greater impact. In one publicised instance in which content providers did bring legal action against a provider of a geoblocking circumvention tool, the case settled before the court could resolve the dispute; the provider agreed to withdraw from the country in which the action was brought.[30]

Given the lack of court decisions in disputes involving the circumvention of geoblocking, the legal status of acts of circumvention and of the provision of circumvention tools remains uncertain. The uncertainty is problematic, both for those who view geoblocking as a viable tool for territorially partitioning the internet and

---

27. E.g., Nutzungsbedingunen für die Nutzung des Videoportals von Sat.1, § 4.1(g), available at http://www.sat1.de/service/nutzungsbedingungen/nutzungsbedingungen-fuer-die-nutzung-des-videoportals-von-sat-1 (accessed 13 January 2018).
28. 17 USC 1201.
29. For a detailed discussion of the legality of circumvention of geoblocking see Trimble, 'The Future of Cybertravel, Legal Implications of the Evasion of Geolocation', 22 Fordham Intell. Prop. Media & Ent. L.J. 567 (2012).
30. Kirk, 'Geoblocking Question Unresolved after New Zealand Lawsuit Ends', PCWorld, 23 June 2015, available at http://www.pcworld.com/article/2939972/geoblocking-question-unresolved-after-new-zealand-lawsuit-ends.html (accessed 13 January 2018). Arguments concerning the circumvention of geoblocking have also emerged in cases in which IP rights infringements were alleged, where plaintiffs sought to show the insufficiency of the geoblocking tools. *Spanski Enterprises v. TV Polska, supra* 23; U.S. District Court for the Central District of California, Case No. 2:17-cv-8041, *The Carsey-Werner Company, LLC v. BBC*.

those who consider circumvention of geoblocking as legitimate spillover, similar to the spillover of physical international travel. In Australia, a report by a governmental commission has called for clarification of the legal status of the circumvention of geoblocking.[31] No such clarification has yet been offered.

Irrespective of whether circumvention of geoblocking is or is not legal, or will or will not become legal, users will likely continue to circumvent geoblocking; thinking that circumvention can be completely eliminated through legal or through technical means, or even through a combination of both, would be naïve. To respond to the availability of geoblocking circumvention tools and acts of circumvention by users, providers and implementers of geolocation and geoblocking technologies seek technological solutions that will prevent or minimise instances of circumvention of the technologies.[32] However, as rapidly as the providers and implementers of geolocation and geoblocking technologies develop such solutions, providers of circumvention tools improve their tools to defeat the solutions.

Some commentators have argued that because geoblocking can be circumvented, it is inevitably ineffective, and the internet can therefore never be territorially partitioned. However, perfect geoblocking (or the physical equivalent – perfectly impermeable physical borders) may not be necessary in order for legal consequences to be associated with the use of geoblocking (or be associated with the existence of physical borders). A door lock is not a technologically perfect barrier to entry, yet the law takes the use of a lock into account for some purposes.[33] Similarly, the use of geoblocking may have legal consequences, even if geoblocking tools never become an absolute means of restricting access to internet content according to the physical location of an internet-connected device.

C. THE LEGALITY OF GEOBLOCKING

I. Mandatory vs. Voluntary Territorial Restrictions

In order to assess the legality of geoblocking, it is useful to split the analysis of legality into two parts: whether the content that is geoblocked is, or is not, legally encumbered by territorial restrictions. As for any means of territorial market partitioning, geoblocking may be employed to limit access to content either because a law mandates certain territorial restrictions on access to the content ('mandatory territorial restrictions'), or because the content provider wants to territorially restrict access to the content for a reason that is unrelated to any of the provider's legal obligations ('voluntary territorial restrictions'). In the first case the content is legally encumbered by territorial restrictions ('territorially encumbered content'), in the second case

---

31. Intellectual Property Arrangements, Australian Government, Productivity Commission Inquiry Report, 23 September 2016, 11, available at https://www.pc.gov.au/inquiries/completed/intellectual-property/report/intellectual-property.pdf (accessed 13 January 2018).
32. FAQ, Digital Element, available at https://www.digitalelement.com/taxonomy_reference/ask-the-expert/ (accessed 11 December 2017).
33. *321 Studios v. Metro Goldwyn Mayer Studios, Inc.*, 307 F. Supp. 2d 1085 (N.D. Cal. 2004), 1095.

the territorial restrictions on content are merely voluntary and the content is legally unencumbered by territorial restrictions ('territorially unencumbered content').

An example of territorially encumbered content is online gambling content that an online gambling provider is licensed to provide only in a particular country for which the provider has been granted a licence. The provider's use of geoblocking to limit access to the online gambling content from other countries will be to comply with online gambling laws; these laws might be the online gambling laws of the other countries where the provider holds no licence (and where the provider therefore may not provide the content), or even the laws of the country that granted the licence, if the laws of that country impose an obligation to comply with other countries' laws.[34] Some jurisdictions make geoblocking mandatory for purposes of compliance with online gambling laws, while other jurisdictions do not specify the means through which territorial limitations should be implemented. Nevertheless, agencies or courts may order providers to employ geoblocking as *the* means to comply with the laws of their country on the internet.

Another example of territorially encumbered content is copyright-protected content for which the copyright owner holds rights in only one country, while another entity holds copyright on the content in other countries. Without permission or a licence to distribute the content in the other countries, the copyright owner may not distribute the content in the other countries. In this situation, the copyright owner might employ geoblocking to comply with territorial restrictions imposed by law – prohibitions that the other countries maintain against distribution of the content without permission or a licence.

With some exceptions, such as some countries' online gambling regulations, geoblocking is not, nor is any other single method, legally required as the only means of territorially limiting activities on the internet.[35] Absent other laws and/or contractual obligations to the contrary, the copyright owner in the example above is not required to employ geoblocking for the purpose of compliance with copyright laws or other territorially defined laws and obligations, and may utilise a means other than geoblocking to territorially limit access to the content. Other means might be, for example, the use of disclaimers, contractual provisions in terms of service, limited language versions, and/or specific country top-level domain names. However, geoblocking is currently the most effective means of imposing territorial restrictions on the internet,[36] and the copyright owner may choose geoblocking, particularly if the copyright owner is concerned about being exposed to liability for copyright infringement in other countries at a time when other countries' laws and practices have not yet clarified whether geoblocking must be employed.[37]

---

34. Trimble, 'Proposal for an International Convention on Online Gambling', in *Pindell/Cabot* (eds.), Regulating Internet Gaming: Challenges and Opportunities, UNLV Gaming Press, 2013, 375–377.
35. See *supra* n. 23 for *Spanski Enterprises v. TV Polska*.
36. See *supra* n. 20 for a new technology that could be more effective than current methods of geoblocking.
37. Trimble, 'To Geoblock, or Not To Geoblock – Is That Still a Question?', Technology & Marketing Law Blog, 9 May 2016, available at http://blog.ericgoldman.org/archives/2017/05/to-geoblock-or-not-to-geoblock-is-that-still-a-question-guest-blog-post.htm (accessed 18 January 2018).

While territorial restrictions might be implemented to comply with laws, geoblocking (or some other means that might be employed to partition markets) might also be used in circumstances when there is no legal obligation to restrict access to content based on territorial requirements. Territorially unencumbered content might be copyright-protected content to which a copyright owner holds rights in multiple countries, or worldwide;[38] if the copyright owner imposes territorial restrictions on access to content from countries for which the owner owns copyright, he will not be implementing the restrictions to comply with legal obligations, unless some other laws incidentally require territorial restrictions on access, such as national censorship laws. The copyright owner could have a number of reasons for imposing territorial restrictions voluntarily; profit maximisation through market partitioning can often be one reason, as discussed in C.III below.

Territorial restrictions on copyright-protected content might be implemented also by a licensee to whom a copyright owner has granted a territorially limited licence; the licensee is legally obligated by the licence to impose territorial restrictions on the content. What might be territorially unencumbered content initially (when copyrights worldwide are owned by a single copyright owner), now becomes territorially encumbered content through the operation of contract law.[39]

II. The Legality of Geoblocking when it Implements Mandatory Territorial Restrictions

The legality of geoblocking can be assessed at two levels. At the first level is the legality of geoblocking tools and their operation, which may themselves raise legal issues: for example, a particular tool might violate privacy laws and rules on personal data protection.[40] At the second level is the legality of the use of geoblocking evaluated in the context of the particular purposes for which the geoblocking is employed.

In cases of mandatory territorial restrictions, the legality of the law that imposes the restrictions and territorially encumbers the content is scrutinised. Laws in which countries mandate territorial restrictions on trade are subject to limitations that countries have negotiated in international trade agreements. For example, World Trade Organization ('WTO') rules limit barriers to cross-border trade;[41] similarly, European Union ('EU') rules on the free movement of goods and services endeavour to keep barriers to cross-border trade within the European Union to a minimum.[42]

---

38. Although rules of copyright ownership are not harmonised among countries and do differ among countries, it is possible that in some circumstances a copyright owner owns copyright in all countries, or at least in all countries in which copyright exists and which adhere to the Berne Convention for the Protection of Literary and Artistic Works.
39. In some jurisdictions, copyright may not be assigned and may only be licensed.
40. See, e.g., U.S. District Court for the Northern District of California, case No. 3:16-cv-03474, Stipulated Order for Permanent Injunction and Civil Penalty Judgment, *United States v. InMobi Pte Ltd.*, 22 June 2016.
41. General Agreement on Tariffs and Trade 1994, Apr. 15, 1994, Marrakesh Agreement Establishing the World Trade Organization, Annex 1A, 1867 U.N.T.S. 187, 33 I.L.M. 1153 (1994) [GATT], Art. XI.
42. Treaty on the Functioning of the European Union, adopted on 13 December 2007, entered into force on 1 December 2009 (OJ C 115/47 of 9 May 2008), Arts. 28 and 56. See also,

Within individual countries, lower-level jurisdictions may also be constrained in creating barriers to intra-country trade for certain reasons; for example, the Dormant Commerce Clause has been applied to minimise barriers to interstate trade within the United States.[43] And other provisions, particularly anti-discrimination provisions, may also prohibit certain barriers to trade imposed by lower jurisdictions within individual countries.[44]

Limitations on cross-border restrictions are not absolute; exceptions are typically carved out for reasons for which territorial restrictions are permissible. These reasons usually include public morality, health, essential security, and other public policy justifications;[45] the protection of IP rights is also among the reasons that countries have accepted as justifications for mandatory restrictions on trade.[46]

Because of the exceptions in international trade treaties that permit countries to maintain trade barriers for IP rights protection, countries' laws might require, for example, that territorial restrictions be placed on the distribution of or access to content in order to protect IP rights. Countries may prohibit the importation or distribution of pirated or counterfeit products whose importation or distribution, or other acts concerning the products, would infringe IP rights in the countries. Countries may also prohibit the importation or distribution of genuine products if the distribution rights to the products have not been exhausted; the use of this option is possible regardless of whether a country adheres to the principle of national exhaustion, or to the principle of international exhaustion.[47]

---

e.g., the North American Free Trade Agreement, U.S.-Can.-Mex., Dec. 17, 1992, 32 I.L.M. 289 (1993), Art. 102(1)(a).

43. '[T]he dormant Commerce Clause, which the Supreme Court has inferred from the text of the clause, prevents a state from enacting regulations that discriminate against out-of-state entities or burden interstate commerce.' *United Healthcare Ins. Co. v. Davis*, 602 F.3d 618 (5th Cir. 2010), 624.
44. E.g., Directive 2006/123/EC of the European Parliament and of the Council of 12 December 2006 on services in the internal market, Article 20. See further section C.IV *infra*.
45. The General Agreement on Tariffs and Trade, Arts. XX and XXI; Treaty on the Functioning of the European Union, Art. 36.
46. The General Agreement on Tariffs and Trade, Art. XX(d).
47. Under the principle of national exhaustion, the first authorised distribution of a copy or a product must occur in the country with the national exhaustion rule in order for the intellectual property right (distribution right, right to sell, right to import) to be exhausted in that country. Under the principle of international exhaustion, the first authorised distribution of a copy or a product will have the identical effect in a country adhering to the international exhaustion rule, regardless of whether the first distribution occurs in that particular country or in some other country in the world. For further details on exhaustion rules, see Christopher Heath, 'Parallel Imports of Patented Goods', chapter 2 of this book. Matters on the internet are complicated by the fact that the operation of the principle of exhaustion has not been fully clarified for digital goods. E.g., *Capitol Records, LLC v. ReDigi Inc.*, 934 F.Supp.2d 640 (SDNY 2013); CJEU C-128/11 *UsedSoft GmbH v. Oracle International Corp.*, ECLI:EU:C:2012:407, 3 July 2012; CJEU C-174/15, *Vereniging Openbare Bibliotheken v. Stichting Leenrecht*, ECLI:EU:C:2016:856, 10 November 2016. Exhaustion of copyright in digital goods is discussed in detail in *Matthias Leistner and Lucie Antoine*, 'Exhaustion and Second-Hand Digital Goods/Contents', chapter 7 of this book.

For instance, provisions of the German Copyright Act on the right to distribute[48] imply a territorial restriction on genuine content that has not been subject to copyright exhaustion: if a copy has not been distributed – with the authorisation of the copyright holder – in Germany, elsewhere in the European Union, or in one of the non-EU countries in the European Economic Area (because Germany adheres to the principle of regional exhaustion),[49] the distribution right has not been exhausted for Germany. If a distributor purchases a copy of a book in the United States, the distributor will not be permitted to distribute the book in Germany without permission or a licence to do so unless copyright to the book has been exhausted in the European Union or in any of the non-EU countries in the European Economic Area.

German law does not require, however, that the distributor in the previous example employ geoblocking to prevent customers who are connected to the internet in Germany from accessing the distributor's US-oriented webpage on which the book in the example is sold, or, in the case of an e-book, from accessing the e-book itself.[50] While the law does not require geoblocking at present, it is unclear whether courts might eventually require its use. In other countries it is equally unclear whether geoblocking needs to be employed. For example, whether the use of geoblocking is mandatory under US copyright law is being debated in two ongoing copyright cases in the United States,[51] and in a third US copyright case the judge recently stated that a party need not geoblock in order to avoid being subject to the personal jurisdiction of a US court.[52]

If the use of geoblocking becomes mandatory – either through statute or court or agency interpretation – the legality of any mandatory uses of geoblocking will depend on a national law's compliance with WTO rules (and possibly the law's compliance with other international agreements), or within national rules in cases of lower-level jurisdictions. National copyright laws fall, in general, within the IP law exception that WTO rules provide;[53] however, it is possible that geoblocking will also be scrutinised against the WTO rules requirement that 'measures and procedures to enforce IP rights do not themselves become barriers to legitimate trade'.[54]

There is no definition of 'legitimate trade' in the context of the WTO rule,[55] and in the absence of any definition, it is impossible to ascertain whether legally

---

48. Urheberrechtsgesetz, § 15 and § 17(1).
49. Urheberrechtsgesetz, § 17(2).
50. On digital exhaustion see *supra* n. 47.
51. See *supra* n. 30.
52. U.S. District Court for the District of Columbia, Case No. 1:16-cv-00159-RDM, *Triple Up Limited v. Youku Tudou Inc.*, memorandum opinion, docket document 15, 24 January 2017.
53. GATT, Art. XX.
54. TRIPS Agreement, Preamble. See also the North American Free Trade Agreement, Art. 1701(1).
55. On the lack of a definition of 'legitimate trade' see, e.g., *de Carvalho*, The TRIPS Regime of Patent Rights, Kluwer Law International, 2010, p. 82. On the meaning of 'legitimate trade' in the TRIPS Agreement see *Gervais*, The TRIPS Agreement: Drafting History and Analysis, Sweet & Maxwell, London, 2012, 159–160; *Malbon/Lawson/Davison*, The WTO Agreement on Trade-Related Aspects of Intellectual Property Rights, Edward Elgar, Cheltenham, 2014, 62–65.

mandated geoblocking is legal under the rule. A narrow interpretation of 'legitimate trade' may limit its applicability to trade in goods that is not illegal under the laws of the country of import,[56] as long as the national laws of that country are compliant with WTO rules.[57] If the national laws of the country are *not* compliant with WTO rules, trade that is illegal under the country's laws could still be 'legitimate' if the trade would be legal under WTO rules. Geoblocking that is used to implement territorial restrictions that are mandated by national laws would therefore create barriers to legitimate trade if the geoblocking prevented access to content where the trade in that content was legal under WTO rules.

Under the above narrow interpretation of the term 'legitimate trade', the legality of geoblocking that is targeted at particular content in order to comply with WTO-compliant national IP laws would depend on whether some other provision of the WTO rules contains an exception that would be defeated through the use of geoblocking. For example, Art. 60 TRIPS addresses the permeability of international borders;[58] the article concerns *de minimis* imports – the importation of 'small quantities of goods of a non-commercial nature contained in travellers' personal luggage or sent in small consignments'. This provision permits countries to make an exception from IP rights enforcement measures for *de minimis* imports; however, the article does not *mandate* that countries introduce the exception. Therefore, even if Art. 60 is expanded through interpretation and extrapolated by analogy to its online equivalent (*de minimis* import of content on the internet), Art. 60 alone, without corresponding national implementation, would not turn geoblocking into a barrier to 'legitimate trade'. Since there are no other provisions in the TRIPS Agreement, or other WTO rules, that create an exception that would allow for a certain degree of permeability of physical borders, it appears that geoblocking that is strictly targeted to implement WTO-compliant national IP laws would not present a barrier to legitimate trade – at least under the narrow interpretation of the term.

Some commentators have argued for a more expansive interpretation of the term 'legitimate trade'; under their interpretation, the term embodies a normative framework through which the WTO dispute settlement body should assess the compatibility of national laws with the TRIPS Agreement on a case-by-case basis.[59] According to this expansive interpretation, to the extent that the TRIPS Agreement gives countries certain leeway in national implementation, the prism of 'legitimate trade' should be used to ascertain whether a country utilises the leeway in a manner that is consistent with the goals of the WTO rules.

---

56. A WTO Director-General referred to trade in 'counterfeit trademark and pirated copyright goods' as an example of 'illegitimate trade'. Azevêdo Highlights 'Dramatic Increase' in Knowledge Component of Trade, WTO News, 20 October 2014, available at https://www.wto.org/english/news_e/spra_e/spra38_e.htm (accessed 26 April 2018).
57. *Malbon/Lawson/Davison*, The WTO Agreement on Trade-Related Aspects of Intellectual Property Rights, Edward Elgar, Cheltenham, 2014, p. 62.
58. On the relationship between 'the objective of avoiding barriers to legitimate trade' and 'enforcement measures applied at the border' see *Kennedy*, WTO Dispute Settlement and the TRIPS Agreement, Cambridge University Press, 2016, p. 215.
59. *Malbon, Lawson and Davison*, The WTO Agreement on Trade-Related Aspects of Intellectual Property Rights, Edward Elgar, Cheltenham, 2014, p. 63.

Under the expansive interpretation, for example, a seizure of goods in a country of transit where the goods are considered to be counterfeit might be considered a barrier to 'legitimate trade' when those goods are non-infringing in both the country of origin and the country of destination. Although no rule in the TRIPS Agreement prohibits seizures of goods in transit, the concept of 'legitimate trade', if interpreted broadly, could serve to prevent seizures in these circumstances.[60] As is discussed in D below, under some circumstances geoblocking could be found to create a barrier to 'legitimate trade' under this expansive interpretation.

III. The Legality of Geoblocking when it Implements Voluntary Territorial Restrictions

Voluntary territorial restrictions can serve many purposes. Market partitioning allows market participants to maximise their profits through the staggered release of content and the provision of localised content, which may include national language versions of content, versions adjusted for content that appeals to local populations, and versions complying with local standards. A territorially targeted release of content can magnify the effects of marketing and enhance consumer confidence in the content. Most importantly, dividing markets by territory enables content owners to price discriminate – they can set different prices for different territories based on local purchasing power and price expectations.

The legality of voluntary territorial restrictions is assessed under national law, with the most significant limitations on voluntary territorial restrictions arising from competition law – which may affect agreements that create and/or maintain territorial restrictions. For example, in the European Union, where vertical agreements[61] are generally permitted, competition law does not allow such agreements to place territorial restrictions on the sales of goods and services;[62] however, the law makes an exception, for example, for a 'restriction of active sales into the exclusive territory [...] reserved to the supplier [...], where such a restriction does not limit sales by the customers of the buyer'.[63] While territorial restrictions of active sales are allowed, the

---

60. On indications that this kind of seizure might be a barrier to legitimate trade, see Promoting Access to Medical Technologies and Innovation, WHO-WIPO-WTO Book, chapter 4, available at https://www.wto.org/english/tratop_e/trips_e/trilatweb_e/ch4c_trilat_web_13_e.htm (accessed 26 April 2018).
61. A 'vertical agreement' is 'entered into between two or more undertakings each of which operates, for the purposes of the agreement on the concerted practice, at a different level of the production or distribution chain [...]' Commission Regulation (EU) No. 330/2010 of 20 April 2010 on the application of Article 101(3) of the Treaty on the Functioning of the European Union to categories of vertical agreements and concerted practices (OJ L102 of 23 April 2010), Art. 1(a).
62. *Ibid.*, Art. 4(b).
63. *Ibid.*, Art, 4(b)(i). '"Active" sales mean actively approaching individual customers by for instance direct mail, including the sending of unsolicited e-mails, or visits; or actively approaching a specific customer group or customers in a specific territory through advertisement in media, on the Internet or other promotions specifically targeted at that customer group or targeted at customers in that territory.' European Commission, Guidelines on Vertical Restraints, SEC(2010) 411, p. 19.

agreements that create and maintain such restrictions must permit passive sales[64] into the territory under the agreements. The rule on passive sales stems from the European Commission's desire to promote EU-wide market integration and allow some competition via passive sales in the interest of 'the elimination of significant price differences between Member States'.[65]

In the online context, according to the European Commission's 'Guidelines on Vertical Restraints', 'having a website is considered a form of passive selling'.[66] Therefore, the Commission would presumably view as anti-competitive, for example, a distribution agreement that required a distributor to geoblock customers located outside of a licensed territory. The geoblocking would mean that these customers would be unable to view the distributor's website, and it would prevent passive sales that should be permissible under EU competition law.[67]

With regard to IP rights, EU competition rules concerning vertical agreements cover only agreements that contain 'ancillary provisions on the assignment or use of intellectual property rights';[68] the rules do not cover provisions on IP rights that 'constitute the primary object of such agreements' and are not 'directly related to the use, sale or resale of goods or services by the buyer or its customers'.[69] Therefore, exclusive licences to reproduce and distribute copyrighted content do not fall under the rules, nor do 'broadcasting contracts concerning the right to record and/or broadcast an event'.[70] Therefore, the rules on vertical agreements do not prevent the use of geoblocking when it is used to implement territorial restrictions based on these licences.

In cases where EU competition rules do apply to the exclusive licensing of IP rights, the exclusive licensing is not considered anticompetitive *per se* under EU law, as long as '[t]he characteristics of the [particular] industry and of its markets in the [European Union] […] serve to show that an exclusive […] licence is not, in itself, such as to prevent, restrict or distort competition.'[71] What the competition law rules call for is an evaluation of whether the imposed territorial restrictions are 'artificial and unjustifiable in terms of the needs of the [particular] industry'.[72] For example, provisions in an exclusive broadcast licence were held anticompetitive when the

---

64. As opposed to 'active sales', '"[p]assive" sales mean responding to unsolicited requests from individual customers including delivery of goods and services to such customers.' *Ibid.*, 19. Using the top-level domain of the exclusive territory would also be considered active selling in the territory. *Funke*, Territorial Restraints and Distribution in the European Union, Distribution and Franchising Committee, ABA Section of Antitrust Law, available at http://www.osborneclarke.com/media/filer_public/73/56/73569cbb-0450-40fe-9fc1-06112e5e049b/territorial-restraints.pdf (accessed 17 January 2018).
65. European Commission, Green Paper on Vertical Restraints in EC Competition Policy, COM(96) 721 final, 22 January 1997, para. 181, p. 53.
66. European Commission (*supra* n. 63), p, 19. However, '[t]he Commission considers online advertisement specifically addressed to certain customers a form of active selling to these customers.' *Ibid.*, 20.
67. *Ibid.*, 19.
68. Commission Regulation (EU) No. 330/2010, Recital 3.
69. *Ibid.*, Art. 2(3).
70. European Commission (*supra* n. 63), p. 14.
71. ECJ C-262/81 *Coditel SA v. Ciné-Vog Films SA*, ECLI:EU:C:1982:334, para. 16.
72. *Ibid.*, para. 19.

provisions included an obligation for satellite broadcast providers not to supply decoding devices that would give access to the exclusively licensed content from outside the licensed territory.[73] The issue that is important for compliance with EU competition rules is whether the use of geoblocking to comply with an exclusive IP licence could be considered excessive under competition law even when geoblocking is applied in a targeted manner, and only to particular content for which territorial restrictions apply.[74]

In a competition law case that concerned exclusive broadcast licences, the European Commission opined in 2015 that the use of geoblocking might be a violation of EU competition law because geoblocking prevents passive sales from geoblocked parts of the European Union.[75] To address the Commission's competition law-related concerns, two of the copyright owners in the case committed not to enter into contractual obligations that would prevent or limit the broadcaster 'from responding to unsolicited requests from consumers residing and located in the [European Economic Area] but outside of such broadcaster's licensed territory'.[76] The Commission made these commitments legally binding upon the two copyright owners in a 2016 decision.[77]

It might be surprising that the European Commission applied the rule on passive sales in a case where not only the sale but also the delivery occurred online. It is questionable whether the passive sales principle should be extended to instances in which the goods being sold are themselves digital and both the sale and the delivery of the goods occur online, because a significant difference exists between online and offline sales of digital goods. For offline sales, physical obstacles will limit the volume of permissible spillover from passive sales; for online sales – and for digital goods delivered online – the physical obstacles disappear, as do any limitations on spillover. Once spillover becomes unlimited, the purpose of exclusive licences is defeated and the copyright owner is deprived of the choice of granting exclusive licences for different territories. The copyright owner might maximise his profits by granting a single exclusive licence for the entire territory in which the competition

---

73. CJEU C-631/11, *Football Association Premier League Ltd. v. QC Leisure*, ECLI:EU:C:2013:387, para. 146.
74. For a detailed discussion of the legality of geoblocking in these circumstances see *Vesela*, Geoblocking Requirements in Online Distribution of Copyright-Protected Content: Implications of Copyright Issues on Application of EU Antitrust Law, 25(3) Michigan State International Law Review 595 (2017).
75. Antitrust: Commission Sends Statement of Objections on Cross-Border Provision of Pay-TV Services Available in UK and Ireland, European Commission, Press Release, 23 July 2015, available at http://europa.eu/rapid/press-release_IP-15-5432_en.htm (accessed 18 January 2018).
76. Commission Decision of 26 July 2016 relating to a proceeding under Article 101 of the Treaty on the Functioning of the European Union and Article 53 of the EEA Agreement (Case AT.40023 – Cross-border access to pay-TV), C(2016) 4740 final, para. 55.
77. *Ibid.* For prior competition law investigations of uses of similar tools of market partitioning, such as DVD region codes, see *Yu*, Region Codes and the Territorial Mess, 30 Cardozo Arts & Ent. L. J. 187, 220–226 (2012).

law rules apply, but it is debatable whether a single exclusive licence promotes competition within the territory.[78]

The key to understanding the above approach that the European Commission has taken toward territorial limitations on broadcast licences (and on geoblocking) is the Commission's larger agenda to create a single European digital market and eliminate intra-EU cross-border barriers to online trade. While competition law may assist in achieving this result in the European Union, EU copyright law continues to present a significant obstacle to reaching the Commission's goal. Therefore the Commission, notwithstanding resistance from EU Member States, has pushed for the creation of a unitary EU copyright,[79] or at a minimum an increase in the level of copyright law harmonisation among the EU Member States.[80] Within this agenda, the Commission has promoted EU-wide licensing through legislation such as the Collective Rights Management Directive,[81] which provides, *inter alia*, for 'multi-territorial licensing of rights in musical works for online use', and the Cross-Border Portability Regulation,[82] which requires that certain content providers provide content to EU residents even when the residents are temporarily present in another EU Member State.

Under copyright law, a problem for broadcasters who do not geoblock is that a broadcaster may be held liable for copyright infringement in countries where the broadcaster makes content available even though the broadcaster has no permission or licence to do so.[83] Absent a collective will among the EU Member States to adopt a unitary EU copyright, the solution to this inherent conflict between competition law and copyright law is to adopt a different rule for selecting the national law that will be applicable in cases of copyright infringement. Currently, with only a single exception – for satellite broadcasting – the law of the place of infringement applies to copyright infringement; for satellite broadcasting, an EU directive provides for the emission principle, under which potentially infringing acts of communication

---

78. Alternatively, a copyright owner may resort to other market partitioning tools. For example, the copyright owner may license a motion picture to a small language market on the condition that the distributor dub the picture (as opposed to adding only subtitles to the picture). Dubbed in the language of the small population, the picture will not be widely distributable outside the licensed market. An open question is whether this is a positive result for the European Union, where language diversity pertains and knowledge of multiple languages should be promoted.

On the evolving opinions of the effects of territorial restrictions on competition in general see, e.g., *Drexl*, 'EU Competition Law and Parallel Trade in Pharmaceuticals: Lessons to be Learned for WTO/TRIPS?', in *Rosén* (ed.), Intellectual Property at the Crossroads of Trade, Edward Elgar, Cheltenham, 2012, pp. 3–24, at pp. 6–7.

79. European Commission, Online Services, Including E-commerce, in the Single Market, SEC(2011) 1641 final, 11 January 2012.

80. European Commission, Towards A Modern, More European Copyright Framework, COM(2015) 626 final, 9 December 2015.

81. Directive 2014/26/EU of the European Parliament and of the Council of 26 February 2014 on collective management of copyright and related rights and multi-territorial licensing of rights in musical works for online use in the internal market (OJ L84 of 20 March 2014).

82. Regulation (EU) 2017/1128 of the European Parliament and of the Council of 14 June 2017 on cross-border portability of online content services in the internal market (OJ L168 of 30 June 2017).

83. CJEU C-170/12. *Peter Pinckney v. KDG Mediatech AG*, ECLI:EU:C:2013:635.

to the public are deemed to occur only in the country from which the broadcast originates (the country of origin principle).[84] The European Commission proposed a regulation in 2016 that would extend the principle of country of origin to 'ancillary online services by broadcasting organisations',[85] thus settling the conflict between competition law and copyright law by enabling the elimination of geoblocking in at least the circumstances covered by the regulation.[86]

While the approach to geoblocking in the European Union is driven by the European Commission's aim of creating a single EU digital market, the approach in the United States focuses on exclusive territorial licences that limit the licensee in licensing to others, which 'raise antitrust concerns only if there is a horizontal relationship among licensors, or among licensees, or between the licensor and its licensee(s).'[87] In cases of exclusive dealing where a licensee is constrained by an exclusive licence, the reasonableness of the arrangement will be evaluated by taking into account both the pro-competitive and anti-competitive effects of such an arrangement.[88] The issue of geoblocking has not yet been specifically raised in an antitrust context in the United States; however, given that US antitrust law is not categorically against absolute territorial limitations, it is likely that, in general, geoblocking would be viewed more favourably by US antitrust law[89] than it is by EU law.

IV. The Anti-Geoblocking Regulation in the European Union

In addition to the EU competition law case mentioned in section C.III above (which is continuing against the remaining parties in the case), the EU anti-geoblocking initiative has entered into the Commission's legislative agenda in yet another form. In May 2016, the European Commission proposed a regulation 'on addressing

---

84. Council Directive 93/83/EEC of 27 September 1993 on the coordination of certain rules concerning copyright and rights related to copyright applicable to satellite broadcasting and cable retransmission (OJ L248 of 6 October 1993), Art. 1(2)(b). The country of origin of the satellite broadcast is 'the Member State where, under the control and responsibility of the broadcasting organisation, the programme-carrying signals are introduced into an uninterrupted chain of communication leading to the satellite and down towards the earth.' *Ibid.*, Art. 1(2)(b).
85. Proposal for a Regulation of the European Parliament and of the Council laying down rules on the exercise of copyright and related rights applicable to certain online transmissions of broadcasting organisations and retransmissions of television and radio programmes, COM(2016) 594 final, 14 September 2016, p. 4.
86. It is presently unclear whether and to what extent copyright owners and broadcasters might be able to contract around the principle of country of origin under the proposed regulation. Report by the European Parliament Committee on Legal Affairs, A8-0378/2017, 27 November 2017, Art. 2(2b), pp. 24–25.
87. Antitrust Guidelines for the Licensing of Intellectual Property, U.S. Department of Justice and the Federal Trade Commission, 12 January 2017, available at https://www.justice.gov/atr/IPguidelines/download (accessed 30 January 2018), p. 21.
88. *Ibid.*
89. On the differences between EU competition law rules and US antitrust rules with regard to passive sales see, for example, Kirsch and Weesner, 'Can Antitrust Law Control E-Commerce? A Comparative Analysis in Light of U.S. and E.U. Antitrust Law', 12 U.C. Davis Journal of International Law and Policy 297 (2006), pp. 323–329.

geo-blocking and other forms of discrimination based on customers' nationality, place of residence or place of establishment within the internal market'.[90] After numerous amendments were introduced in the legislative process, the regulation was adopted in February 2018 and published on 2 March 2018 as Regulation (EU) 2018/302.

The regulation, one part of the EU's Digital Single Market Strategy, targets 'unjustified geo-blocking',[91] which the regulation defines as geoblocking employed to discriminate in violation of the anti-discrimination provision of the EU directive on services in the internal market. The Services Directive provision prohibits discrimination among service recipients based on their nationality or place of residence, but still allows for 'differences in the conditions of access where those differences are directly justified by objective criteria'.[92] According to the Explanatory Memorandum accompanying the proposal, the regulation was designed to clarify what the 'objective criteria' are and when the differences are not justifiable.[93] In the end, the adopted regulation aims to prevent unjustified discrimination generally, not only for differences that are deemed unjustified according to the Services Directive.

The regulation prohibits traders from discriminating among their customers with respect to the customers' access to traders' online interfaces and to goods and services.[94] Traders must also not discriminate against their customers as to conditions for payment transactions.[95] But not all geoblocking is prohibited as discriminatory; in addition to leaving some situations open for disparate treatment of customers from different countries, the regulation permits geoblocking when geoblocking is used to implement mandatory territorial restrictions.[96]

One controversial amendment that was introduced in the legislative process but was ultimately cut from the adopted version would have prohibited discrimination in the provision of 'electronically supplied services the main feature of which is the provision of access to and use of copyright-protected works or other protected subject matter […], provided that the trader has the rights or has acquired the licence to use such content for the relevant territories.'[97] This provision would have meant, for example, that a copyright owner could not geoblock users from an EU country to implement voluntary territorial restrictions on access to copyrighted content to which the copyright owner holds copyright in that same country. The provision was subject to heavy criticism and was ultimately deleted from the proposal. The adopted

---

90. Proposal for a Regulation, COM(2016) 289 final, 25 May 2016.
91. Ibid., p. 2.
92. See supra n. 44.
93. See supra n. 90, p. 2.
94. Regulation (EU) 2018/302 of the European Parliament and of the Council of 28 February 2018 on addressing unjustified geo-blocking and other forms of discrimination based on consumers' nationality, place of residence or place of establishment within the internal market and amending Regulations (EC) No 2006/2004 and (EU) 2017/2394 and Directive 2009/22/EC, Articles 3 and 4.
95. Ibid., Article 5.
96. Ibid., Articles 3(3) and 4(5).
97. Report of the Committee on the Internal Market and Consumer Protection, A8-0172/2017, 27 April 2017, pp. 23–24. For an earlier draft wording see Draft Report, 2016/0152(COD), 19 December 2016, p. 45, and the Opinion of the European Parliament Committee on Legal Affairs, 2016/0152(COD), 4 April 2017, p. 34–35.

regulation calls only for a future evaluation to be conducted to determine whether a prohibition on discrimination should cover the provision of copyright-protected content where 'the trader has the requisite rights for the relevant territories.'[98]

The evolution of the language in the drafts of the proposal evidenced the difficulty in completely eliminating geoblocking. The proposal had only focused on the tool – geoblocking – to pursue its objectives, which have at their core the substantive legal issues that should be addressed directly. It appears that the starting point for the proposal was the desire to eliminate geoblocking altogether, and later the need for exceptions continued to shape the proposal. The regulation is EU-specific and results from the very specific agenda that is being driven by the European Commission, and it is difficult to imagine that the approach taken could easily be transplanted to a different setting – unless another setting would also warrant the creation of 'leaky' borders.

D.   GEOBLOCKING AND THE FUTURE OF TRADE

Geolocation is now a standard feature on the internet,[99] and in at least some industries geoblocking seems to be widely used. If geoblocking becomes ubiquitous, its impact on trade – both cross-border trade and intra-country trade – will be significant. Widespread implementation of geoblocking could transform the internet into an environment where trade is less free than it is in the physical world.

Geoblocking could be perceived as the ultimate means of erecting impermeable borders on the internet. This perception is incorrect; as discussed in section B.IV above, countervailing tools tend to be available that enable users to circumvent geoblocking. However, the use of circumvention tools is an extraordinary step that goes beyond the ordinary use of the internet; circumvention is possibly illegal, and the continuous improvements that come about in geoblocking tools may make circumvention difficult. The perception might be that geoblocking is harder to circumvent than other means that are used for market partitioning and that through the use of geoblocking internet actors may achieve '*absolute* territorial exclusivity'[100] – the kind of exclusivity that has prompted the European Commission to investigate whether the use of geoblocking, in particular cases, violates EU competition law, as discussed in section C.III above.

---

98. *Supra* note 94, Article 9(2), and already Proposal, Presidency, 14780/17, 27 November 2017, p. 33.
99. In the United States, several bills were introduced in the US Congress with legislation that would provide for location privacy rules; none of the bills were passed. The legality of the use of location data for the purpose of delivering targeted content and its limits were clarified by court decisions. E.g., *In re iPhone Application Litig.*, 844 F.Supp.2d 1040 (NDCA 2012); U.S. District Court for the Northern District of California, case No. 3:16-cv-03474, *United States v. InMobi Pte Ltd.*, Stipulated Order for Permanent Injunction and Civil Penalty Judgment, 22 June 2016.
100. Commission Decision of 26 July 2016 relating to a proceeding under Article 101 of the Treaty on the Functioning of the European Union and Article 53 of the EEA Agreement (Case AT.40023 – Cross-border access to pay-TV), C(2016) 4740 final, para. 44 (emphasis added).

Some of the emerging geoblocking tools may raise additional concerns for cross-border trade. One technology has already been developed that would add geolocation information to internet protocol packets, which are the packets that carry data on the internet; through use of the technology, packets would contain information about the location of the devices used by the sender and the recipient of the packet.[101] Packets geotagged with this information could be routed on a particular path, depending on the location of the origin of a packet and its destination, and could also be blocked in transit if, for example, a country chose not to allow a packet to pass through switches located in its territory.

A country that would prohibit the routing of certain packets through equipment located in its territory could be in violation of free trade rules. This situation would be similar to the situation in a case involving the transit of pharmaceuticals through Schiphol Airport in the Netherlands; the pharmaceuticals were being shipped from India to Brazil – two countries where the pharmaceuticals were not protected by patents – through the Netherlands, where the owner of a Dutch patent on the pharmaceuticals requested that Dutch customs seize the pharmaceuticals in transit.[102]

In this case, under the expansive interpretation of the term 'legitimate trade' (discussed in section C.II above), it could be argued that the seizure, though it did not violate the TRIPS Agreement, amounted to a barrier to 'legitimate trade'. Similarly, some might consider that a country would be raising barriers to 'legitimate trade' if that country prevented internet protocol packets from transiting through its territory because the packets carried content that infringed IP rights in the country of transit, even if the content were non-infringing in both the country of origin and the country of destination of the packets.

Another characteristic of geoblocking that could make it a potent barrier to trade is the level of granularity at which geoblocking may be employed, as discussed in section B.II above. For example, content could be delivered to internet users residing in a high-rent apartment complex for a different price than that same content delivered to internet users residing in a neighbouring low-rent apartment complex. Competition rules might be adapted to mitigate anti-competitive results that this conduct might cause. However, because the internet enables internet actors to adopt integrated business models and eliminate distributors, *de facto* anti-competitive conduct might not always fall under the purview of competition law – for example, when a copyright owner uses geoblocking to implement voluntary territorial restrictions on the copyright owner's own content.

In the physical world, the effects of voluntary territorial restrictions might be partly mitigated through the operation of the exhaustion doctrine.[103] If in the apartment complex example above, it were not digital content that was being distributed but rather a physical book, a person from one apartment complex could buy the book and resell it to a person in the other apartment complex. Because of the exhaustion

---

101. See *supra* n. 20.
102. WTO DS408, *European Union and a Member State – Seizure of Generic Drugs in Transit*, 2010.
103. On the interplay between the exhaustion doctrine and competition law in the European Union see *Drexl*, *supra* n. 78, pp. 3–4.

doctrine, no authorisation or licence from the copyright owner would be necessary for the resale.[104]

In the online world, the effects of voluntary territorial restrictions that are imposed through geoblocking might not be subject to the same mitigation that applies to the physical book, because the exhaustion doctrine might not apply – either because the doctrine does not apply to digital content at all (as seems to be the case – for now – in the United States),[105] or because the online content is considered to be only licensed and not sold.[106]

New theories might be developed to prevent trade from being hindered by uses of geoblocking if the uses are considered to be damaging, and the current environment seems to be particularly inclined to constrain profit-maximising behaviour by IP rights owners, including behaviour that is considered undesirable voluntary market partitioning.[107] Justice Breyer, writing for the majority of the U.S. Supreme Court in *Kirtsaeng*, noted that the US Constitution's IP Clause, which is the basis for federal copyright legislation in the United States, 'nowhere suggests that [the] limited exclusive right should include a right to divide markets or concomitant right to charge different purchasers different prices for the same book, say to increase or to maximize the gain.'[108] While *Kirtsaeng* concerned market partitioning at the international level, the observation about the US Constitution's IP Clause could apply equally to market partitioning within the United States. Similarly, the Court of Justice of the European Union refused to adopt the notion that copyright owners are entitled to a 'premium [that] goes beyond what is necessary to ensure *appropriate* remuneration for those right holders',[109] and the European Commission, in its decision against Paramount Pictures International Limited and Viacom Inc. (discussed in section C.III above), noted that IP rights holders have no guarantee that they will have an 'opportunity to demand the highest possible remuneration'; instead 'they are ensured […] only appropriate remuneration for each use of the protected subject matter'.[110]

---

104. Because the exhaustion doctrine may mitigate the effects of territorial restrictions, traders might attempt to prevent its application: 'Trade-restrictive licensing practices become a problem particularly in the case that one or more states have adopted the principle of international exhaustion, since the right holder will try to fill the gap created by the exhaustion of his right through the inclusion of, for example, an export ban in the licence contract.' Gallego, 'The Principle of Exhaustion of Rights and Its Implications for Competition Law', 34(5) IIC 473 [2003], p. 475.
105. *Capitol Records, LLC v. ReDigi Inc.*, 934 F.Supp.2d 640 (SDNY 2013).
106. On sale versus licence in the context of copyright exhaustion see *Vernor v. Autodesk*, 621 F.3d 1102 (9th Cir. 2010); CJEU C-128/11, *UsedSoft GmbH v. Oracle International Corp.*, ECLI:EU:C:2012:407.
107. On other considerations that weigh in favour of some market partitioning see *Drexl, supra* n. 78, pp. 5–18.
108. *Kirtsaeng v. John Wiley & Sons, Inc.*, 568 U.S. 519, 552 (2013).
109. CJEU C-403/08, *Football Association Premier League Ltd v. QC Leisure*, ECLI:EU:C:2011:631, para. 116 (emphasis added).
110. Commission Decision of 26 July 2016 relating to a proceeding under Article 101 of the Treaty on the Functioning of the European Union and Article 53 of the EEA Agreement (Case AT.40023 – Cross-border access to pay-TV), C(2016) 4740 final, recital 41.

E. CONCLUSION

The internet is no longer a borderless medium on which content moves freely without territorial restrictions. Some countries have walled their part of the internet to prevent certain content from entering their territory, some internet service providers have been recruited to implement restrictions on content in a territorial manner, and some individual internet actors have used geolocation and geoblocking tools to select the users who may access the actors' content, based on a user's physical location. It would be unrealistic to expect that the trend of internet territorialisation will cease and that the internet will return to its initial borderless state. The challenge is to ensure that the internet does not become an environment where free trade not only does not flourish, but where it faces obstacles greater than the obstacles that free trade encounters in the physical world.

Technological capabilities that make it possible to place effective territorial restrictions on the internet at different levels of granularity, including at levels much more precise than at the level of any existing jurisdiction, will magnify the importance of questions about rationales for permitting territorial restrictions – particularly the restrictions that content providers might impose on territorially unencumbered content. The answers to these questions will be important for both trade law and competition law.[111]

---

111. On the need for coordination between competition law and trade law see *Abbott/Singham*, 'Competition Policy and International Trade Distortions', in *C. Herrmann* et al. (eds.), European Yearbook of International Economic Law (EYIEL), vol. 4, 2013, 23–37. On the lack of 'comprehensive body of competition law within the framework of the WTO' see *Gallego* (*supra* n. 104), p. 476.

CHAPTER 4
The Registration of Descriptive Terms in International Trade

Anke Moerland

A. INTRODUCTION

The Agreement on Trade-related Aspects of Intellectual Property Rights[1] (hereinafter TRIPS) sets out minimum standards for the protection and enforcement of intellectual property (IP) rights. This is the primary goal of TRIPS. What is, however, paid less attention to, is the aim that IP rules in themselves should not become barriers to trade. The circumstances surrounding the TRIPS negotiations, in particular the dispute between the European Communities (EC) and the United States (US) regarding *Certain Aramid Fiber* (GATT Panel, *US – Section 337*),[2] indicate that all negotiating parties had an interest in stipulating in TRIPS that IP enforcement measures should not become barriers to (legitimate) trade (see chapter 1). The first recital of the preamble as well as Art. 41.1 second sentence TRIPS reflect this aim. Recital 1 reads as follows:

> 'Desiring to *reduce distortions and impediments to international trade*, and taking into account the need to promote effective and adequate protection of intellectual property rights, and to *ensure that measures and procedures to enforce intellectual property rights do not themselves become barriers to legitimate trade*;' [emphasis added]

Even though the second part of Recital 1 TRIPS (and Art. 41.1) only addresses measures enforcing IP rights, the aim of avoiding barriers to legitimate trade may not be limited

---

1. Agreement on Trade-Related Aspects of Intellectual Property Rights, Annex 1C of the Marrakesh Agreement Establishing the World Trade Organization, signed on 15 April 1994, 33 I.L.M. 1197 (1994).
2. GATT Panel, *United States – Section 337 of the Tariff Act of 1930* (L/6439 – 36S/345 of 16 January 1989).

to IP enforcement measures. Arguably, the entire World Trade Organisation (WTO) system is based on reducing barriers to international trade, as evidenced in the first part of Recital 1 of the TRIPS Preamble (see emphasis). The fact that enforcement measures have been particularly highlighted may mainly be due to the negotiating circumstances (in particular the *Certain Aramid Fiber* dispute, which concerned border measures)[3] as well as the need for TRIPS proponents to justify the inclusion of an international IP agreement in the trade context[4] – enforcement, and in particular border measures, are one of the most evident examples of IP rules that could impede international trade and may therefore have received prominent attention.

This chapter focuses on descriptive terms registered as trade marks and generic terms registered as geographical indications (GIs). It addresses the question as to whether the rules for registering and opposing the registration of descriptive and generic terms under domestic trade mark and GI law (as imposed by trade agreements) create barriers to legitimate trade and how such effects could be addressed. In order to further define under which conditions such rules would be classified as barriers to legitimate trade, two examples will illustrate situations that regularly occur in international trade.[5]

I. Rapadura

Rapadura is the Brazilian word for dried sugar cane juice. The German company Rapunzel Naturkost AG had registered 'Rapadura' as a word mark in Germany in 1989 in class 30 for whole cane sugar.[6] From 2000 onwards, the Brazilian government requested the German company to renounce the trade mark in light of international trade rules, and in particular because Brazilian producers and exporters have experienced severe impediments and economic damage due to the registered trade mark.[7] The period for opposition had already expired and therefore legal tools were no longer available to the Brazilian government.

The effect of a foreign language term being registered as a trade mark in Germany for example is that Brazilian producers who want to describe their products by using the Brazilian original name cannot do so because a registered trade mark is protected against use in the course of trade of identical names for identical or similar products where such use would result in a likelihood of confusion.[8] Consumers

---

3. See *M. Kennedy*, 'Avoiding Barriers to Legitimate Trade: Objectives and Obligations', chapter 1 of this book.
4. *P. Drahos*, 'Expanding Intellectual Property's Empire: the Role of FTAs', GRAIN [2003]; *D. Matthews*, Globalising Intellectual Property Rights: The TRIPs Agreement, New York 2002; *J. Braithwaite and P. Drahos*, Global Business Regulation, Cambridge 2000.
5. *C. Heath and T. Prüfer*, 'Fremdsprachige Bezeichnungen als Marke', in *Ohly, Bodewig, Dreier, Götting, Haedicke and Lehmann* (eds.), Festschrift für Gerhard Schricker, Munich 2005, 791–800, p. 792.
6. German DPMA register number 1143537, applied for on December 30, 1988, registered on 24 July 1989 and cancelled on 1 January 2009.
7. bio-markt.info, Rapunzel: Streit um RAPADURA 2006, available at <http://bio-markt.info/kurzmeldungen/Rapunzel_Streit_um_RAPADURA%C2%AE.html> (accessed 3 January 2018).
8. Art. 16 TRIPS.

would indeed be confused about the origin of sugar cane products carrying the same name, having gotten accustomed to 'Rapadura' being used as a trade mark, rather than as a descriptive term. As a result of the Brazilian government's efforts, in 2008, Rapunzel renounced the trade mark 'Rapadura' and registered the word mark 'Rapunzel Rapadura', thereby alleviating the problems posed by the protection of the sole foreign language term.

II.   Feta

The question as to whether the term 'feta' has a generic meaning, or indeed refers to the source and origin of this particular cheese, has been subject to debate in several countries, including in the European Union.[9] In the European Union, 'feta' is protected as a designation of origin (PDO), with the territory of production being located in Greece.[10] While the European Court of Justice (ECJ, now CJEU) found that the term had not become generic within the EU (with the exception of Denmark),[11] this is not generally the case for other countries. In Canada for example, 'feta' refers to a 'type' of cheese, namely a cheese made of a mixture of goat and sheep milk which is stored in brine. It is not associated with a particular origin, such as Greece. Most 'feta' cheese on the Canadian market is domestically produced.[12]

The Canada-EU Comprehensive Economic Trade Agreement (CETA),[13] which provisionally entered into force on 21 September 2017,[14] stipulates that the term 'feta' must be protected as a geographical indication.[15] This general rule means that producers who do not comply with the product specifications set out in the PDO registration cannot use the term 'feta' for the presentation or designation of their product on the EU and Canadian markets. However, the agreement provides for certain exceptions to this general rule. According to Art. 20.21.2, current users who have used the term prior to 18 October 2013, can continue using it in Canada for products in the class of 'cheeses'. New entrants can also use the term 'feta', however accompanied

---

9. See for an overview of the debate *D. Gangjee*, 'Say Cheese? A Sharper Image of Generic Use Through the Lens of Feta', 5 European Intellectual Property Review (EIPR) 172 [2007].
10. Commission Regulation (EC) No 1829/2002 of 14 October 2002 amending the Annex to Regulation (EC) No 1107/96 with regard to the name 'Feta', OJ L 277/10 (15 October 2002).
11. Joined Cases ECJ C-465/02 and ECJ C-466/02 *Federal Republic of Germany and Kingdom of Denmark v. Commission of the European Communities* [2006] ETMR 16, ECLI:EU:C:2005:804, paras. 85-88, 98.
12. G. Christides, 'Feta cheese row sours EU-Canada trade deal', BBC News Europe, 14 December 2013.
13. Comprehensive Economic and Trade Agreement (CETA) between Canada, of the one part, and the European Union and its Member States, of the other part, OJ L11/23 of 14 January 2017.
14. Council Decision (EU) 2017/38 of 28 October 2016 on the provisional application of the Comprehensive Economic and Trade Agreement (CETA) between Canada, of the one part, and the European Union and its Member States, of the other part, OJ L11/1080 of 14 January 2017.
15. See Art. 20.19 jo. Annex 20-A Canada-EU CETA.

by a) a qualifier such as 'kind', 'type', 'style', 'imitation' or the like, and b) a legible and visible indication of the geographical origin of the product concerned.[16]

The consequence of this agreement is that in Canada, producers can no longer describe the type of cheese with the relevant term used in the common language other than under the conditions listed above. This presents an obstacle for Canadian producers to market their products under the same conditions as EU producers of 'feta' cheese: they will have to adapt their labelling and thereby risk losing consumers who have become used to the product 'feta', rather than 'feta'-like cheese.

III.   A Barrier to Legitimate Trade

Where trade mark and GI rules create impediments for competitors from abroad to put their own products on the domestic and/or foreign market, one would generally regard such rules as a barrier to trade. The qualification that a barrier may be created to 'legitimate' trade is difficult and ambiguous. The term has not been defined in the TRIPS context (see the discussion in chapter 1 of this book). It entails a normative judgment that should balance the underlying values and interests.

Inspiration on how the concept could be understood may come from intra-Community trade where a similar concept exists. A barrier to trade within the EU would be a restriction to the free movement of goods, which entails that quantitative restrictions on imports are prohibited, unless they are justifiable.[17] Where products are limited or restricted from entering other markets, these can be classified as barriers to trade and according to EU law should be prohibited. Intellectual property rights, for example trade mark rules, can create quantitative restrictions on the importation of products if e.g. foreign language terms are registered as a trade mark in the country of importation and the trade mark holder enforces his rights against imported products that use those terms on their products. The same is true where generic terms are protected as geographical indications: those producers that do not fulfil the product specifications cannot market their product using the same or similar indication. The effect is that imported or domestic products are limited or restricted from entering the market. Whether such IP rules create barriers to legitimate trade depends on whether they are justifiable or not.

In order to ensure the free movement of goods, the founding fathers of the European Community had to strike a balance between the free circulation of goods legitimately placed on the market on the one hand, and the need 'to ensure that the social, artistic, economic and technological benefits which flow from intellectual property laws are not substantially damaged' on the other.[18] Hence, they included one exception dealing with intellectual property rights in the list of exceptions that can justify an impediment of the free movement of goods. Art. 36 Treaty on the Functioning of the European Union (TFEU) sets out:

---

16. See Art. 20.21.1 Canada-EU CETA.
17. Art. 34 Consolidated version of the Treaty on the Functioning of the European Union (TFEU), adopted on 13 December 2007, entered into force on 1 December 2009 (OJ C 115/47 of 9 May 2008).
18. G. *Tritton*, Intellectual Property in Europe, 3rd ed., London 2008, para. 7-001.

'The provisions of Articles 34 and 35 shall not preclude prohibitions or restrictions on imports, exports or goods in transit justified on grounds of [...] the protection of industrial and commercial property. Such prohibitions or restrictions shall not, however, constitute a means of arbitrary discrimination or a disguised restriction on trade between Member States.'

Two rules can be deduced from this exception. First, the protection of industrial and commercial property can serve as a justification for a restriction on the internal market. Second, for a restriction to be justified, however, it must not constitute a means of arbitrary discrimination or a disguised restriction on trade between the Member States. Linking this terminology to the international framework, one could interpret the term 'legitimate' in a similar manner: a barrier to legitimate trade exists if the measure creates arbitrary discrimination or a disguised restriction on trade and hence cannot be justified.

Looking at the EU framework for further guidance as to when the exercise of IP rules constitutes an arbitrary discrimination or a disguised restriction to trade, in *Deutsche Grammophon*, the ECJ held that the exception for IP rules is justified if it is applied 'for the purpose of safeguarding rights which constitute the specific subject-matter of such property'.[19] Importantly, while the Court found that generally for IP rights, the specific subject-matter is the exclusive right to first place a product on the market,[20] another consideration is the question of whether the exercise of IP rights is consistent with the policy and rationale behind the right.[21] This aim is evident in subsequent case law where the 'specific subject-matter' doctrine has become a more fluid concept, refined on a case-by-case basis. In particular, in *Boehringer v. Swingward (No. 2)*, the specific subject-matter of a trade mark was held to be the guarantee of the origin of the products.[22]

This analysis of when a restriction to the free movement of goods would be justifiable is relevant, even though it is clear that under EU law, recourse to Arts. 34–36 TFEU is no longer permitted in view of the complete and exhaustive harmonisation of trade mark rights.[23] It nevertheless provides us with guidelines for what should be taken into consideration in order to decide as to whether a restriction of the free movement of goods is justified. Applying this to the international level, international trade should be without distortions or impediments, unless a restriction of international trade can be justified. Whether a restriction is justified, and thereby does not create a barrier to legitimate trade, should be based on the question of whether the relevant rule is applied so as to safeguard the specific subject-matter of the property. When deciding on the specific subject-matter, one should also take into account the policy and rationale of the right. This contribution will hence aim at assessing whether the

---

19. ECJ C-78/70 *Deutsche Grammophon GmbH v. Metro-SB-Grossmarkte GmbH & Co*, KG [1971] E.C.R. 487; [1971] C.M.L.R. 631, para. 11.
20. Joined cases ECJ C-15-16/74 *Centrafarm BV v. Sterling Drug Inc* and *Centrafarm v. Winthrop* [1974] E.C.R. 1147; [1974] 2 C.M.L.R. 480.
21. *Ibid.*
22. ECJ C-348/04 *Böhringer Ingelheim KG v. Swingward Ltd* [2007] 2 C.M.L.R. 52, [2007] E.T.M.R. 775, para. 14.
23. ECJ C-355/96 *Silhouette International Schmied GmbH & Co KG v. Hartlauer Handelsgesellschaft mbH* [1998] E.C.R. I-4799; [1998] E.T.M.R. 539.

restriction for importers to market their products using descriptive, foreign language terms (in case such terms were protected as a trade mark) or for local producers to use the generic term (which under the EU agreement is no longer considered generic) can be justified by the specific subject-matter, policy and rationale of the relevant provision of trade mark or GI law. The applicable trade mark rules for the registration of descriptive terms on the EU level are Art. 4.1.c TMD[24] and Art. 7.1.c EUTMR[25] and on the international level Art. 15 TRIPS and Art. 6*quinquies* Paris Convention.[26] The applicable GI rules for generic terms are Art. 6 EU Regulation 1151/2012[27] on the EU level, Art. 24.6 TRIPS, Art. 6*quinquies* Paris Convention and relevant provisions in bilateral trade agreements on the international level.

Section B of this chapter will address the registration of descriptive (foreign language) terms under trade mark law, and whether the application of EU law constitutes a barrier to legitimate trade. The analysis of the EU legal framework will be the starting point, on the basis of which the consequences of the current EU trade mark rules for competitors will be assessed. The chapter will further suggest ways to address the barriers to trade created by the EU trade mark rules by drawing comparisons with other legal systems as well as international treaties. Section C will subsequently focus on the protection of generic terms according to GI rules; it will assess what the applicable rules in EU bilateral trade agreements regarding generic terms are, what consequences traders face and whether their application constitutes a barrier to legitimate trade.

B. THE PROTECTION OF FOREIGN DESCRIPTIVE TERMS AS TRADE MARKS

When a foreign name such as 'Rapadura' is registered for a national or EU trade mark, the relevant trade mark office needs to assess all absolute grounds of refusal set out in the TMD or EUTMR.[28] Two grounds of refusals are incorporated in both

---

24. Directive (EU) 2015/2436 of the European Parliament and of the Council of 16 December 2015 to approximate the laws of the Member States relating to trade marks (hereinafter TMD), OJ L 336/1 of 23.12.2015, entered into force 12 January 2016, applicable as of 15 January 2019.
25. Regulation (EU) 2017/1001 of the European Parliament and of the Council of 14 June 2017 on the European Union trade mark (codification) (hereinafter EUTMR), OJ L 154/1 of 16.6.2017, entered into force 6 July 2017, applicable as of 1 October 2017. Note that the relevant provisions of the Directive and Regulation assessed in this contribution are very similar. This contribution will generally refer to the provisions of the TMD, only where the equivalent provisions differ from each other, will the provisions of the EUTMR be referred to.
26. Paris Convention for the Protection of Industrial Property, adopted in Paris on 20 March 1883, entered into force on 7 July 1884; last revised at the Stockholm Revision Conference, adopted in Stockholm on 14 July 1967 and entered into force 26 April 1970, 828 U.N.T.S. 305 (hereinafter Paris Convention).
27. Regulation (EU) No 1151/2012 of the European Parliament and of the Council of 21 November 2012 on quality schemes for agricultural products and foodstuffs, OJ L 343/1 of 14.12.2012, entered into force on 3 January 2013.
28. In the case of 'Rapadura', this was the German Patent and Trade Mark Office (DPMA) as a German trade mark was applied for. In case of applications for EU trade marks, this is

instruments which seem to be most relevant for foreign language terms: descriptive marks and marks registered in bad faith.

I. Absolute Ground of Refusal Regarding Signs Designating Characteristics of the Goods or Services

Where the proposed word mark describes a certain kind, quality, quantity or other characteristic of the product for which the trade mark is applied for, it cannot be registered. Art. 4.1.c TMD[29] states:

> 'The following shall not be registered or, if registered, shall be liable to be declared invalid:
>
> [...]
>
> (c) trade marks which consist *exclusively* of signs or indications which *may* serve, in trade, to designate the kind, quality, quantity, intended purpose, value, geographical origin, or the time of production of the goods or of rendering of the service, or other characteristics of the goods or services;' (emphasis added)

The ECJ has clarified a number of ambiguities regarding this provision, which are also relevant for foreign language terms.

A clear limit to this ground of refusal regards its subject-matter: it only applies to signs and indications which exclusively consist of descriptive terms.[30] Where a descriptive term is accompanied by an arbitrary or fanciful term or combined with a visual sign, the mark would be registrable, unless any of the other grounds of refusal poses problems. This is why the trade mark 'Rapadura Rapunzel' does not fall under this ground of refusal because the foreign language term is accompanied by a distinctive element, being Rapunzel.

The provision is interpreted rather broadly with regard to the terminology '*may* serve, in trade, to designate': there is no need that the term is actually being used already on the market. It is sufficient that it may be used in the future to describe a certain characteristic. When assessing Art. 4.1.c TMD, the competent authority must:

> 'determine whether a trade mark for which registration is sought currently represents, in the mind of the relevant class of persons, a description of the characteristics of the goods or services concerned or whether it is reasonable to assume that that might be the case in the future.'[31]

---

the European Union Intellectual Property Office (EUIPO).

29. Art. 7.1.c EUTMR sets out the same substantive rule. German Trade Mark law provides for essentially the same rule in § 8 para. 2 no. 2 and 3 German Markengesetz.
30. There is no limitation to the type of characteristics being described: they do not have to be commercially essential. This was clarified by the ECJ in ECJ C-363/99 *Koninklijke KPN Nederland v. Benelux-Merkenbureau* (*Postkantoor*) [2004] E.C.R. I-1619; [2004] E.T.M.R. 57, para. 102.
31. ECJ C-363/99, para. 56, referring to ECJ C-108/97 *Windsurfing Chiemsee Produktions- und Vertriebs GmbH v. Boots- und Segelzubehör Walter Huber* [1999] E.C.R. I-2779; E.T.M.R. 585, para. 31

It thereby involves an assessment of whether the sign is commonly used or capable of being used in the future to describe a characteristic in the mind of the relevant consumers; if one of the possible meanings *can* be used to designate a characteristic of the goods or services, this would be sufficient for the ground of refusal to apply.[32]

This rather broad interpretation is fully in line with the public interest that the provision intends to protect. According to the ECJ in *Chiemsee*, it serves the public interest of leaving terms free to be used by all traders and thereby prevents descriptive signs from being reserved to one undertaking only.[33] In other words, it entails a right of economic operators to describe the same characteristics of their own goods or services[34] 'without fear of infringement'.[35] This is also described as the 'protective function' of trade mark law: the provision limits the risk of anti-competitive effects, by avoiding that language is being monopolised by one business to the detriment of others.

At the same time, the provision aims at guaranteeing the 'distinguishing function' of trade marks. Terms that do not (any longer) distinguish the goods of one undertaking from those of another cannot be registered as trade marks because their meaning is purely descriptive of a characteristic or has become the generic name for the type of goods involved.[36]

Another important condition that the ECJ has clarified relates to the understanding by the consumer: the relevant public must 'immediately and without further reflection' be able to understand that the sign is a description of a characteristic of the goods or services applied for.[37] Merely evoking or alluding to certain characteristics rather than a direct designation would not be sufficient to fall under this ground of refusal.[38] While the consumer needs to directly understand the term to be descriptive, he does not have to understand exactly which characteristic is described. In the *Doublemint* case, the ECJ held that even though 'double mint' could be interpreted as twice as much mint or two different flavours of mint, this did not matter since the consumer would understand the term to be descriptive of a characteristic of the chewing gum.[39]

Applying these conditions to foreign language terms, it poses the question of who the relevant public is that needs to understand the foreign language terms to describe characteristics of the goods or services applied for. Who would need to recognise that 'Rapadura' describes a type of whole cane sugar, 'Cupuaçu' a characteristic of fruit juice, 'Citrus Paradisi' the flavour of mineral waters and fruit juices, and 'datschnije' a way of producing and origin of vegetables?[40]

---

32. ECJ C-191/01 *OHIM v. Wrigley (Doublemint)* [2003] E.C.R. I-12447; [2004] E.T.M.R. 9, para. 32.
33. ECJ C-191/01, para. 25.
34. ECJ C-363/99 *Postkantoor*, para. 55.
35. *Tritton* (*supra* n. 18), para. 3-080.
36. In the *Chiemsee* case, the Court first assessed the protected function, but later on also considered whether the mark is able to distinguish the products from others, see ECJ C-108/97, para. 37.
37. T-259/99 *DKV v. OHIM (Eurohealth)* [2001] E.C.R. II-1645, para. 35.
38. *Tritton* (*supra* n. 18), para. 3-080.
39. ECJ C-191/01, para. 35.
40. Examples reported in *Heath/Prüfer* (*supra* n. 5), 792. 'Cupuaçu' is the Brazilian word for the cocoa plant and has been registered for fruit juice, 'Citrus Paradisi' is Latin for grapefruit

1. *The Relevant Public Following ECJ* **Matratzen Concord** *[2006]*

In its *Chiemsee* judgment in 1999, the ECJ held that when assessing whether terms designate a specific characteristic to the relevant public, the class of persons that should be considered is the trading community and the average consumers 'in the territory in respect of which registration is applied for'.[41] In the case at hand, a national trade mark was at issue, therefore the respective territory was that of the relevant Member State. In case an EU trade mark is applied for, it would be the traders and consumers in a part of the Union.[42] Such a part of the Union could be a single Member State,[43] but according to the General Court, it could also be a smaller area, like a sub-region.[44] Applying the rule established in *Chiemsee* to foreign language terms, it depends on the knowledge and experiences of traders and consumers in the specific Member State (or part of the Union) whether they already understand, or are reasonably assumed to understand in the future, the meaning of the foreign terms.

The limitation of the relevant public to the Member State where registration is sought for a national trade mark was confirmed by the ECJ in 2006 in a prominent case dealing with foreign language terms. Hukla Germany SA had registered the word 'Matratzen' (German for mattresses) for beds, mattresses, sofas, etc. in Spain in product class 20 of the Nice Classification.[45] In an action for cancellation of the national trade mark 'Matratzen' initiated by Matratzen Concord AG, the Provincial Court of Barcelona considered whether the protection of foreign terms as trade marks did not unjustifiably restrict the free movement of goods given that the trade mark holder of 'Matratzen' was in a position to restrict the import of mattresses from German-speaking Member States.[46] Furthermore, the Court considered whether generic words from languages of the Member States should remain available to be used by any undertaking established in these States.[47] The latter arguably is based on the protection of the public interest as stipulated in Art. 4.1.c of the TMD – to avoid descriptive terms from being monopolised by one undertaking.

The ECJ, however, did not follow the concerns formulated by the referring Court. It made clear that according to the applicable Trade Mark Directive,[48] none of the grounds of refusal prevents foreign terms from being registered:[49]

---

and was registered for mineral waters and fruit juices, 'datschnije' is the Russian word for home-grown products, from the garden or cottage.
41. ECJ C-108/97, para. 29. Confirmed in ECJ C-421/04 *Matratzen Concord AG v. Hukla Germany SA (Matratzen)* [2006] E.C.R. I-2303; [2006] E.T.M.R. 48, para. 24.
42. See Art. 7.2 EUTMR.
43. ECJ C-25/05 *P August Storck KG v. OHIM* [2006] E.C.R. I-5739, para. 83.
44. T-72/11 *Sogepi Consulting y Publicidad v. OHIM (Espetec)*, Judgment of the General Court (Seventh Chamber) of 13 September 2012, OJ C 113 of 9.4.2011, para. 35.
45. Nice Agreement Concerning the International Classification of Goods and Services for the Purposes of the Registration of Marks of 15 June 1957, as revised and amended.
46. ECJ C-421/04, para. 14.
47. ECJ C-421/04, para. 13.
48. Council Directive 89/104/EEC of 21 December 1988 to approximate the laws of the Member States relating to trade marks, OJ 1989 L 40, p. 1.
49. The arguments raised by the referring Court were based on former Arts. 28 and 30 EC Treaty, which address the freedom of movement of goods. Since that is primary law

'Article 3(1)(b) and (c) of the Directive [Article 4.1.b and c TMD] does not preclude the registration in a Member State, as a national trade mark, of a term borrowed from the language of another Member State in which it is devoid of distinctive character or descriptive of the goods or services in respect of which registration is sought, unless the *relevant parties in the Member State* in which registration is sought are capable of identifying the meaning of the term.'[50] [emphasis added]

In other words, in the absence of a specific ground of refusal for foreign language terms,[51] Art. 4.1.c TMD cannot be interpreted to cover words that are descriptive in their home language where that language is generally not known to traders and consumers in the Member State of registration. According to the ECJ,

It is possible that, because of linguistic, cultural, social and economic differences between the Member States, a trade mark which is devoid of distinctive character or descriptive of the goods or services concerned in one Member State is not so in another Member State.[52]

Hence, as Advocate General A. Jacobs suggested, the relevant competent authority needs to determine in each case whether traders and consumers of the relevant product in the territory of registration are capable of identifying the meaning of the term, now or in the future.[53] The Court thereby focuses almost exclusively on the distinguishing function of Arts. 4.1.b and c TMD: if traders and consumers do not understand the meaning, the mark is distinctive and therefore should be protectable. While this may be intuitive for Art. 4.1.b,[54] it disregards the protective function of Art. 4.1.c TMD, which is to leave terms free for all traders to use.

2. Barrier to Legitimate Trade? Consequences for Traders

From the above, it is clear that the ECJ has assessed the *concrete* understanding of the relevant group of persons of the foreign language terms used in a sign. Does the application of such a concrete understanding of the relevant public by traders and consumers constitute a legitimate barrier to trade? I argue that it does, for the following reason. The way the ECJ has applied Art. 4.1.c TMD in the *Matratzen* judgment above does not safeguard the specific subject-matter of trade marks. Arguably, the specific subject-matter of trade mark law in general, and more specifically of Art. 4.1.c TMD, is to guarantee that trade marks serve as indications of origin and that descriptive

---

and in an area exhaustively harmonised, the harmonising law needs to be assessed, the referring Court's arguments were not further addressed, even though they indeed address the problem of creating barriers to trade.

50. ECJ C-421/04 *Matratzen Concord AG v. Hukla Germany SA (Matratzen)* [2006] E.C.R. I-2303; [2006] E.T.M.R. 48, para. 26.
51. ECJ C-421/04, para. 22.
52. ECJ C-421/04, para. 25.
53. Opinion of Advocate General Jacobs ECJ C-421/04 *Matratzen Concord AG v. Hukla Germany SA*, delivered on 24 November 2005, [2006] E.C.R. I-2306, para. 56.
54. Art. 4.1.b reads as follows: '1. The following shall not be registered or, if registered, shall be liable to be declared invalid: [...] (b) trade marks which are devoid of any distinctive character'.

terms should be kept free for all traders to be used to describe their products. By protecting foreign language terms as trade marks, this specific subject-matter is not guaranteed and thereby should be classified as a barrier to legitimate trade.

According to the ECJ in *Chiemsee*, the public interest behind the prohibition to register a descriptive trade mark is that the term should be kept free for all undertakings to describe the kind, nature, origin or other characteristics of their product.[55] Another public interest of the provision is that of indicating origin.[56] These public interests constitute the specific subject-matter of trade marks that the provision is meant to protect. It is argued that where the concrete understanding of foreign language terms by the relevant public is assessed, the application of the provision does not safeguard this specific subject-matter. First, limiting the understanding to consumers and traders in the national market does not guarantee that the term is kept free for all potential traders. Only if all traders with various linguistic backgrounds are considered as the relevant public, can one ensure that all potential traders can make use of the terms to describe their products. Secondly, neither does it guarantee that such terms fulfil the function of indicating an origin: traders and consumers participating in trade on the national market but originating from a different linguistic background would not experience a term that describes a certain characteristic of the product as functioning as a trade mark. They would not perceive the term as an indicator of origin that would enable them to distinguish the product from other products of its kind.

The consequence of applying a concrete understanding of foreign language terms by the relevant public is that to the extent that traders and consumers of a Member State are sufficiently unfamiliar with foreign languages such as Brazilian or Russian, and are likely to be unfamiliar with those languages in the future, the signs are not considered to be descriptive and can therefore be registered as trade marks. These terms will then benefit from the usual scope of protection granted to trade marks. In the EU framework, identical or similar foreign language terms used on the packaging of a similar product are very likely to infringe the trade mark holder's rights based on Art. 10.2.a or 10.2.b TMD.[57]

Such a breach of Art. 10.2.a or b TMD can only be remedied if one of the justifications applies. A relevant justification is found in Art. 14.1.b TMD:

> '1. A trade mark shall not entitle the proprietor to prohibit a third party from using, in the course of trade: [...]; (b) signs or indications which are not distinctive or which concern the kind, quality, quantity, intended purpose, value, geographical origin, the time of production of goods or of rendering of the service, or other characteristics of goods or services;'

Art. 14.2 TMD makes this limitation of the trade mark holders' rights conditional upon the fact that the use made by the third party is in accordance with honest practices in industrial or commercial matters. In other words, foreign traders, wishing to describe a characteristic of their product by using a registered trade

---

55. ECJ C-108/97, para. 30.
56. In addition, the ECJ also considered the distinguishing function of Art. 4.1.c TMD, see ECJ C-108/97, para. 37.
57. See Art. 9.2.a or b EUTMR for the equivalent provisions.

mark in accordance with honest commercial practices, could invoke Art. 14 TMD in national court proceedings to justify a breach of Art. 10.2.a or b TMD. In fact, the ECJ in *Matratzen* itself suggested this recourse for traders that would be affected by the effects of its judgment.[58] Advocate General Jacobs in his Opinion in the same case explained the rationale behind Art. 14 TMD, by referring to the ECJ judgment *BMW*.[59] Accordingly, the provision is meant to 'reconcile the fundamental interests of trade-mark protection with those of free movement of goods': the free movement of goods is ensured for cases of descriptive use of trade marks by limiting the rights of the trade mark holder in such situations.[60] An example would be a catalogue in the German language that refers to mattresses.[61]

However, relying on a justification to achieve market entry, rather than addressing the undesirable effect of the *Matratzen* judgment at the registration stage, presents a number of problems. First, the condition of being compliant with 'honest practices in industrial and commercial matters' was interpreted rather narrowly by the ECJ in *Budweiser*, reflecting 'an expression of the duty to act fairly in relation to the legitimate interests of the trade-mark proprietor.'[62] The legitimate interests of the trade mark owner hence have to be respected. It is at least doubtful whether the use of a descriptive term that is otherwise used as a trade mark to indicate origin respects the interests of the trade mark owner sufficiently, since consumers may be confused about the origin of the product, which exactly contravenes the legitimate interests of the trade mark holder. Secondly, as Heath and Prüfer point out, the third party needs to bear the risk of facing infringement proceedings in a foreign and possibly unknown legal system. Calculating the legal costs involved in such proceedings will be difficult, leaving the third party with the risk of incurring more costs than its imports are worth.[63] Due to these difficulties, I will argue in the next session that foreign language terms should not be registered as trade marks in the first place, thereby reducing the need to invoke Art. 14.1.b TMD in such situations.

3. The Way Forward: Assessing Multiple Languages

Instead of applying the concrete understanding of the relevant public, as suggested by the ECJ in the *Matratzen* judgment, the more appropriate understanding would be an *abstract* one, as to whether the term is able to be used to describe the product. If the term indeed is descriptive, no matter whether consumers are likely to understand it now or in the future,[64] traders from different parts of our globalised world may

---

58. ECJ C-421/04, para. 31.
59. ECJ C-63/97 *Bayerische Motorenwerke AG v. Deenik* [1999] E.C.R. I-905, [1999] E.T.M.R. 339, para. 62.
60. ECJ C-421/04 Opinion of Advocate General Jacobs delivered on 24 November 2005, [2005] E.C.R. I-2306, para. 62.
61. ECJ C-421/04 Opinion of AG Jacobs, para. 64.
62. ECJ C-245/02 *Anheuser-Busch Inc. v. Budějovický Budvar, národní podnik* [2004] E.C.R. I- 10989, para. 82.
63. *Heath/Prüfer*, Aus der Matratzengruft, section 4.c (manuscript on file with the author).
64. Art. 4.1.c does not require the term to be understood by the relevant public; it differs from e.g. Art. 4.1.g TMD, which clearly refers to the public's understanding of a mark in order to determine whether the public is deceived. That provision reads as follows: '4. 1. The

experience obstacles when marketing their product by describing it with exactly that term. According to the protective function, all traders should be able to do so, without fear of infringement.

Would every language then have to be taken into consideration? If the public interest as explained in the *Chiemsee* decision and following cases[65] is interpreted broadly, all possible languages which traders could use to describe their products on the national or EU market would be covered. Such an interpretation is supported by the relevant international treaty, the Paris Convention.[66] It contains a provision in Art. 6 *quinquies* B, which also excludes trade marks from registration in case they are

> 'devoid of any distinctive character, or consist exclusively of signs or indications which may serve, in trade, to designate the kind, quality, quantity, intended purpose, value, place of origin, of the goods, or the time of production, or have become customary in the current language or *in the bona fide and established practices of the trade of the country where protection is claimed.*' [emphasis added].

The provision was introduced and further amended during the Revision Conferences of The Hague (1925) and London (1934). It highlights two aspects that are relevant for foreign language terms. First, according to the Guide on the application of the Paris Convention published by BIRPI in 1969,[67] Art. 6*quinquies* B is meant to guarantee that descriptions remain in the public domain, 'even where the description as such is not known to the general public and [...] [may therefore not be] devoid of any distinctive character.'[68] In other words, the protective function was clearly seen to be at the heart of the provision when it was included in the Paris Convention.

Secondly, the notion that where a term has 'become customary in the current language or in the bona fide and established practices of the trade of the country where protection is claimed' indicates that the assessment of the relevant public, and hence the languages that need to be considered, is not limited to the current language. It should also take into consideration the practices, and arguably languages, that are commonly used in trade in which the country is involved. According to Ladas, the provision would include a multiple language exception.[69]

Incorporating this background into the EU context, it may not be sufficient to limit the relevant public to the consumers and traders in the respective Member State. Rather, it should be the group of traders and consumers that are engaged in

---

following shall not be registered or, if registered, shall be liable to be declared invalid: [...] g) trade marks which are of such a nature as to deceive the public, for instance, as to the nature, quality or geographical origin of the goods or service'.
65. This reasoning was applied by ECJ in several following cases, ECJ C-363/99 *Postkantoor*, ECJ C-191/01 *Doublemint*.
66. Note that the TRIPS Agreement does not include a provision on descriptive terms; for grounds of refusal, it refers to the Paris Convention in Art. 15.2 TRIPS.
67. G. H. C. Bodenhausen, Guide to the Application of the Paris Convention for the Protection of Industrial Property, United International Bureaux for the Protection of Intellectual Property (BIRPI), 1969.
68. *Bodenhausen* (*supra* n. 67), p. 116.
69. S. *Ladas*, Patents Trade Marks and Related Rights: National and International Protection, 1975, 1236.

the marketing and consumption of products of the same or similar product category on the national or EU market. Two suggestions follow from this analysis.

First, central to the analysis should be the international niche market, in which the specific product is traded and offered for sale. This implies a move away from the national consumers and traders to the international consumers and traders of the specific product, who also conduct business in the respective Member State. The focus on the international market of the specific product is much more aligned with culturally and linguistically diversified societies, where it is very difficult to establish the knowledge of the average consumer of the relevant product.[70] 'Rapadura' in this context is likely to be offered for sale by traders with a connection to Brazil and purchased by consumers with a sensitivity for organic and natural products. Where the term carries a generic or descriptive meaning for such an international community, it should not be registered so that other traders can continue to offer such products to potential markets.

Secondly, and in addition to the previous condition, the scope of the relevant market should encompass those countries with which the relevant country or regional entity has concluded international trade agreements.[71] For Member States of the EU, the most relevant international trade agreements are those concluded within the framework of the WTO.[72] So when determining where international traders may come from, WTO membership (or potentially other important free trade agreements) should be guiding. Accordingly, traders from WTO Members should be able to use their own language to describe and market their products in a Member State of the European Union; as a result, terms borrowed from a language of another WTO Member should not be registered. Such an approach has the benefit of covering most actual and possible future trading relationships, similar to the broad meaning of the wording 'may serve' in Art. 4.1.c TMD.

An example of a country that already takes multiple languages into consideration is the United States. According to the Trademark Act of 1946 Section 2(e)(1), marks that are 'merely descriptive of the goods' should be prohibited from registration.[73] In order to establish whether foreign language terms are descriptive, the doctrine of foreign equivalents requires the applicant of foreign language terms to provide the examiner with a translation of the foreign word into English. If the ordinary American purchaser would translate the term into English, and the literal and direct English translation is descriptive, the term will not be protected as a trade mark.[74] According to the USTPO, the 'ordinary American purchaser' includes 'all American purchasers, including those proficient in a non-English language who would ordinarily

---

70. C. Heath and D. Marie-Vivien, 'Geographical Indications and the Principles of Trade Mark Law – A Distinctly European Perspective', 46 International Review of Intellectual Property and Competition Law (IIC) 7 [2015] 819–842, p. 829.
71. Heath/Prüfer, Aus der Matratzengruft, section 4a.
72. Needless to say other trade agreements concluded by the EU would also be relevant for determining trading relationships. However, it is likely that most trading partners are also Members of the WTO.
73. 15 U.S.C. § 1052, Section 2(e)(1).
74. USTPO, Trademark Manual of Examining Procedure, October 2017, section 1207.01(b)(vi) on Doctrine of Foreign Equivalents, available at https://tmep.uspto.gov/RDMS/TMEP/current#/current/d1e2.html (accessed 31 January 2018).

be expected to translate words into English.'[75] Only where the foreign language is a dead or obscure language will the doctrine not be applied.[76]

Judging from the guidelines for trade mark examiners in the US, the purpose of the US doctrine of foreign equivalents is to extend protection to US consumers who speak languages other than English and thereby minimise confusion among them.[77] It is not evident that the purpose is to keep terms free for all traders, coming from current or potential trading partners of the US, to acknowledge international trading circles and keeping those terms free for traders using their own mother tongue to describe their products. Nevertheless, the doctrine consists of a useful tool that can be used by the EU to institutionalise the translation of foreign language terms into the official language(s) of the Member State(s) in order to avoid the registration of foreign language terms.

II. Absolute Ground of Refusal Regarding Registrations Made in Bad Faith

Foreign language terms could also be covered by another ground of refusal when applied for registration with a Member State.[78] Other than arguing that the term is descriptive, one could resort to Art. 4.2 TMD, in case a registration has been made in bad faith:

> '2. A trade mark shall be liable to be declared invalid where the application for registration of the trade mark was made in bad faith by the applicant. Any Member State may also provide that such a trade mark is not to be registered.'

Where Member States have made available this ground of refusal at the registration stage, a trade mark which is applied for in bad faith cannot be registered. According to settled case-law of the CJEU, the concept of 'bad faith' should be interpreted as 'an autonomous concept of European Union law which must be given a uniform interpretation in the European Union'.[79] The existence of bad faith is subject to an overall assessment, taking into account all factors relevant to the particular case:

---

75. USTPO, section 1210.10 on Doctrine of Foreign Equivalents.
76. USTPO, section 809 on Translation and Transliteration of Non-English Wording in Mark.
77. This is supported by T. Merante, 'A Mark for All Languages: The Doctrine of Foreign Equivalents in Trademark Law', in blog by Journal of Intellectual Property & Entertainment Law (JIPEL) [2017], available at < http://blog.jipel.law.nyu.edu/2015/10/a-mark-for-all-languages-the-doctrine-of-foreign-equivalents-in-trademark-law/ > (accessed 1 February 2018).
78. Note that the relevant provision Art. 52.1.b in the EUTMR only presents an absolute ground of invalidity. Hence it cannot be invoked during the registration phase, or in opposition of an application.
79. ECJ C-320/12 *Malaysia Dairy Industries Pte. Ltd v. Ankenaevnet for Patenter og Varemaerker*, para. 29. In that case, Art. 4.4.g of Directive 2008/95 was assessed, identical to Art. 5.4.c TMD, which reads as follows: '4. Any Member State may provide that a trade mark is not to be registered or, if registered, is liable to be declared invalid where, and to the extent that: [...] (c) the trade mark is liable to be confused with an earlier trade mark protected abroad, provided that, at the date of the application, the applicant was acting in bad faith.' In para. 25 of the judgment, the CJEU establishes that 'terms of a provision of European

'[S]uch as, inter alia, whether the applicant knew or should have known that a third party was using an identical or similar sign for an identical or similar product (see, to that effect, Case C-529/07 *Chocoladefabriken Lindt & Sprüngli* [2009] E.C.R. I-4893, paragraphs 37 and 40 to 42).'[80]

In case the applicant knew or should have known about a third party's use of an identical or similar sign for an identical or similar product, and if the applicant's intention at the filing date was to prevent that third party from continuing to use its sign, the element of bad faith is likely to be established. However, in a case like 'Rapadura', no third party had used that word for marketing similar products on the German market before Rapunzel registered the term, so the guidelines given in the *Lindt* case would not help. Looking for further guidance when interpreting 'bad faith', a decision by the Board of Appeal of OHIM in 2001 suggested that 'bad faith' involves 'actual or potential fraud, intent to deceive or to mislead or any other injurious intent'.[81] Using this broad notion of bad faith, a situation where the registration of a foreign language term leads to an undue monopolisation of the use of and trade in the product, rather than its denomination, should be classified as having been made in bad faith. Therefore, I propose an additional criterion to assess registrations made in bad faith: the registration of a mark may not create the objective and non-negligible possibility of hindering legitimate trade. If such a non-negligible possibility exists (in cases of undue monopolisation) the registration should be classified as being made in bad faith and therefore should be denied.

1. Undue Monopolisation of a Product and Consequences for Traders

When does the registration of a foreign language term lead to undue monopolisation? Such a situation arose with regard to Zefir (Russian: Зефи́р), a type of soft cake made by whipping fruit and berry purée (mostly apple purée) with sugar and egg whites.[82] The shape of this confectionery was subject to a GOST standard in the former USSR. In other words, in the former area of USSR, all Zefir cakes were and continue to be produced according to this standard: it is the typical form for such cakes. The Düsseldorf Court of Appeal, being confronted with a trade mark application for the form of this sugar cake, noted that the registration of the typical shape for a foreign

---

Union law which makes no express reference to the law of the Member States for the purpose of determining its meaning and scope must normally be given an independent and uniform interpretation throughout the European Union; that interpretation must take into account the context of the provision and the objective of the relevant legislation (see, inter alia, Case C-482/09 *Budějovický* Budvar [2011] ECR I-8701 paragraph 29)'. Since there are no express references to the law of Member States in Art. 4.2 TMD either and since the context of the provision and the objective of the legislation should be very similar to the analysis of Art. 5.4.c TMD in *Malaysia Dairy*, it is argued that a similar interpretation should be applied to the concept of bad faith in both provisions.

80. ECJ C-320/12, para. 36.
81. Cancellation Division OHIM, *R. v. Lancome Parfums et Beauté & CIE's Trade Mark; Laboratoires Décléor's Application for Cancellation* [2001] E.T.M.R. 89, as retrieved from Tritton (*supra* n. 18), para. 3.111.
82. See *Wikipedia*, Zefir (food) 2017, available at < https://en.wikipedia.org/wiki/Zefir_(food) > (accessed 24 January 2018).

speciality can have 'no other reason but to monopolise the product in Germany to exclude other undertakings [...] from the further distribution of this product in Germany'.[83] As a result, the application was denied on the basis of a registration made in bad faith.[84]

Where other traders are prevented, without due cause, from marketing the type of product to which the trade mark registration applies, the term or shape should not be registered (if available as an absolute ground of refusal) or be declared invalid. Traders would not only be prevented from using a specific sign or shape (which is normally the case when a trade mark is being protected), but here the trade mark registration would have the effect of monopolising trade in that particular product: only the trade mark holder would be allowed to offer that product on the market where registration has occurred.

Four situations come to mind when the registration of foreign terms would prevent other traders from putting their products on the market: 1) the registered term is the same as the name of the product in the foreign language ('Rapadura'), 2) the registered shape is the same as the typical shape of a foreign speciality ('Zefir'), 3) the registered term is the same as a characteristic of the product in the foreign language which is commonly used to describe the product ('datschnije' – from the garden or cottage),[85] or 4) the registered term is the same as an ingredient of the product, that according regulations for consumer food information may even have to be mentioned on the packaging ('garum armoricum', the Latin generic name of a fish extract).[86] Even though the two last-mentioned have not been denied registration by the respective courts on the basis of bad faith, such situations arguably could fall under the scope of this ground of refusal, as an element of undue monopolisation is involved.

2. Barrier to Legitimate Trade?

In order to avoid registered trade marks becoming barriers to legitimate trade, bad faith registrations should be refused in the mentioned cases. As mentioned, the element of 'bad faith' covers situations where a party unduly wants to deceive, injure or mislead other parties involved in trade of the same or similar products through

---

83. Düsseldorf Court of Appeal from 30 December 2002, 20 U 120/02, as retrieved in Heath, Marie-Vivien (supra n. 70), p. 827.
84. The applicable German law was Art. 8.2.4 of the German Trade Mark Act.
85. The term datschnije was registered with the German Patent Office for conserved vegetables (classes 29. 30 and 31). The trade mark owner claimed in front of the Provincial Court (Landesgericht) Hamburg that a Baltic importer of 'ogurzi datschnije' (cucumber from the garden) was infringing her trade mark. The Court found an infringement and rejected the counterclaim that the trade mark was descriptive in the first place. See LG Hamburg from 27 June 2003, Az 416 O 21/03 (unpublished), retrieved in Heath, Marie-Vivien (supra n. 70), p. 827.
86. Decision of the Paris District Court (Tribunal de grande instance) 6 March 2014 – Case Nos. RG 2011/16210; M20140240, reported in 46 IIC 7 [2015], pp. 872-875. The Court denied registrability of the Garum Amicorum because it is the Latin generic name of a fish extract from the Armorica region that the relevant public (pharmacists) understand to be a generic term that is devoid of any distinctive character. It was not denied on the basis of bad faith.

monopolisation. By its very nature, such conduct is bound to prevent legitimate trade. Furthermore, such registrations would not serve the functions of trade mark law and hence should be classified as creating barriers to legitimate trade. The main purposes of trade mark protection are 1) to enable consumers to distinguish products from one undertaking from those of another, as well as 2) to keep descriptive and generic words/forms free to be used by all. Where deceptive, misleading or generic signs are registered, consumers are deceived or misled and other traders are prevented from using the terms for the same type of product.

In order to avoid foreign language terms being registered as trade marks without the necessary consideration, the application file for 1) an EU trade mark or 2) a national trade mark should contain the mandatory requirement to provide a translation of the foreign language term into an official language. For the EU, my suggestion would be to provide a translation into one of the five official languages of the EUIPO (English, French, German, Italian and Spanish). The requirement of providing a translation should be broad, encompassing the translation of any language, even if it is a dead language such as Latin. Such an obligation would help the trade mark examiners to identify foreign language terms and, at the same time, where the applicant fails to provide the translation, the registration should be considered as having been made in bad faith.

C. PROTECTION OF GEOGRAPHICAL INDICATIONS THAT ARE CONSIDERED GENERIC

A similar risk of creating barriers to legitimate trade occurs in the field of geographical indications, where names of products are protected as geographical indications in a free trade agreement, even though such names may have become generic in the partner country. Domestic producers in the partner country then find themselves in a position where they risk infringement procedures if they market their products under the generic name.

In the following, the free trade agreements (FTAs)[87] that the EU has concluded with partner countries during the last decade will be analysed regarding 1) the definition of generic terms, 2) their automatic protection, 3) limitations to protection, 4) the scope of protection, including applicable exceptions, and 5) the justification regarding the use of generic terms. The protection (or exceptions from protection) granted to generic terms will then be assessed as to their consequences for traders and whether they can be classified as barriers to legitimate trade. The following FTAs form part of the analysis: CARIFORUM-EC EPA (2008);[88] EU-South Korea FTA (2011);[89]

---

87. For simplicity, all agreements are referred to as free trade agreements, even though they have different names.
88. Economic Partnership Agreement between the CARIFORUM States, of the one part, and the European Community and its Member States, of the other part, OJ L 289/I/3 of 30.10.2008, provisionally applied since 29 December 2008. CARIFORUM stands for the Caribbean Forum of African Caribbean and Pacific states and includes fifteen countries.
89. Free Trade Agreement between the European Union and its Member States, of the one part, and the Republic of Korea, of the other part, OJ L 127/6 of 14.5.2011, provisionally applied since July 2011.

EU-Peru/Colombia TA (2012);[90] EU-Central America AA (2012);[91] EU-Canada CETA (2014); EU-Singapore FTA (2014);[92] EU-Vietnam FTA (2015);[93] and Draft India-EU BTIA (2010).[94]

I.   Definition of Generic Terms

Generic terms are generally understood as 'indications that are identical with the term customary in common language as the common name for such goods or services', as defined in TRIPS.[95] This definition is also included in the CARIFORUM-EC EPA and the EU-Singapore FTA; the other agreements contain no definition. Taking the examples of 'camembert' or 'brie', those names can be argued to have become commonly used terms that consumers use to refer to types of cheese, rather than to their origin. In other words, they lose their geographic link and acquire another meaning based on qualities rather than on specific origin.[96]

Whether a term has lost its direct link with the geographical origin must be established according to certain factors. The FTAs mentioned above do not specify such factors; hence, domestic rules should be resorted to. In the EU, Art. 41.2 EU Regulation 1151/2012 on GI protection for foodstuffs provides that all relevant factors need to be taken into account for establishing genericity, in particular: (a) the existing situation in areas of consumption; and (b) the relevant national or Union legal acts. Regarding point (a), Art. 3.1 of the predecessor Regulation 2081/92[97] provided some more guidance in that 'the existing situation in the Member State in which the name originates and areas of consumption, [and] the existing situation in other Member

---

90. Trade Agreement between the European Union and its Member States, of the one part, and Colombia and Peru, of the other part, OJ L 357/3 of 21.12.2012, provisionally applied as of July 2013.
91. Agreement establishing an Association between the European Union and its Member States, on the one hand, and Central America on the other, OJ L 346/3 of 15.12.2012, provisionally applied as of 1 August 2013.
92. Free Trade Agreement between the European Union and the Republic of Singapore, initialled in October 2014, awaiting ratification by parties. Text available at http://trade.ec.europa.eu/doclib/press/index.cfm?id = 961 (accessed 2 February 2018).
93. Free Trade Agreement between the European Union and the Socialist Republic of Vietnam, initialled in February 2016, awaiting ratification by parties. Text available at http://trade.ec.europa.eu/doclib/press/index.cfm?id = 1437 (accessed 2 February 2018).
94. The area of GI is not addressed in the 2013 draft, therefore the earlier draft of the India-EU Broad-based Trade and Investment Agreement (BTIA) from July 2010 has been used; see https://www.bilaterals.org/?eu-india-fta-consultation-draft-on (accessed 1 February 2018).
95. Art. 24.6 TRIPS Agreement. Almost identical definitions are incorporated in Art. 145.C.1 CARIFORUM-EC-EPA and Art. 11.22.5 and 11.22.6 EU-Singapore FTA. Note that Art. 11.22.6 also addresses names contained in a GI, rather than only the entire GI. Within the EU framework, a very similar definition can be found in Art. 3.6 EU Regulation 1151/2012 (see *supra* n. 27).
96. M. Blakeney, The Protection of Geographical Indications, Cheltenham, UK; Northampton, MA, USA 2014, para. 3.82.
97. Council Regulation (EEC) No 2081/92 of 14 July 1992 on the protection of geographical indications and designations of origin for agricultural products and foodstuffs. Official Journal L 208/1 of 24.07.1992.

States' should be taken into account. In order to assess 'the existing situation', the ECJ held in *Bayerisches Bier* that relevant factors include the places of production, the consumption of the product and the perception of the product by the consumer, both inside the Member State which obtained the registration and outside of it.[98] In its earlier *Parmesan* judgment, the ECJ had already made clear that quotations from dictionaries and specialist literature were not sufficient to support the generic nature of a term. Rather, information on the quantity of imported 'Parmigiano Reggiano' cheese into Germany was necessary for the Court to make an assessment of the genericity of 'Parmesan' in Germany, as compared to the consumption of cheese marketed under 'Parmesan' in Germany.[99] Regarding point (b), the legislative history of the domestic or international protection of a product also needs to be taken into consideration to determine whether a term has become generic.[100]

This guidance for establishing genericity is certainly not binding on the negotiating partner of an FTA; it, however, shows how cautious the ECJ is in acknowledging the existence of the generic character of a term. So far, the ECJ has not yet found any of the terms that came up for decision to be generic. Reasons for this caution are policy-driven: the EU wants to maintain possibilities, especially for businesses in less favoured areas of the EU,[101] and prevent 'the disappearance of th[e] reputation [that a GI has acquired] as a result of popularisation through general use outside its geographical area'.[102] The likelihood that a term will be found generic in a dispute between the EU and its negotiating partner would hence be rather low, if EU rules are applied.

Not only does the approach taken by the ECJ render the likelihood of finding genericity of a term rather small; in fact, in some agreements a provision is contained that prohibits GIs that are protected according to the FTA from becoming generic as long as they are protected in their country of origin.[103] This means that GIs that are protected according to the FTA[104] cannot be found to have become generic in the partner country, for as long as they are protected in their home country. This

---

98. ECJ C-343/07 *Bavaria NV, Bavaria Italia Srl v. Bayerischer Brauerbund eV* [2009] E.C.R. I-5491, para. 101, citing ECJ C-132/05 *Commission of the European Communities v. Federal Republic of Germany* [2008] E.C.R. I-957, para. 53.
99. ECJ C-132/05 *Commission of the European Communities v. Federal Republic of Germany* [2008] E.C.R. I-957, paras. 54–56.
100. In T-291/03 *Consorzio per la tutela del formaggio Grana Padano v. OHIM* [2007] E.C.R. II-3081, para. 78, the Court of First Instance established that 'grana' has not become generic since the protection of 'grana padano' was meant to cover all granas. In ECJ C-343/07, the ECJ held that among other things that because five bilateral agreements existed that protected the name 'Bayerisches Bier' as a geographical name, the name had not become generic. See para. 109.
101. See Recital 2 of EU Regulation 1151/2012.
102. ECJ C-343/07 (*supra* n. 98), para. 106.
103. See Art. 207h EU-Peru/Colombia FTA; Art. 246.2 EU-Central America AA; Art. 9.4.2 draft EU-India BTIA (as proposed by the EU).
104. The terminology of the provisions suggests that it only regards those GIs listed in the FTA. See section C.II.

provision also exists in EU law[105] as well as in the Lisbon Agreement.[106] It may be logical to avoid protected GIs being able to become generic, due to the above cited policy rationale. However, its effect seems to be contrary to the reason why generic terms are treated differently than other terms: they refer to a type of product rather than to a specific geographical origin, and therefore do not fulfil the essence of why we protect GIs in the first place. Arguably, terms that have already been used (and protected) for several years risk becoming the commonly used term for a type of product in everyday language. However, according to the above-cited provision, they cannot become generic. As a consequence, those words that in fact are used in a generic way, but are protected in the home country, cannot be excluded from protection. The effect on other traders is that those not complying with the product specifications are prevented from using the term to indicate the type of product they sell.

II. Recognition and Automatic Protection of Geographical Indications in Annexes

Whether a term is considered generic is already agreed upon during the FTA negotiations. As part of the negotiations, the parties draft lists with their most important geographical indications that they want to be protected in the other territory, which will be included as Annexes to the agreements. At the moment when these lists are drafted and submitted to the other party, each of them needs to assess whether the terms may be considered generic in their territory. Once the list is final, the included terms are recognised as GIs[107] and therefore will be protected according to the agreed level of protection.[108] These principles of recognition and automatic protection require the assessment of genericity to be approached strategically, as part of the FTA negotiations.

Looking at the list of terms included in recent EU FTAs, the following terms are treated differently from other terms, because of their generic character: Nürnberger

---

105. See Art. 13.2 EU Regulation 1151/2012.
106. Art. 6 Lisbon Agreement for the Protection of Appellations of Origin and Their International Registration, October 31, 1958, as revised, July 14, 1967, 923 U.N.T.S. 205 (hereinafter Lisbon Agreement).
107. Most agreements require a system of registration and protection to contain elements such as a register, an administrative process verifying that GIs fulfil the definition of a GI, an internal objection procedure and procedures for rectification and termination of entries. See Art. 6.2 EU-Vietnam FTA as an example.
108. See Art. 6.3 jo. Annex GI – I EU-Vietnam FTA; Art. 11.17.3 jo. Annex 11-B EU-Singapore FTA; Art. 20.19 jo. Annex 20-A EU-Canada CETA; Art. 208 jo. Annex XIII EU-Peru/Colombia TA; Art. 245.1 jo. Annex XVII EU-Central America AA; Art. 10.19 jo. Annex 10-B EU-South Korea FTA; Arts. 9.2.3 and 9.2.4 of the draft EU-India BTIA. Note that the CARIFORUM-EC EPA does not yet contain a list of GIs that should be protected by both sides; an agreement to that effect still has to be negotiated, before the protection agreed upon in the EPA will be applied to those GIs. See Arts. 145.A.2 and 145.E CARIFORUM-EC EPA.

Bratwürste,[109] Feta,[110] Jambon de Bayonne,[111] Beaufort,[112] Asiago,[113] Munster,[114] Fontina,[115] Gorgonzola,[116] and Champagne.[117] As set out below,[118] these terms are protected, but in certain FTAs only to a limited extent. Their inclusion in the FTAs has been described as 'claw back' provisions, with which the EU aims at clawing back the use of terms that have become generic in other countries. In contrast, Parmesan, Valencia Orange, Black Forest Ham, Tiroler Bacon, Bavarian Beer, Munich Beer,[119] are excluded from protection entirely, leaving their use free. In the EU-Canada FTA, Noix de Grenoble and Budejovicke[120] are also excluded from protection.

When the lists have been approved by both sides, and the FTA has been concluded, changes to the lists are only possible according to the procedure for amendments, usually carried out by Trade Committees or Working Groups.[121] What is clear, however, is that trying to get a term excluded from the list *ex post* because of its generic character may be very difficult, with little bargaining room available when only one term is under consideration, as compared to a full list.

---

109. See Annex XVII EU-Central America AA; Annex XVII EU-Central America AA; Annex 20-A EU-Canada CETA; Annex 11.A, number 17 EU Singapore FTA; Annex GI-I, number 14 EU-Vietnam FTA.
110. See Annex 10-A EU-South Korea FTA; Annex XVII EU-Central America AA; Annex XIII EU-Peru/Colombia FTA; Annex 20-A EU-Canada CETA; Annex 11.A, number 31 EU-Singapore FTA; Annex GI-I, number 98 EU-Vietnam FTA.
111. See Annex 10-A EU-South Korea FTA; Annex XVII EU-Central America AA; Annex XIII EU-Peru/Colombia FTA; Annex 20-A EU-Canada CETA; Annex 11.A, number 113 EU-Singapore FTA; Annex GI-I, number 65 EU-Vietnam FTA.
112. See Annex 20-A EU-Canada CETA;
113. See Annex 10-A EU-South Korea FTA; Annex XVII EU-Central America AA; Annex 20-A EU-Canada CETA; Annex 11.A, number 127 EU-Singapore FTA; Annex GI-I, number 114 EU-Vietnam FTA.
114. See Annex 20-A EU-Canada CETA;
115. See Annex 10-A EU-South Korea FTA; Annex XVII EU-Central America AA; Annex 20-A EU-Canada CETA; Annex 11.A, number 128 EU-Singapore FTA; Annex GI-I, number 116 EU-Vietnam FTA.
116. See Annex 10-A EU-South Korea FTA; Annex XVII EU-Central America AA; Annex XIII EU-Peru/Colombia FTA; Annex 20-A EU-Canada CETA; Annex 11.A, number 129 EU-Singapore FTA; Annex GI-I, number 117 EU-Vietnam FTA.
117. See Annex 10-B EU-South Korea FTA; Annex XVII EU-Central America AA; Annex XIII EU-Peru/Colombia FTA; Annex GI-I, number 78 EU-Vietnam FTA.
118. See section C.III.
119. Note that the terms Parmigiano Reggiano, Cítricos Valencianos, Schwarzwälder Schinken, Tiroler Speck, Münchener Bier and Bayerisches Bier in their original language are protected as GIs and also included in the according lists in the FTAs.
120. These two terms are not included in Annex 20-A of the EU-Canada CETA and were praised as a negotiating victory on the side of Canada. See *S. Lester, B. Mercurio and L. Bartels*, Bilateral and Regional Trade Agreements: Commentary and Analysis, 2016, p. 340. Budějovické pivo is protected in Annex 10-A EU-South Korea FTA, Annex XVII EU-Central America AA and Annex 11.A, number 4 EU-Singapore FTA; Českobudějovické pivo is protected in Annex 10-A EU-South Korea FTA, Annex XIII EU-Peru/Colombia FTA and Annex GI-I, number 10 EU-Vietnam FTA.
121. See Art. 10.25 EU-South Korea FTA; Art. 247 EU-Central America AA; Art. 209 EU-Peru/Colombia TA; Art. 20.22 EU-Canada CETA; Art. 11.18 EU-Singapore FTA; Art. 6.4 and 6.11 EU-Vietnam FTA; Art. 9.3 draft EU-India BTIA.

In order to make sure not to overlook terms that could be considered generic, a negotiating partner should have an objection procedure in place through which the listed terms are scrutinised. Most FTAs require an internal objection procedure as an element of the system of registration and protection of GIs,[122] but not all.[123] Completing this procedure is also important because some FTAs,[124] 'in principle', do not allow adding GIs already registered in either party at the date of signing to the Annex. Hence, where words are excluded from the list after having been opposed successfully in an internal objection procedure, those terms 'in principle' will not be protected in the negotiating partner's territory. The wording is particularly ambiguous as it is unclear under which conditions one would be able to deviate from 'in principle'. In any case, adding already protected GIs at a later stage to the list is subject to a high threshold. Negotiating partners should use this provision to their advantage.

III. Limitations to Claiming back Prior Uses

Where negotiation dynamics and bargaining power do not allow for exclusion of generic terms from the lists, a second best option is to limit the extent of their protection. Such limitations have been prominently included in the EU-Canada CETA and to a lesser extent in the EU-Vietnam FTA. Accordingly, the protection has been postponed or limited because of their currently generic nature in the partner country.

(1) **Use allowed with qualifiers**: Current users[125] in Canada can continue using Asiago, Feta, Fontina, Gorgonzola and Munster for their products. New entrants, however, must add a qualifier such as 'kind', 'type', 'style', 'imitation' or the like, as well as a clear indication of the geographical origin.[126]

(2) **Concurrent trade marks**: In Canada, any person has the right to register a trade mark containing or consisting of Valencia Orange, Black Forest Ham, Tiroler Bacon, Parmesan, St. George Cheese, Bavarian Beer and Munich Beer (as well as their French version) on condition that they do not mislead the public.[127]

(3) **Grandfathering**: Persons who have made commercial use in Canada of the term Nürnberger Bratwürste, as well as Beaufort and Jambon de Bayonne, for at least five or ten years respectively before 18 October 2013, can continue to use the terms.[128] A similar rule is included in the EU-Vietnam FTA with

---

122. See Art. 10.18.3, 10.18.4 and 10.18.6 EU-South Korea FTA; Art. 244.2 and 245.1 EU-Central America AA; Art. 208 EU-Peru/Colombia TA; Art. 11.17.2 EU-Singapore FTA; Art. 6.2 EU-Vietnam FTA; Arts. 9.2.3, 9.2.4 and 9.3 of the draft EU-India BTIA.
123. The EU-Canada CETA does not establish elements that a system of registration and protection of GIs needs to fulfil as it does not provide for such a system. Only the listed GIs are protected according to the specified level; no other GIs than those contained in Annex 20-A will be protected in Canada as GIs. See Art. 20.17.
124. Such a provision in included in the FTAs concluded with Vietnam and Canada. See Art. 20.22.2 EU-Canada CETA; Art. 6.4.2 EU-Vietnam FTA.
125. Art.. 20.21.2 specifies that this regards persons or their successors who have made commercial use of those indications preceding the date of 18 October 2013.
126. Art. 20.21.2 EU-Canada CETA.
127. See Art. 20.21.11 EU-Canada CETA.
128. See Art. 20.21.3 and 4 EU-Canada CETA.

regard to Asiago, Feta, Gorgonzola and Fontina: where persons have used the terms in good faith before 1 January 2017, they can continue to use them.[129]

(4) **Transitional periods**: The use of the terms listed under point (3) will only be prohibited in Canada after a transitional period of five years from the date of entry into force of the agreement.[130] In the EU-Vietnam FTA, a transitional period of ten years has been included for the term 'champagne' for persons who made actual commercial use in good faith of this indication for wine products.[131]

(5) **Excluded from protection**: Certain terms have been excluded from protection altogether:[132] 'comté' for food products when referred to a county (e.g. 'Comté du Prince-Edouard'), 'beaufort' in association with cheese products produced in the proximity of Beaufort range.

(6) **Use of components allowed**: Only the multi-part terms like Brie de Meaux, Gouda Holland, Edam Holland and Mortadella Bologna are protected, as opposed to the single components Brie, Gouda, Edam and Mortadella, which can still be used.[133]

IV. Scope of Protection of Generic Terms

For those generic terms not benefitting from a limitation as described above, the general level of protection for geographical indications applies to the listed terms. This protection usually involves the protection of registered GIs against (1) the indication of an area of origin other than the true place of origin, in a manner that misleads the public as to the geographical origin of the product, as well as (2) other abusive practices that would constitute an act of unfair competition within the meaning of Art. 10*bis* Paris Convention.[134] In addition, most agreements extend the higher level of protection for wines and spirits as included in TRIPS[135] to foodstuffs and agricultural products, creating equal protection among them.[136] As a consequence, producers

---

129. See Arts. 6.5a.1 and 2 EU-Vietnam FTA.
130. See Arts. 20.21.3 and 4 EU-Canada CETA.
131. Art. 6.5a.3 EU-Vietnam FTA.
132. Art. 20.21.12 EU-Canada FTA.
133. Annex 20-A EU-Canada CETA.
134. See Art. 22.2 TRIPS, which is incorporated in recent FTAs: Art. 6.5.1.b and c EU-Vietnam FTA; Art. 11.19.1 EU-Singapore FTA; Art. 20.19.2b and c EU-Canada FTA; Art. 246.1.a and 246.1.c EU-Central America AA; Art. 10.21.a and 10.21.c EU-South Korea FTA; Art. 145.B.3.a CARIFORUM-EC EPA. Note that Art. 210.1.d and e EU-Peru/Colombia FTA and Art. 9.4.1.c and d draft EU-India BTIA (as proposed by the EU) include a similar standard to the TRIPS rule. However, they also include the scope of protection applied by the EU internally, regarding any (direct or indirect) commercial use, see Art. 210.1.a EU-Peru/Colombia FTA and Art. 9.4.1.a draft EU-India BTIA (as proposed by the EU). See Art. 13.1.a EU Regulation 1151/2012.
135. Art. 23.1 TRIPS requires that wines and spirits not originating in the place indicated by the GI to be prohibited, even where the true origin of the goods is indicated or used in translation or accompanied by expressions such as 'kind', 'types', 'style', 'imitation' or the like.
136. See Art. 6.5.1 EU-Vietnam FTA; Art. 11.19.2 and 3 EU-Singapore FTA; Art. 20.19.3 EU-Canada FTA; Art. 246.1.b EU-Central America AA; Art. 10.21.b EU-South Korea FTA;

who do not comply with the product specifications set out in the GI registration cannot use the protected term for the presentation or designation of their product.

However, similar to trade mark protection, certain terms are excluded from protection because they do not fulfil the functions of geographical indications. Generic terms no longer indicate origin, which is the prime function of geographical indications, and therefore should not be protected. The TRIPS exception excluding generic terms from GI protection is optional, meaning that WTO Members can choose to apply it.[137] Only two recent EU FTAs[138] have also included the optional exception. Nevertheless, the fact that an FTA does not repeat the TRIPS exception does not affect a WTO Member's discretion to implement the exception foreseen by TRIPS: they remain free to exclude generic terms from protection in their domestic laws.

Where countries have chosen to exclude generic terms from GI protection, the question arises as to whether the exception can apply to the terms listed in the Annexes to the FTAs. Generally, the exception applies to all terms that were found to be generic. Whether a term is considered generic is a separate matter, as discussed above.[139] In fact, the terms contained in the lists of GIs have already been recognised as GIs by both parties and thereby have (implicitly) been denied generic character. Whether those terms also cannot benefit from the exception in the future, when they may have become generic, depends on whether the FTA and/or domestic law stipulate that protected GIs cannot become generic.[140] Some FTAs, such as those concluded with Peru, Colombia, Central America and possibly India,[141] contain a provision to that end; this indeed means that the listed GIs cannot become generic in the future. For the negotiating partners who have not included such a provision in their domestic law, the exception may be applicable to the listed terms in the future, following domestic law on how to establish genericity and after having followed the procedure for removing the relevant term from the Annex with the list of protected GIs.

In summary, even though the number of terms that may benefit from a generic terms exception is limited through the Annex with the list of protected GIs and in some FTAs through a provision limiting the finding of genericity in the future, such an exception is still applicable to all terms that are not listed in the Annex. For countries who want to set up a well-functioning GI system that does not create barriers to legitimate trade, such an exception is necessary in order to exclude customary words from protection. The protection of generic terms would not help consumers to identify the origin of products, nor does it ensure that customary words remain free for all traders to use.

V. Use of Generic Terms Defence

The final possibility for generic terms to be used by other traders even if they are protected as a GI is a justification included in two FTAs regarding the use of generic

---

   Art. 145.B.3.b CARIFORUM-EC EPA; Art. 9.4.1.b draft EU-India BTIA (as proposed by the EU).
137. Art. 24.6 TRIPS, see *supra* n. 95.
138. See Art. 145.C.1 CARIFORUM-EC EPA and Arts. 11.22.5 and 11.22.6 EU-Singapore FTA.
139. See *supra* section C.II.
140. See *supra* section C.I.
141. See *supra* n. 103.

terms: even where a protected GI contains a name that is considered generic, other traders should be able to use it.[142] This rule represents a justification at the infringement stage and is also foreseen in the EU context.[143] So after a GI was registered, use of a term would in principle constitute a breach of the scope of protection for GIs, unless the justification can be used. Procedurally, this means a trader can invoke the justification in an infringement procedure that the GI owner has initiated. The disadvantages of such a 'last resort' provision have been discussed in relation to the equivalent rule under EU trade mark law, Art. 14.1.b TMD:[144] being involved in proceedings in a foreign legal system puts a high burden on traders, both in relation to expertise as well as costs. Notably, there is no equivalent to Art. 14.2 TMD which required that the use of the term under trade mark protection has to be in accordance with fair commercial practices. This could imply that the defence available in the GI context may be easier to be invoked as compared to Art. 14.1.b TMD, but there is no evidence of that so far.

VI.   A Barrier to Legitimate Trade? Consequences for Traders

The variety of rules regarding generic terms in the various recently concluded EU FTAs means that traders in partner countries of the EU who want to use generic terms are confronted with several questions. The following table summarises them.

	1. Step: List contains generic terms	2. Step: Limits to claiming back	3. Step: Exception for generic terms	4. Step: Prohibition that GIs cannot become generic	5. Step: Generic use defence
CARIFORUM-EC EPA			√		
EU-SK FTA	√				
EU-Peru/ Colombia FTA	√			√	√
EU-CA AA	√			√	
EU-Canada CETA	√	√			√
EU-Singapore FTA			√		
EU-Vietnam FTA	√	√			
Draft EU-India BTIA				√	

First, a trader will have to verify whether the generic term he uses is indeed covered in the Annex of the relevant agreement and therefore protected as a GI under the terms of the agreement. If the term is not covered, he is free to use the term. Should at a later stage the equivalent term be applied for GI protection in the partner country, the trader needs to check whether domestic law provides for an exception of generic

---

142. See Art. 246 EU-Central America AA; Art. 20.21.7 EU-Canada CETA.
143. Art. 41.1 EU Regulation 1151/2012.
144. See *supra* section B.I.2.

terms in the registration process of a GI. If it does, he could invoke the genericity of the term in an opposition procedure, if genericity constitutes a ground for opposition.

If the term is contained in the list annexed to the relevant agreement, a trader in the second step needs to check whether any limitations are established in the FTA that would phase out or require additional indications for using the generic term. Such limitations so far have only been included in two agreements, but may be included in future agreements.

Thirdly, if the term is protected in full, or the limitations are no longer applicable, the trader could review whether domestic law contains an exception for generic terms, under its provisions of invalidity of GIs. The fact that only two FTAs include the provision does not mean that domestically, the rule has not been included in other partner countries, as it is based on an optional TRIPS exception. In case the exception is present, a trader could try to invalidate the GI at a later stage, arguing that the term has become generic. Whether the assessment of genericity will be successful is unclear, since at the moment of FTA negotiations both parties agreed to them being protected as GIs and therefore (implicitly) denied their generic character. However, the generic nature of a term may change over time and, therefore, genericity could be found at a later point in time.

The assessment of genericity in the future under step 3 is only useful if no provision is contained in the FTA that prohibits GIs from becoming generic (step 4). Two free trade agreements contain this provision, which is also found in EU law and under the Lisbon Agreement. If a trader is confronted with this rule, the term is protected according to the scope of protection set out in the FTA, which usually follows the TRIPS standard and equates the protection for foodstuffs and agricultural products with the protection foreseen for wines and spirits in TRIPS.

As a last remedy (step 5), a trader should check whether a justification is contained in domestic law that allows him to use the generic term even though it is protected as a GI. Two agreements foresee this justification; it comes with certain costs but may constitute a final remedy for traders to continue using generic terms for their products.

Whether these consequences for traders should be regarded as barriers to legitimate trade should be answered by taking into consideration the specific subject-matter of GI protection, and in particular the policy and rationale behind the exception for generic terms. Perhaps even more for geographical indications than for trade marks, the specific subject-matter is the protection of indications of origin that allow consumers to easily identify the origin of products. The particular rationale behind the exception for generic terms is similar to its equivalent provision under trade mark law: Art. 24.6 TRIPS and Art. 6*quinquies* Paris Convention show a similarity in language used.[145] Borrowing from ECJ jurisprudence,[146] generic terms are excluded from trade mark, or GI protection for that matter, in order to prevent the registration of signs or indications that are not capable of distinguishing the goods and services of one undertaking from those of another. As a consequence, it is

---

145. D. J. Gervais, The TRIPS Agreement: Drafting History and Analysis, London 1998, para. 2.231.
146. ECJ C-517/99 *Merz & Krell GmbH & Co v. Deutsches Patent- und Markenamt* [2001] E.C.R. I-6959; [2002] E.T.M.R. 21, para. 28.

argued that protecting GIs in partner countries, the terms of which can be considered generic in those countries and thereby fail to distinguish the origin of the products, should not be registered and protected as GIs. The fact that recent EU FTAs do so can be considered a barrier to legitimate trade.

D. CONCLUSIONS

This contribution aimed at showing how the registration of descriptive and generic terms as trade marks or geographical indications creates barriers to legitimate trade. Where terms are protected that should, according to the public interest behind the relevant law, be excluded from protection, traders face impediments that cannot be justified. The effects for foreign traders in the case of trade mark-protected foreign language terms, and for domestic traders in the case of GI-protected generic terms are argued to be equivalent to creating barriers to legitimate trade.

Legitimate trade has been defined for the purpose of this contribution on the basis of the objective that the WTO system pursues: the reduction of barriers to international trade, in particular measures that create arbitrary discrimination or disguised restrictions on trade. Whether a restriction is justified, and thereby does not create a barrier to legitimate trade, depends on whether the measure is applied in a way that safeguards the specific subject-matter of the property, taking into account the policy and rationale of the right.

Foreign language terms have been registered in the EU, based on jurisprudence of the ECJ, in particular the *Matratzen* judgment. According to the ECJ in that judgment, the most relevant ground of refusal regarding descriptive terms does not apply to foreign language terms: where foreign terms are generally not known to traders and consumers in the Member State where registration is being sought, the term is not descriptive and does not need to be refused.

This application of the law arguably is not in line with the specific subject-matter of trade mark law, and in particular against the public interest that Art. 4.1.c TMD serves. According to the ECJ in *Chiemsee*, descriptive terms should remain free to be used by all traders and thereby should not be reserved to one undertaking only. Where foreign language terms are protected as trade marks, foreign traders will not be able to market their products by describing them in their own language. Relying on a justification in infringement proceedings does not offer an adequate alternative due to the costs involved in legal proceedings in a foreign country.

I have suggested that the original wording in Art. 6*quinquies* B Paris Convention and the public interest as noted in *Chiemsee* should prevail in determining whether foreign language terms are regarded as being descriptive. Accordingly, all traders should be able to use their own languages to describe their products. Central to the analysis should be the international niche market that deals in and consumes the specific product, also in the respective Member State. It is proposed that national and the EU trade mark offices check terms applied for trade mark protection against their meaning in the most common foreign languages. Arguably, the languages spoken in WTO Members cover most current and potential traders. The doctrine of foreign equivalents in the US may serve as an inspiration for a tool on how to address the issue. Such a practice could be facilitated by including a mandatory requirement in the application file to provide the translation of a foreign language term in the national language in case of a national trade mark application, and in case of an EU trade mark application, into one of the five official languages of the EUIPO (English, French, German, Italian and Spanish). Failure to do so should be classified as a registration made in bad faith.

The determination of whether a term should be protected in a partner country of the EU as a geographical indication is very much a political decision: it is during FTA negotiations that lists of terms are drawn up that will be protected as GIs in the future in the partner country. These lists also contain generic terms, as it has been an explicit goal of the EU to 'claw back' terms originating in the EU but at the same time being used as the common name for the type of product in partner countries. As a consequence, domestic traders in the partner countries will no longer be able to use the generic term (or only in a limited way).

From a GI law perspective, generic terms should not be protected because they do not indicate origin. Rather than referring to the link between the product and its origin, they refer to types of products. Since the origin function is central to GI law and to the exception of generic terms in particular, the protection of generic terms through FTAs is argued to create a barrier to legitimate trade.

While the best solution would be to exclude generic terms from the lists of FTAs, this may not be feasible in terms of negotiation dynamics and bargaining power. A second-best option would then be to limit the extent of their protection, in the way the EU-Canada CETA and the EU-Vietnam FTA, for example, have included grandfathering provisions and transitional periods.

In addition, negotiating partners need to be cautious of a provision included so far in two agreements: the prohibition that an already protected GI can become generic. This would enlarge the effect of the protection of terms in the lists to any future situation. Arguably, terms protected now may in the future be used in a more generic way, meaning that at one point they would be classified as having generic character. In case a country provides for the exclusion of generic terms from protection in their domestic law, such terms could become freely usable after a finding of genericity.

Finally, for all cases where terms are (still) protected as GIs, a third-best option is a justification regarding the use of generic terms: accordingly, even where a GI contains a name that is considered generic, other traders should be able to use it. While this justification can only be invoked in infringement proceedings, it may create the only final possibility for domestic traders not complying with the product specifications of the GI to continue using the generic term.

CHAPTER 5
The Seizure of Goods in Transit – Can EU Trade Mark Legislation Serve as a Model?

Martin Senftleben

A. INTRODUCTION

In the field of enforcement, the potential clash between free trade rules and the aim to ensure effective protection of intellectual property (IP) clearly comes to the fore: while Art. V of the General Agreement on Tariffs and Trade (GATT 1994)[1] explicitly recognizes the freedom of transit, Art. 51 of the Agreement on Trade Related Aspects of Intellectual Property Rights (TRIPS)[2] eschews an explicit prohibition of customs measures against counterfeit and pirated goods in transit.[3] As Art. 9(4) of the EU Trade Mark Regulation (EUTMR)[4] and Art. 10(4) of the Trade Mark Directive (TMD)[5] show, this back door to transit seizures remains a lasting temptation for lawmakers

---

1. General Agreement on Tariffs and Trade: Multilateral Trade Negotiations Final Act Embodying the Results of the Uruguay Round of Trade Negotiations, done at Marrakesh on 15 April 1994, 33 I.L.M. 1125 (1994).
2. Agreement on Trade-Related Aspects of Intellectual Property Rights, Annex 1C of the Marrakesh Agreement Establishing the World Trade Organization, signed on 15 April 1994, 33 I.L.M. 1197 (1994).
3. According to Art. 51, footnote 13 TRIPS, '[i]t is understood that there shall be no obligation to apply [customs] procedures to imports of goods put on the market in another country by or with the consent of the right holder, or to goods in transit.' While this provision leaves no doubt that there is no international obligation, it does not inhibit WTO Members from going beyond the international minimum standard of protection in the field of IP enforcement by providing for customs measures against goods in transit.
4. Regulation (EU) 2017/1001 of the European Parliament and of the Council of 14 June 2017 on the European Union trade mark (codification), OJ L 154/1 of 16 June 2017.
5. Directive (EU) 2015/2436 of the European Parliament and of the Council of 16 December 2015 to approximate the laws of the Member States relating to trade marks, OJ L 336/1 of 23 December 2015.

seeking to offer broad IP protection. Even though a past controversy about the in-transit seizure of generic drugs in the Netherlands almost reached the WTO panel stage,[6] the EU legislator opted for the introduction of new trade mark rights against goods in transit. This grant of rights raises complex questions of compliance with the international guarantee of free transit.

However, the risk of an impediment to world trade is not confined to the EU territory. Trans-regional repercussions of an evolving EU practice of seizing goods in transit cannot be ruled out. Other regional agreements, such as the Trans-Pacific Partnership Agreement (TPP)[7] also reflect a growing interest in the extension of enforcement measures to goods in transit. Art. 18.76.5 TPP stipulates that each Contracting Party

> 'shall provide that its competent authorities may initiate border measures ex officio with respect to goods under customs control that are:
>
> (a) imported;
> (b) destined for export; or
> (c) in transit;
>
> and that are suspected of being counterfeit trademark goods or pirated copyright goods.'

This provision only concerns an optional seizure of goods in transit ('may initiate border measures') that remains at the discretion of customs authorities.[8] Moreover, the status of the TPP is unclear after the U.S. withdrew from the negotiation process.[9] This development, however, need not be the end of new enforcement standards on both sides of the Pacific. The remaining negotiation partners – Australia, Brunei, Canada, Chile, Japan, Malaysia, Mexico, New Zealand, Peru, Singapore and Vietnam – have resurrected the trade deal by establishing the Comprehensive and Progressive

---

6. *Request for Consultations by India*, European Union and a Member State – Seizure of Generic Drugs in Transit (WT/DS408/1), World Trade Organization (WTO), 19 May 2010; *Request for Consultations by Brazil*, European Union and a Member State – Seizure of Generic Drugs in Transit (WT/DS409/1), WTO, 19 May 2010.
7. For the text of the TPP, see https://ustr.gov/trade-agreements/free-trade-agreements/trans-pacific-partnership/tpp-full-text (accessed on 9 May 2018).
8. In practice, instances where customs authorities take action on their own initiative may be relatively scarce. EU statistics show that the number of *ex officio* actions has decreased considerably in recent years. See the overview given in *European Commission*, Report on EU Customs Enforcement of Intellectual Property Rights – Results at the Border 2014, Luxembourg: Publications Office of the European Union 2015, available at http://ec.europa.eu/taxation_customs/customs/customs_controls/counterfeit_piracy/statistics/index_en.htm, (accessed 9 May 2018), p. 10, showing low percentages of *ex officio* actions in recent years: 2.62% in 2012, 3.06% in 2013 and 1.73% in 2014. *European Commission*, Report on EU Customs Enforcement of Intellectual Property Rights – Results at the Border 2011, Luxembourg: Publications Office of the European Union 2012, 9, shows a percentage of 26.50% in 2008, 9.62% in 2009, 4.02% in 2010, and 2.80% in 2011. Cf. O. Vrins, 'Regulation 608/2013: Towards a more effective customs enforcement of intellectual property rights?', 39 BMM Bulletin 118 [2013], 122–123.
9. Cf. *BBC News*, 'TPP: What is it and why does it matter?', 23 January 2017, available at http://www.bbc.com/news/business-32498715 (accessed 9 May 2018).

5. The Seizure of Goods in Transit

Agreement for Trans-Pacific Partnership (CPTPP). The CPTPP incorporates the majority of the previous TPP provisions, including Art. 18.76.5 TPP which sets forth the competence of customs authorities to take measures against goods in transit.[10] Hence, there seems to be sufficient support for the seizure of goods in transit in the region. The adoption of the CPTPP may lead to a proliferation of enforcement measures against in-transit goods.

If an acceptable practice evolves under Art. 9(4) EUTMR and Art. 10(4) TMD, the EU approach may thus find followers. A continuous expansion of the practice of transit seizures, however, may blur the territorial limits of intellectual property rights and place a heavy burden on world trade.[11] Against this background, the question arises as to which developments led to the adoption of a new right against goods in transit in the EU (following section B). It is also important to clarify which safeguards the new EU legislation contains against an encroachment upon the international freedom of transit (section C), and whether these safeguards can be deemed sufficient (section D). The analysis will show whether the EU approach can serve as a model for other regions (sections E and F).

B. NEW RIGHT AGAINST GOODS IN TRANSIT IN THE EU

With the inclusion of Art. 9(4) EUTMR and Art. 10(4) TMD in the portfolio of harmonised trade mark rights, the European Commission sought to neutralise the implications of the jurisprudence of the Court of Justice of the European Union (CJEU).[12] In *Philips and Nokia*, the CJEU found that goods placed under a suspensive customs procedure could not, 'merely by the fact of being so placed, infringe intellectual property rights applicable in the European Union.'[13] The Court also made it clear that

---

10. See the text of the CPTPP and the background information provided by the Canadian government at *Canadian Government*, Comprehensive and Progressive Agreement for Trans-Pacific Partnership, available at https://www.international.gc.ca/trade-commerce/trade-agreements-accords-commerciaux/agr-acc/cptpp-ptpgp/index.aspx?lang=eng (accessed 9 May 2018). For comments on the transit provision in the TPP, see K. Weatherall, 'TPP – Australian Section-by-Section Analysis of the Enforcement Provisions', Legal Studies Research Paper No. 13/84, Sydney: Sydney Law School 2013, pp. 35–37.
11. M.R.F. Senftleben, 'Wolf in Sheep's Clothing? Trade Mark Rights Against Goods in Transit and the End of Traditional Territorial Limits', 47(8) International Review of Intellectual Property and Competition Law 941 [2016], pp. 957–958.
12. *European Commission*, Proposal for a Directive of the European Parliament and of the Council to Approximate the laws of the Member States Relating to Trade Marks, COM(2013) 162 final, 2013/0089 (COD) of 27 March 2013; *European Commission*, Proposal for a Regulation of the European Parliament and of the Council Amending Council Regulation (EC) No 207/2009 on the Community Trade Mark, COM(2013) 161 final, 2013/0088 (COD) of 27 March 2013, p. 9. R. Knaak, A. Kur and A. von Mühlendahl, 'Study on the Functioning of the European Trade Mark System', Max Planck Institute for Intellectual Property & Competition Law Research Paper No. 12-13, Munich: Max Planck Institute 2011, para. 2.31 and 2.177; F. Eijsvogels, 'The new Customs Regulation, the Commission's proposals relating to trademarks and transit – Back to previous Dutch practice?', 39 BMM Bulletin 135 [2013], p. 140.
13. CJEU, 1 December 2011, C-446/09 and C-495/09, *Philips and Nokia*, [2011] E.C.R. I-12435, ECLI:EU:C:2011:796, para. 56. Cf. H. Große Ruse-Khan, 'An international trade perspective

intellectual property rights could only be infringed 'where, during their placement under a suspensive procedure [...], or even before their arrival [...], goods coming from non-member States are the subject of a commercial act directed at European Union consumers, such as a sale, offer for sale or advertising.'[14] As a result, customs authorities could legitimately take steps against goods in transit only if there was material indicating that one or more of the operators involved in the manufacture, consignment or distribution of the goods were about to direct the goods towards EU consumers or were disguising their commercial intentions.[15] Such a suspicion could follow from the fact that the destination of the goods was not declared whereas the suspensive procedure requested required such a declaration, the lack of precise or reliable information as to the identity or address of the manufacturer or consignor of the goods, a lack of co-operation with the customs authorities, or the discovery of documents or correspondence suggesting that the goods would be diverted to EU consumers.[16]

However, an abstract consideration that fraudulent diversion to EU consumers could not be ruled out was not sufficient. Otherwise, all goods in external transit or customs warehousing could be detained 'without the slightest concrete indication of an irregularity'.[17] Such a situation would give rise to a risk that customs actions in the EU would be random and excessive. In this regard, the CJEU recalled explicitly that 'imitations and copies coming from a non-member State and transported to another non-member State may comply with the intellectual property provisions in force in each of those States.'[18] In light of the EU objective to develop world trade through the progressive abolition of restrictions on trade,[19] it was essential that goods be able to pass in transit, via the EU, from one non-Member State to another 'without

---

on transit seizures', 39 BMM Bulletin 142 [2013], p. 145. As to previous case law, see CJEU, 27 October 2003, case C-115/02, *Administration des douanes v. Rioglass*, [2003] E.C.R. I-12705, ECLI:EU:C:2003:587, paras. 27–29; CJEU, 18 October 2005, case C-405/03, *Class International*, [2005] E.C.R. I-08735, ECLI:EU:C:2005:616, para. 47, 50 and operative part; CJEU, 9 November 2006, case C-281/05, *Montex Holdings*, [2006] E.C.R. I-10881, ECLI:EU:C:2006:709, para. 34. For an overview of relevant CJEU decisions, see *Senftleben* (*supra* n. 11), pp. 943–945; R. Knaak, 'Customs Regulation', in M. Vivant (ed.), European Case Law on Infringements of Intellectual Property Rights, Brussels: Larcier/Bruylant 2016, 139, pp. 148–149.
14. CJEU, 1 December 2011, C-446/09 and C-495/09, *Philips and Nokia*, [2011] E.C.R. I-12435, ECLI:EU:C:2011:796, para. 57.
15. German Federal Court of Justice, 21 March 2007, I ZR 246/02, *Diesel II*, Gewerblicher Rechtsschutz und Urheberrecht 2007, 876, paras. 18–19; German Federal Court of Justice, 21 March 2007, I ZR 66/04, *Durchfuhr von Originalware*, Gewerblicher Rechtsschutz und Urheberrecht 2007, 875, paras. 12–14. As to the Benelux territory, see Court of Appeal of The Hague, 30 October 2012, *Bacardi v. TOP Logistics*, ECLI:NL:GHSGR:2012:BY1494, para. 35. With regard to the guidelines given by the CJEU, see CJEU, 9 November 2006, case C-281/05, *Montex Holdings*, [2006] E.C.R. I-10881, ECLI:EU:C:2006:709, para. 19.
16. CJEU C-446/09 and C-495/09, paras. 60–61.
17. CJEU C-446/09 and C-495/09, para. 62.
18. CJEU C-446/09 and C-495/09, para. 63.
19. See Art. 206 of the Treaty on the Functioning of the European Union, OJ C 115/47 of 9 May 2008 (consolidated version).

that operation being hindered, even by a temporary detention, by Member States' customs authorities.'[20]

As the European Commission explained during the EU trade mark law reform,[21] the CJEU decision in *Philips and Nokia* had met with 'strong criticism from stakeholders as placing an inappropriately high burden of proof on rights holders, and hindering the fight against counterfeiting.'[22] It was evident that there was 'an urgent need to have in place a European legal framework enabling a more effective fight against the counterfeiting of goods as a fast-growing activity.'[23] These arguments paved the way for the adoption of Art. 9(4) EUTMR and Art. 10(4) TMD which entitle the trade mark proprietor

> 'to prevent all third parties from bringing goods, in the course of trade, into the Member State where the trade mark is registered without being released for free circulation there, where such goods, including packaging, come from third countries and bear without authorization a trade mark which is identical to the trade mark registered in respect of such goods, or which cannot be distinguished in its essential aspects from that trade mark.'

In light of the fact that an earlier seizure of generic drugs in transit had exposed the EU to harsh criticism at the international level,[24] this constitutes a bold legislative step. The previous debate about customs measures had been triggered by the seizure of a shipment of the generic drug Losartan on its way from India to Brazil by customs authorities in Amsterdam. As a justification for the customs measure, the Dutch authorities could point to European patent rights of DuPont and Merck Sharp & Dohme. These rights, however, enjoyed protection neither in Brazil nor in India. The seizure itself rested on the so-called 'manufacturing fiction' allowing Dutch customs authorities to assume that goods in transit had been produced in the country of transit (instead of the country of origin) when assessing an infringement of intellectual property rights. The Dutch Supreme Court had established the manufacturing fiction in *Philips v. Postech* – a case concerning the seizure of recordable CDs which had been in transit via the Netherlands on their way from Taiwan to Switzerland. Seeking

---

20. CJEU C-446/09 and C-495/09, para. 63.
21. *Supra* n. 4 and 5.
22. *European Commission* (*supra* n. 12), p. 9. Cf. *Knaak/Kur/von Mühlendahl* (*supra* n. 12), para. 2.31 and 2.177; *Eijsvogels* (*supra* n. 12), p. 140.
23. European Commission (*supra* n. 12), p. 9.
24. See the references *supra* n. 6. Cf. H. Große Ruse-Khan (*supra* n. 13), p. 142; H. Große Ruse-Khan and T. Jäger, 'Policing Patents Worldwide? EC Border Measures Against Transiting Generic Drugs under EC and WTO Intellectual Property Regimes', 40 IIC 502 [2009], pp. 510–520; H. Große Ruse-Khan, 'A Trade Agreement Creating Barriers to International Trade? ACTA Border Measures and Goods in Transit', 26 American University International Law Review 646 [2011], p. 646; S.P. Kumar, 'International Trade, Public Health, and Intellectual Property Maximalism: The Case of European Border Enforcement and Trade in Generic Pharmaceuticals', 5 Global Trade and Customs Journal 155 [2010], p. 155; B. Mercurio, '"Seizing" Pharmaceuticals in Transit: Analysing the WTO Dispute that wasn't', 61 International and Comparative Law Quarterly 389 [2012], p. 389; K. Weatherall, 'Politics, Compromise, Text, and the Failures of the Anti-Counterfeiting Trade Agreement', 33 Sydney Law Review 230 [2011], pp. 249–253; S. Rinnert, 'Beschlagnahme von Generika im Transit', Gewerblicher Rechtsschutz und Urheberrecht – International Teil 2011, p. 901.

to offer Philips the opportunity to invoke patent rights enjoying protection in the Netherlands against the goods in transit, the Dutch Supreme Court held in *Philips v. Postech* that the infringement analysis could be based on the assumption that the CDs had been produced in the Netherlands.[25]

Opposing the application of the manufacturing fiction in the *Losartan* case, India, Brazil, several other developing countries and the Indian producer Dr Reddy's Laboratories qualified the transit seizure of Losartan as an attempt to artificially extend the territorial scope of EU patent rights and impede international trade.[26] In May 2010, India and Brazil formally complained before the WTO about the seizure of generic medicines in transit in the EU.[27] Ultimately, the case did not lead to a panel report under the WTO dispute settlement system. In light of the CJEU decision in *Philips and Nokia*, there seemed to be little doubt that incidents, such as the seizure of Losartan in Amsterdam, belonged to the past. In the amended EU Customs Regulation No 608/2013, it was stated in Recital 11 that the seizure of medicines in transit required a 'substantial likelihood of diversion of such medicines onto the market of the Union' – a standard that seemed to reflect the outcome of the *Philips and Nokia* case.[28]

C. SAFEGUARDS AGAINST EXCESSIVE MEASURES

Considering these developments, it is surprising that the amendment to the EU trade mark law has led to a new right of trade mark owners to take measures against goods in transit. Despite the international criticism triggered by the seizure of goods in transit in the *Losartan* case, EU policy makers decided to adopt Art. 9(4) EUTMR and Art. 10(4) TMD. In these new provisions, the requirement of the conflicting sign being 'identical to the trade mark registered in respect of such goods, or which cannot be distinguished in its essential aspects from that trade mark' makes it clear that the drafters intended to confine the scope of the provision to counterfeit goods. The formulation corresponds with the international definition of 'counterfeit trademark

---

25. Dutch Supreme Court, 19 March 2004, Nederlandse Jurisprudentie 2007, no. 585. Cf. P.J. Sciarone, Het arrest van de Hoge Raad inzake Philips/Postech en de Losartan-affaire – Deel I, Berichten industriële eigendom, 2012, p. 2 (4–6); S. Rinnert, Die neue Customs-IP-Enforcement-Verordnung, Gewerblicher Rechtsschutz und Urheberrecht, 2014, p. 241 (242–243). As to the adequacy of the manufacturing fiction, see the doubts expressed by C. Heath, 'Customs Seizures, Transit and Trade – In Honour of Dieter Stauder's 70th Birthday', 41 IIC 881 [2010], pp. 893–895.
26. Große Ruse-Khan (*supra* n. 13), p. 143.
27. See *Requests for Consultations by India and Brazil* (*supra* n. 6). The practice of in-transit seizure in the EU was not confined to the *Losartan* case. By contrast, further cases affecting goods in transit had arisen at the time. See the overview provided by Heath (*supra* n. 25), pp. 883–886; S.P. Kumar, Border Enforcement of Intellectual Property Rights Against In-Transit Generic Pharmaceuticals: An Analysis of Character and Consistency, European Intellectual Property Review 506 [2010], p. 506; F.M. Abbott, 'Seizure of Generic Pharmaceuticals in Transit Based on Allegations of Patent Infringement: A Threat to International Trade, Development and Public Welfare', 1 WIPO Journal 43 [2009], p. 47.
28. Große Ruse-Khan (*supra* n. 13), p. 144.

5. The Seizure of Goods in Transit

goods' in Art. 51, footnote 14 TRIPS which accompanies the TRIPS provisions on border measures.

Admittedly, the *Losartan* case concerned patent rights. Art. 9(4) EUTMR and Art. 10(4) TMD deal with trade mark rights. While a patent protects a product incorporating a new technical solution as such, a trade mark only protects a sign identifying the commercial source of that product. This difference may have led EU policy makers to believe that, in practice, it would be easier to keep a sufficient distance from an EU trade mark than to invent around a patent that is protected in the EU. However, this assumption is doubtful in the case of generic medicine and the legitimate resale of genuine pharmaceutical products after the exhaustion of trade mark rights – cases where a reference to the trade-marked name of the original product may be necessary to inform consumers appropriately.[29]

The assumption is also doubtful because trade mark rights increasingly acquire the status of products in their own right. As a result of substantial investment in marketing and advertising, the mark becomes a central part of the product, if not the main product feature in the eyes of consumers.[30] Moreover, the basic problem

---

29. Not surprisingly, this kind of case generated quite some case law. In particular, see CJEU, 11 July 1996, C-427/93, C-429/93 and C-436/93, *BMS/Paranova*, [1996] E.C.R. I-03457, ECLI:EU:C:1996:282, para. 79; CJEU, 12 October 1999, C-379/97, *Upjohn*, [1999] E.C.R. I-06927, ECLI:EU:C:1999:494, para. 28 and 42; CJEU, 26 April 2007, C348/04, *Boehringer Ingelheim and Others*, [2007] E.C.R. I-03391, ECLI:EU:C:2007:249, para. 36; CJEU, 22 December 2008, C-276/05, *The Wellcome Foundation*, [2008] E.C.R. I-10479, ECLI:EU:C:2008:756, para. 23; CJEU, 28 July 2011, C-400/09 and C-207/10, *Orifarm and Others*, [2011] E.C.R. I-07063, ECLI:EU:C:2011:519, para. 36. For an overview of issues in the area of repackaging, see *M. Marell, M.R.F. Senftleben and M. Rieger-Jansen*, 'Trademark Enforcement Issues in the Pharmaceutical Industry', in *J. de Werra* (ed.), Intellectual Property in the Pharmaceutical Industry, Zurich: Schulthess 2012, p. 127 (139–141).
30. With regard to the formal recognition of these enhanced functions of trade marks, see CJEU, 18 June 2009, C-487/07, *L'Oréal/Bellure*, [2009] E.C.R. I-05185, ECLI:EU:C:2009:378, para. 58. As to the discussion about the legitimacy of protecting brand experience and goodwill, see *M.A. Lemley and M.P. McKenna*, 'Owning Mark(et)s', 109 Michigan Law Review 137 [2010], p. 137; *B. Beebe*, 'Intellectual Property Law and the Sumptuary Code', 123 Harvard Law Review 809 [2010], pp. 848–859; *M.R.F. Senftleben*, 'The Trademark Tower of Babel – Dilution Concepts in International, US and EC Trademark Law', 40 IIC 45 [2009], p. 59; *L. Bently, J. Davis and J.C. Ginsburg* (eds.), Trade Marks and Brands – An Interdisciplinary Critique, Cambridge: Cambridge University Press 2008, p. 241; *G.B. Dinwoodie and M.D. Janis*, 'Dilution's (Still) Uncertain Future', 105 Michigan Law Review First Impressions 98 [2006], p. 98; *B. Beebe*, 'Search and Persuasion in Trademark Law', 103 Michigan Law Review 2020 [2005], p. 2020; *M. Strasser*, 'The Rational Basis of Trademark Protection Revisited: Putting the Dilution Doctrine into Context', 10 Fordham Intellectual Property, Media & Entertainment Law Journal 375 [2000], p. 375; *R.S. Brown*, 'Advertising and the Public Interest: Legal Protection of Trade Symbols', 108 Yale Law Journal 1619 [1999], pp. 1619–1620; *M. Lemley*, 'The Modern Lanham Act and the Death of Common Sense', 108 Yale Law Journal 1687 [1999], pp. 1694–1698; *G.S. Lunney, Jr.*, 'Trademark Monopolies', 48 Emory Law Journal 367 [1999], pp. 437–439; *R.C. Dreyfuss*, 'We Are Symbols and Inhabit Symbols, so Should we be Paying Rent? Deconstructing the Lanham Act and Rights of Publicity', 20 Columbia-VLA Journal of Law & Arts 123 [1996], p. 128; *R.C. Dreyfuss*, 'Expressive Genericity: Trademarks as Language in the Pepsi Generation', 65 Notre Dame Law Review 397 [1990], pp. 413–414. As to the foundations of the dilution doctrine, see

remains the same irrespective of differences in the configuration of patent and trade mark rights: a territorially limited intellectual property right enjoying protection in the EU is used as a universal yardstick to determine whether goods in transit constitute 'counterfeit' goods. Although the goods are destined for another country, the question of counterfeiting is thus answered on the basis of the rights portfolio in the EU. In consequence, a manufacturer of goods seeking to ensure a smooth transit via the EU will have to avoid a conflict with an EU trade mark right even though he may be free to use an identical or very similar sign in the country of final destination.

The territorial scope of trade mark rights enjoying protection in the EU is thus artificially extended. If this strategy of enhancing the impact of EU trade mark rights on world trade is applied systematically, a certain degree of *de facto* protection of EU trade marks beyond the borders of the European Union can hardly be denied. Concerns about an encroachment upon the international guarantee of the freedom of transit are thus not unfounded – even if Art. 9(4) EUTMR and Art. 9(4) TMD 'merely' concern trade mark rights which serve as identifiers of commercial source.

Considerations of this kind are not completely absent from the context surrounding the new trade mark right. In light of the concerns about an undue curtailment of the international freedom of trade, the EU legislator sought to soften the effect of the new transit provisions. Apart from granting an exclusive right, Art. 9(4) EUTMR and Art. 10(4) TMD also stipulate that the entitlement of seizing goods in transit shall lapse

> 'if during the proceedings to determine whether the registered trade mark has been infringed, initiated in accordance with the provisions of Regulation (EU) No 608/2013 concerning customs enforcement of intellectual property rights, evidence is provided by the declarant or the holder of the goods that the proprietor of the registered trade mark is not entitled to prohibit the placing of the goods on the market in the country of final destination.'

EU law thus seeks to safeguard the freedom of trade by imposing the obligation on a trader confronted with a transit seizure to show that the owner of a trade mark right in the EU does not have a corresponding right in the country of final destination. While this additional rule may have been deemed a sufficient concession during the legislative process, it may raise more problems than it solves in practice.

I. Burden of Proof

The distribution of the burden of proof set forth in Art. 9(4) EUTMR and Art. 10(4) TMD is remarkable. On its merits, it reflects a bias in favour of the owner of trade mark rights in the EU. For the purposes of Art. 9(4) EUTMR and Art. 10(4) TMD, there seems to be a presumption that trade mark rights enjoying protection in (a part of) the EU also enjoy protection in other parts of the world. Given this presumption, the declarant or the holder of the seized goods has to carry the burden of proving that such a right does not exist in the country of final destination. Art. 9(4) EUTMR and Art. 10(4) TMD require evidence 'that the proprietor of the registered trade mark

---

F.I. Schechter, 'The Rational Basis of Trademark Protection', 40 Harvard Law Review 813 [1927], p. 813.

is not entitled to prohibit the placing of the goods on the market in the country of final destination.'

With this distribution of the burden of proof, Art. 9(4) EUTMR and Art. 10(4) TMD depart from the standard rule that the right holder – in this case the trade mark proprietor – must present all necessary evidence to support his infringement claim. As the goods are merely in transit in the EU and the infringement would finally take place in the country of final destination, it would have been more consistent to impose the burden of producing evidence of infringement in the country of final destination on the EU trade mark owner. Given the fact that intellectual property rights are territorially limited, goods that appear as 'counterfeit trademark goods' in light of EU trade mark rights may nonetheless be legitimate abroad if the right holder failed to secure corresponding trade mark rights in the country of final destination.[31]

Irrespective of these concerns about an unjustified bias in favour of EU trade mark owners, the distribution of the burden of proof can be explained with practical considerations. If the transit seizure really concerns counterfeit goods, the declarant or the holder of the goods is unlikely to take any steps. Practically speaking, it may thus make sense to impose the burden of proving the absence of infringement on the affected trader in order to separate the wheat from the chaff. If the declarant or the holder of the goods makes an effort to demonstrate non-infringement in the country of final destination, this fact alone might already indicate that the affected trader is not a counterfeiter.

Nonetheless, the fact remains that, on its merits, the responsibility for keeping international trade intact is to be borne by the trader who is confronted with a transit seizure in the EU.[32] This trader must produce proof of the absence of a trade mark infringement in the country of final destination. Moreover, a relatively light burden of proof would already have been sufficient to achieve the objective of separating the wheat from the chaff. In particular, it would have been sufficient to oblige the declarant or the holder of the goods to show that the trade mark at issue has not been registered in the country of final destination.

Nonetheless, the open wording of Art. 9(4) EUTMR and Art. 10(4) TMD ('that the proprietor of the registered trade mark is not entitled to prohibit the placing of the goods on the market in the country of final destination') leaves room for a much broader interpretation of the trader's onus of proof. Taken to the extreme, evidence of a missing entitlement in the country of final destination may be understood to require a comprehensive legal analysis, including the question of trade mark protection against confusion because of mere similarity of signs, protection against dilution based on a mere risk of calling to mind the protected mark, and the inapplicability of limitations of trade mark rights that may tip the scales in favour of the declarant or holder of the seized goods. However, a requirement to conduct such a broad analysis would create a sharp contrast with the starting point of the transit seizure. As explained, the new right against goods in transit only covers counterfeit goods bearing an essentially identical sign. Questions of mere similarity or mere association with the trade mark seem extraneous and unjustified against this background.

---

31. H. Große Ruse-Khan, The Protection of Intellectual Property in International Law, Oxford: Oxford University Press 2016, pp. 295–296; Heath (supra n. 25), p. 897.
32. See also the critical comments by Große Ruse-Khan (supra n. 31), pp. 295–296.

Under a maximalist approach, the burden of proof may also be understood to include the question of a potential encroachment upon unregistered trade mark rights, such as rights concerning well-known marks in the sense of Art. 6*bis* Paris Convention (hereinafter PC).[33] As Art. 6*bis* PC leads to protection even if there is no registration,[34] it can be particularly difficult to ascertain the protection status in the country of final destination. In a country following the WIPO Joint Recommendation Concerning Provisions on the Protection of Well-Known Marks,[35] the threshold for acquiring protection as a well-known mark will be quite low.[36] Art. 16(2) TRIPS stipulates that, in determining whether a trade mark is well-known, 'Members shall take account of the knowledge of the trademark in the relevant sector of the public, including knowledge in the Member concerned which has been obtained as a result of the promotion of the trademark.' Hence, the inquiry can hardly be confined to clear-cut cases of famous marks that can be expected to be known by the general consuming public all around the globe. The trade mark proprietor in the EU may thus use the legal uncertainty surrounding the determination of protection as a well-known mark in the country of final destination to make the process of proving the absence of trade mark infringement particularly burdensome. The EU trade mark owner may also prolong that process by invoking protection on the basis of Art. 6*bis* PC or Art. 16(2) TRIPS to cast doubt on mere register evidence produced by the declarant or holder of the goods.

II. Reference to International Freedom of Trade

It seems that the drafters of Art. 9(4) EUTMR and Art. 10(4) TMD felt uneasy about this configuration of the exclusive right against transit goods themselves. They included several additional safeguards in the recitals accompanying the grant of the new exclusive right. Recital 15 EUTMR and Recital 21 TMD not only reflect the aim to 'strengthen trade mark protection and combat counterfeiting more effectively' but also underline that this aim is to be achieved

---

33. For the text of the Paris Convention for the Protection of Industrial Property (1971), see http://www.wipo.int/treaties/en/ip/paris/ (accessed on 9 May 2018). As to the complexity of identifying well-known marks and country differences, see *World Intellectual Property Organization*, WIPO Joint Recommendation Concerning the Protection of Well-Known Marks, WIPO publication No. 833, Geneva: WIPO 2000; *A. Kur*, Die WIPO-Vorschläge zum Schutz bekannter und berühmter Marken, Gewerblicher Rechtsschutz und Urheberrecht 1999, p. 866. As to different concepts of 'well-known' marks in international, EU and US law, see *Senftleben* (*supra* n. 30), pp. 50–55.
34. As to the scope of protection envisaged at the international level, see Art. 16(2) and (3) TRIPS and *World Intellectual Property Organization* (*supra* n. 33).
35. *World Intellectual Property Organization* (*supra* n. 33).
36. As to the level of international harmonisation of the standard of 'well-known' and remaining differences at the national level, see *Kur* (*supra* n. 33), p. 866; *Senftleben* (*supra* n. 30), p. 45; *J.T. McCarthy*, 'Dilution of a Trademark: European and United States Law Compared', 94 Trademark Reporter 1163 [2004], p. 1163; *B. Beebe*, 'A Defense of the New Federal Trademark Antidilution Law', 16 Fordham Intellectual Property, Media & Entertainment Law Journal 1143 [2006], pp. 1146–1147 and 1174.

'in line with international obligations of the Member States under the World Trade Organisation (WTO) framework, in particular Article V of the General Agreement on Tariffs and Trade on freedom of transit and, as regards generic medicines, the 'Declaration on the TRIPS Agreement and public health' adopted by the Doha WTO Ministerial Conference on 14 November 2001.'

The reference to the Doha Declaration is understandable in light of the aforementioned *Losartan* case that gave rise to the described delicate debate about shipments of generic medicines at the international level. It also forges a link with Recital 11 of the EU Customs Regulation No 608/2013 which confirms, in light of the Doha Declaration, 'WTO Members' right to protect public health and, in particular, to promote access to medicines for all.'

The direct reference to Art. V GATT 1994, however, is surprising. With this reference to an international free trade norm, Recital 15 EUTMR and Recital 21 TMD subject the application of the new exclusive right against goods in transit to a scrutiny in light of international trade standards. As the application of the new right against goods in transit should be 'in line with international obligations of the Member States under the World Trade Organisation (WTO) framework', it can be argued that the right cannot be invoked if this would lead to an encroachment upon Art. V GATT 1994. Recital 23 TMD indicates in this respect that EU policy makers saw the opportunity for the declarant or the holder of the seized goods to prove non-infringement in the country of final destination and, as a result, eliminate the trade mark proprietor's entitlement to seizure, as a way of reconciling 'the need to ensure the effective enforcement of trade mark rights with the necessity to avoid hampering the free flow of trade in legitimate goods'. In light of the described concerns about an overly broad interpretation of the trader's onus of proof, the question arises as to whether this safeguard is sufficient to ensure compliance with Art. V GATT 1994.

D. COMPLIANCE WITH INTERNATIONAL GUARANTEE OF FREE TRANSIT

The regulation of the freedom of transit in Art. V GATT 1994 commences in paragraph 1 with the following definition of 'traffic in transit':

'[g]oods (including baggage), and also vessels and other means of transport, shall be deemed to be in transit across the territory of a contracting party when the passage across such territory, with or without trans-shipment, warehousing, breaking bulk, or change in the mode of transport, is only a portion of a complete journey beginning and terminating beyond the frontier of the contracting party across whose territory the traffic passes. Traffic of this nature is termed in this Article "traffic in transit".'

Based on this definition, Art. V(2) GATT 1994 establishes the general rule of freedom of transit by positing that

'[t]here shall be freedom of transit through the territory of each contracting party, via the routes most convenient for international transit, for traffic in transit to or from the territory of other contracting parties. No distinction shall be made which is based on the flag of vessels, the place of origin, departure, entry, exit or destination, or on any circumstances relating to the ownership of goods, of vessels or of other means of transport.'

In *Colombia – Ports of Entry*, a WTO Panel made clear that this international obligation required 'unrestricted access via the most convenient routes' for transit goods whether or not the goods had been trans-shipped, warehoused, break-bulked, or had changed modes of transport. Goods in transit from any WTO Member had to be allowed entry for the passage of goods whenever destined for the territory of a third country.[37] This freedom, however, is not absolute. Art. V(3) GATT 1994 makes it clear that

> '[a]ny contracting party may require that traffic in transit through its territory be entered at the proper custom house, but, except in cases of failure to comply with applicable customs laws and regulations, such traffic coming from or going to the territory of other contracting parties shall not be subject to any unnecessary delays or restrictions […].'

On the one hand, Art. V(3) GATT 1994 thus offers room to argue that the new EU trade mark right against goods in transit is part of the applicable set of 'customs laws and regulations' with which traders shipping goods through the EU have to comply.[38] On the other hand, Art. V(3) GATT 1994 leaves little doubt that this freedom has its limits: 'unnecessary delays or restrictions' are unacceptable and amount to a violation of the international guarantee of free transit. Hence, it may be argued that the procedure following the seizure of goods in transit leads to unnecessary delays or restrictions because it imposes the burden on affected traders to provide evidence of non-infringement in the country of final destination – potentially including evidence of the absence of sign similarity or association, and protection on the basis of Art. *6bis* PC and Art. 16(2) TRIPS.[39]

The delay caused by a transit seizure can be considerable anyway. In the *Losartan* case, for instance, the generic drugs at issue had first been held up temporarily in the Netherlands. Subsequently, they were returned to India instead of ensuring shipment to the intended final destination which was Brazil.[40] Not surprisingly, the issue of unnecessary delays and restrictions of international trade featured prominently in India's formal request for consultations before the WTO.[41] As explained above, the CJEU itself emphasised in *Philips and Nokia* that, considering the policy objective to abolish trade restrictions, goods had to be able to pass in transit via the EU 'without that operation being hindered, even by a temporary detention, by Member States' customs authorities.'[42]

Another reference point for casting doubt upon compliance of the new trade mark right against goods in transit can be found in Art. V(4) GATT 1994. According to this provision, '[a]ll charges and regulations imposed by contracting parties on traffic in transit to or from the territories of other contracting parties shall be reasonable, having regard to the conditions of the traffic.' This further international rule offers

---

37. WTO Panel, *Colombia – Ports of Entry* (WT/DS366/R of 27 April 2009), para. 7.401.
38. However, see the serious doubts expressed by *Große Ruse-Khan (supra* n. 13), p. 147.
39. *Große Ruse-Khan (supra* n. 31), pp. 297–299.
40. *Große Ruse-Khan (supra* n. 13), p. 142.
41. *Request for Consultations by India (supra* n. 6), p. 2.
42. CJEU C-446/09 and C-495/09, para. 63.

the possibility of arguing that the new trade mark right against goods in transit in the EU constitutes an unreasonable regulation: due to the territorial nature of trade mark rights, the EU can hardly have a legitimate interest in applying its territorially limited rights to goods that are not destined for EU consumers. The new trade mark right appears as a disproportionate attempt to embark on unjustified world policing[43] – unjustified because the effort made to stop counterfeit goods is primarily based on trade mark rights existing in the EU. The whole question of counterfeiting is viewed through the prism of a protected legal position in the EU – as if legal protection in the EU automatically implied legal protection around the globe.

I. Broader GATT Context

In light of Art. V GATT 1994, Art. 9(4) EUTMR and Art. 10(4) TMD are thus exposed to a serious risk of challenge based on the international guarantee of the freedom of transit. The consideration of the broader treaty context in which Art. V GATT 1994 is embedded, does not change this outcome of the analysis. Admittedly, Art. XX(d) GATT 1994 offers room for the adoption and enforcement of measures

> 'necessary to secure compliance with laws or regulations which are not inconsistent with the provisions of this Agreement, including those relating to [...] the protection of patents, trademarks and copyrights, and the prevention of deceptive practices [...].'

As the TRIPS Agreement constitutes Annex 1C to the Marrakesh Agreement Establishing the World Trade Organization and thus the 1994 GATT treaty package, it can hardly be deemed inconsistent to ensure the protection of trade marks in the EU. Art. 41(1) TRIPS further supports this argument by establishing the international obligation of contracting parties to

> 'ensure that enforcement procedures as specified in this Part are available under their law so as to permit effective action against any act of infringement of intellectual property rights covered by this Agreement, including expeditious remedies to prevent infringements and remedies which constitute a deterrent to further infringements.'

Even this escape route, however, does not offer full clarity about the compliance of Art.9(4) EUTMR and Art. 10(4) TMD with international law. First, the scope of Art. 41(1) TRIPS is explicitly confined to 'enforcement procedures as specified in this Part'. This is a reference to Part III of the TRIPS Agreement dealing with 'Enforcement of intellectual property rights'. Within Part III, there are provisions, such as Art. 51 TRIPS, which explicitly set forth measures against counterfeit goods. These provisions, however, are silent on goods in transit.[44] Instead, Art. 51 TRIPS refers to the risk of 'release into free circulation' which, by definition, would not arise in the

---

43. Cf. *Große Ruse-Khan/Jäger* (*supra* n. 24), p. 502.
44. *Große Ruse-Khan* (*supra* n. 31), p. 309. As pointed out by *Eijsvogels* (*supra* n. 12), p. 141, the application of Arts. 51 and 52 TRIPS in respect of goods in transit would require a 'manufacturing fiction' allowing the qualification of the country of transit as 'country of importation'.

EU in the case of goods in transit. Art. 51 TRIPS also reflects the possibility of taking measures against counterfeit goods 'destined for exportation' from the territory of a contracting party, such as the EU or an EU Member State. However, goods in transit are not 'destined for exportation'. They are simply on their way through the EU. The accompanying footnote 13 makes it clear that Art. 51 TRIPS should not be understood to oblige WTO Members to apply procedures for suspending the release of goods 'to imports of goods put on the market in another country by or with the consent of the right holder, or to goods in transit.' Legitimate parallel trade and goods in transit are thus explicitly kept outside the scope of the international obligation.

II. No Circular Line of Reasoning

More generally, Art. 41(1) TRIPS provides that enforcement procedures 'shall be applied in such a manner as to avoid the creation of barriers to legitimate trade and to provide for safeguards against their abuse.' Similarly, the application of Art. XX(d) GATT is subject to the proviso that the protection of patents, trade marks and copyrights, and the prevention of deceptive practices does not lead to measures 'applied in a manner which would constitute [...] a disguised restriction on international trade [...]'.

These provisions prevent a circular line of reasoning. Under Art. 1(1) TRIPS, WTO Members are free to implement more extensive protection than required by the TRIPS Agreement, 'provided that such protection does not contravene the provisions of this Agreement'. In principle, the EU thus enjoys the freedom of providing for protection against goods in transit even though this protection is not reflected in the TRIPS Agreement itself.[45] This freedom, however, must not be misused to frustrate objectives underlying the Agreement. As Art. 41(1) TRIPS and the broader GATT context demonstrate, the avoidance of barriers to legitimate trade is one of these objectives. Goods that appear as 'counterfeit trademark goods' from an EU perspective may be legitimate from the perspective of foreign trade mark systems. Hence, the EU is not free to impose its own assessment of counterfeit goods on other countries.

If Art. 10(4) EUTMR and Art. 9(4) TMD are regarded as a 'barrier to legitimate trade' or a 'disguised restriction on international trade', a potential attempt to justify the new exclusive right of EU trade mark owners in light of the enforcement provisions of the TRIPS Agreement is thus doomed to fail from the outset.[46] As Henning Große Ruse-Khan concludes, 'good arguments support a finding that an expansion of IP rights to cover as infringement the mere transit of goods without any further connection to the territory of the IP-granting state, in particular any evidence for the goods being diverted onto the domestic market, is inconsistent with Art. V GATT. Such an expansion in itself can further not be justified under Art. XX(d) GATT as it is not necessary to secure compliance with TRIPS.'[47]

---

45. *Eijsvogels, supra* n. 12, p. 141.
46. In this sense *Große Ruse-Khan* (*supra* n. 31), p. 309. Cf. also *Große Ruse-Khan/Jäger* (*supra* n. 24), pp. 524–530, who see the TRIPS Agreement as an international 'ceiling' barring the adoption of border measures against goods in transit.
47. *Große Ruse-Khan* (*supra* n. 13), p. 148.

III. Cautious Approach Required

The new exclusive right of trade mark proprietors in the EU against goods in transit thus raises complex questions of compliance with the international guarantee of freedom of transit. In light of the applicable international provisions, the status of the new trade mark right in the EU is ambiguous. It is conceivable that the invocation of the right will be challenged at the WTO on the ground that it leads to an unjustified impediment of international trade. As the new EU trade mark legislation requires the application of Art. 9(4) EUTMR and Art. 10(4) TMD in line with international standards, in particular Art. V GATT 1994, courts in the EU will have to cope with the complexity of the international legal framework and develop workable solutions by applying an amalgam of EU and international law. The final result – and perhaps the most practical solution – may be an exclusive right with a limited scope. Given the serious risk of an encroachment upon the international freedom of transit, a cautious approach is advisable when applying Art. 9(4) EUTMR and Art. 10(4) TMD.

In particular, courts will have to take into account the necessity test following from Art. XX(d) GATT. As explained, a transit seizure must be 'necessary' to secure compliance with domestic laws protecting trade mark rights in order to be justified under international law. However, the necessity test of Art. XX(d) GATT 1994 cannot be met in the case of goods destined for a country outside the EU. By definition, an encroachment upon EU trade mark rights is excluded in such a case.[48] A seizure of transit goods can only be necessary if there is a substantial likelihood of diversion onto the EU market. Hence, the new right granted in Art. 9(4) EUTMR and Art. 10(4) TMD can hardly go beyond the standard of protection reached in the *Philips and Nokia* decision of the CJEU.[49]

As a broader scope of application is nonetheless the very purpose of the new exclusive right,[50] the described prohibition of unnecessary delays or restrictions following from Art. V(3) GATT 1994 must be taken particularly seriously. Art. V(3) GATT 1994 precludes the imposition of a heavy burden of proof with regard to non-infringement in the country of final destination. As explained above, proof including the absence of sign similarity or association, and protection on the basis of Art. 6*bis* PC or Art. 16(2) TRIPS is unnecessary and disproportionate. To achieve the practical result of identifying counterfeit goods, it is sufficient to oblige the declarant or holder of the goods to actively take *some* steps against the transit seizure. There is no need to impose an obligation to embark on a broad and costly legal analysis. Hence, the burden of proof must be limited, for instance, by confining the inquiry to trade marks registered in the country of final destination.

IV. Medicinal Products

Considering the explicit reference to the Doha Declaration in Recital 15 EUTMR, Recital 21 TMD and Recital 11 EU Customs Regulation No 608/2013, a cautious approach observing – to the greatest extent possible – the limits set forth in *Philips and Nokia*

---

48. Cf. *Große Ruse-Khan* (*supra* n. 13), p. 148; *Große Ruse-Khan* (*supra* n. 31), p. 310.
49. CJEU C-446/09 and C-495/09, para. 57.
50. See the references *supra* n. 12.

is of even greater importance when the goods at issue are medicinal products.[51] Not surprisingly, Recital 19 EUTMR and Recital 25 TMD insist on appropriate measures to ensure the smooth transit of generic medicines. These recitals make clear that with respect to international non-proprietary names (INNs), the trade mark proprietor should not have the right to prevent a third party from bringing transit goods into the EU on the basis of similarities between the INN for the active ingredient in the medicines and the trade mark.

At the international level, the need to keep INNs free has explicitly been recognised. In 1993, the World Health Assembly endorsed resolution WHA46.19[52] which states that trade marks should not be derived from INNs and INN stems should not be used as trade marks. It was recognised in this context that use of INNs should remain in the public domain because a practice of using INNs as trade marks could frustrate the rational selection of INNs and ultimately compromise the safety of patients by promoting confusion in drug nomenclature. Lists of Proposed and Recommended INNs are published regularly following meetings of the World Health Organization INN Expert Group.[53]

Hence, the clarification in Recital 19 EUTMR and Recital 25 TMD that a transit seizure cannot be based on similarities between an INN and a protected trade mark seeks to exclude the strategic use of drug brand names which are based on the INN for the active ingredient in the medicine, as a weapon against generic drugs in transit using the same INN.[54] Producers of generic medicines should not be forced to avoid the use of an INN to ensure the smooth transit via the EU.

While this objective is laudable,[55] the need to highlight this self-evident result in Recital 19 EUTMR and Recital 25 TMD sheds light on the inroads made into the freedom of transit. The freedom of using INNs might be preserved. Outside the field of INNs, however, producers of generic medicines will have to take EU trade marks into account to avoid a delay of the shipment through the EU. To ensure a smooth transit without burdensome procedures and a lengthy exchange of arguments about trade mark protection in the country of final destination, a producer of generic medicines will have to check which pharmaceutical trade marks enjoy protection

---

51. Cf. *Große Ruse-Khan/Jäger* (*supra* n. 24), pp. 530–533.
52. For the text of this resolution, see http://apps.who.int/medicinedocs/en/d/Jh1806e/11.html (accessed 9 May 2018).
53. With regard to trade marks and INNs, see *WIPO*, Trademarks and International Nonproprietary Names for Pharmaceutical Substances (INNs), (SCT/24/5 of 31 August 2010, SCT/19/4 of 27 May 2008, and SCT/18/6 of 12 September 2007), available at: www.wipo.int/sct (accessed 9 May 2018). Lists of Recommended and Proposed INNs are available at: www.who.int/medicines/publications/druginformation/ innlists/en/index.html (accessed 9 May 2018). For a discussion of the impact of brand names on therapeutic standards, see *J.A. Greene*, What's in a Name? Generics and the Persistence of the Pharmaceutical Brand in American Medicine, 66 Journal of the History of Medicine and Allied Sciences 468 [2011], p. 468.
54. Cf. *Große Ruse-Khan* (*supra* n. 13), p. 146; *S.M. Flynn and B. Madhani*, 'ACTA and Access to Medicines', WCL Research Paper No. 2012-03, Washington: American University 2011, available at http://ssrn.com/abstract=1980865 (accessed 9 May 2018).
55. It remains to be seen whether the recital will lead to sufficient room for the use of INNs. Cf. the critical comments by *Große Ruse-Khan* (*supra* n. 31), pp. 294–295.

in the EU, and refrain from the use of (essentially) identical signs insofar as this is possible without compromising the adequacy of consumer information. The EU thus imposes its own trade marks as a reference point for judging the legitimacy of trade marks used on medicinal products for other countries where the EU trade marks involved do not necessarily enjoy protection.

E. GUIDELINES FOR OTHER REGIONS

In light of the international guarantee of free transit in Art. V GATT 1994, the new trade mark rights against goods in transit granted in Art. 9(4) EUTMR and Art. 10(4) TMD are highly problematic. The seizure of goods in transit runs counter to the principle of independence of protection and the territorial restriction of IP rights to the country where they have been granted.[56] With the introduction of measures against goods in transit on the basis of domestic trade mark rights, the EU disregards the freedom of other WTO Members to take sovereign decisions about a trade mark's protection status. As Frederick Abbott has rightly pointed out, the enforcement of domestic IP rights against goods in transit leads to an undesirable 'long-arm' extension of jurisdiction.[57] Against this background, a particularly cautious approach is necessary in the EU – an approach based on a restrictive interpretation of the new right in line with the international obligation to guarantee the freedom of transit.[58] Recital 15 EUTMR and Recital 21 TMD lay the groundwork for this cautious approach. As the verdict of incompliance with Art. V GATT 1994 is hanging above the EU trade mark rights like the sword of Damocles, policy makers in other regions should refrain from copying the EU approach. The risk of unjustifiable inroads into the international freedom of transit is too great.

Nonetheless, the fact remains that Art. 51, footnote 13 TRIPS does not categorically ban customs measures against goods in transit. Footnote 13 merely makes it clear that 'there shall be no obligation to apply such procedures [...] to goods in transit.' Considering the context and negotiation history of the provision, this seems to reflect an option for WTO Members to extend border measures to goods in transit: they can decide to enhance IP protection in this way, but they are not bound to do so.[59] Hence, the GATT/TRIPS architecture does not prevent WTO Members from making an attempt to accomplish the squaring of the circle: the seizure of goods in transit without encroaching upon the freedom of transit.

Despite all described flaws, it is conceivable that Art. 9(4) EUTMR and Art. 10(4) TMD set in motion a learning process that will bring the international IP community

---

56. As to the recognition of the principle of independence in international trade mark protection, see Art. 6(3) PC. Cf. the critical comments about an extension of protection beyond the territorial borders of the country granting IP rights by *Heath* (supra n. 25), p. 897.
57. *Abbott* (supra n. 26), p. 49. See also the critical comments about extra-territorial protection by H. Ullrich, 'Technology Protection According to TRIPs: Principles and Problems', in *F.-K. Beier and G. Schricker* (eds.), From GATT to TRIPs – The Agreement on Trade-Related Aspects of Intellectual Property Rights. Weinheim: VCH Verlagsgesellschaft 1996, p. 357 (365).
58. *Senftleben* (supra n. 11), pp. 957–958.
59. *Kumar* (supra n. 27), pp. 516–518.

closer to the solution of this puzzle. The above analysis provides several insights in this regard. First, it shows the crucial importance of confining the transit seizure and corresponding rules to 'counterfeit trademark or pirated copyright goods' in the sense of Art. 51 TRIPS. This is the treaty context surrounding footnote 13. As the described experiences with pharmaceutical products show,[60] it is not advisable to allow transit seizures on the basis of patent rights. With the explicit reference to the Doha Declaration,[61] EU legislation seeks to avoid any interference with legitimate trade in generic drugs. When it comes to fake drugs, customs measures against 'counterfeit trademark goods' seem sufficient. The packaging of fake drugs will normally reproduce the patent owner's trade mark to mislead consumers.

Secondly, the legal analysis in transit cases should remain strictly confined to the question of whether the goods at issue fall within the counterfeit and piracy concepts laid down in Art. 51, footnote 14 TRIPS. To avoid a lengthy legal dispute and impermissible delays in the sense of Art. V(3) GATT 1994, it is not advisable to require the declarant or holder to provide a comprehensive legal analysis including the question of trade mark protection against confusion because of mere similarity of signs, and protection against dilution based on a mere risk of calling to mind the protected mark. With regard to limitations of trade mark protection that may support the activities of the declarant or holder, it should be sufficient to provide evidence of the existence of relevant exemptions in the country of final destination to dispel the assumption that the trade mark proprietor can take steps against the marketing of the goods. In addition, the legal analysis should not be extended to the question of a potential encroachment upon unregistered trade mark rights, such as rights concerning well-known marks in the sense of Art. 6*bis* PC.[62]

In copyright cases, the analysis should focus on clear-cut cases of copying all (or almost all) protected features of the affected article. The analysis should not include specific, individual (design) features and the question as to whether these individual features – when viewed in isolation – are original enough to attract copyright protection under the originality test applied in the country of final destination.[63] With regard to limitations of copyright protection, it should again be sufficient to provide evidence of the existence of exemptions in the destination country that are capable of dispelling the assumption of piracy.

---

60. See the references *supra* n. 6 and 26.
61. Recital 15 EUTMR and Recital 21 TMD.
62. Cf. *Senftleben* (*supra* n. 11), p. 957.
63. The question of sufficient originality can raise considerable difficulty when focusing on small parts of protected works. According to CJEU, 16 July 2009, C-5/08, Infopaq International, [2009] E.C.R. I-06569, ECLI:EU:C:2009:465, paras. 38–39, the assessment of infringement claims concerning individual parts of protected works leads to the question whether the copied part – viewed in isolation – can be deemed original enough to attract copyright protection. Even in cases where a work in its entirety undoubtedly enjoys copyright protection due to its originality, the copyright protection of potentially small, individual parts of the work may be doubtful and require a detailed legal analysis in light of the threshold criteria applied in the country of final destination. To avoid this complex analysis and the risk of unnecessary delays that are prohibited under Art. V(3) GATT, it is preferable to exclude these cases from the outset.

A third guideline follows from the foregoing analysis of the new EU provisions. As Vincenzo Di Cataldo has emphasised, the link between the legal basis for an in-transit seizure in the EU and the rights portfolio in the country of final destination is insufficient: '[n]othing allows one to infer, from the existence of a trade mark in a country, the existence of a right on the same trade mark in a different country.'[64] As explained above, it is a serious flaw of current EU legislation that the burden of establishing a link with the legal situation in the destination country is imposed on the declarant or holder of the goods in transit. As Vincenzo Di Cataldo points out, this configuration of the EU system disregards the principle of proximity of evidence. The trade mark proprietor is ideally placed to provide evidence of a trade mark registration in the country of final destination (the proprietor can be expected to know best about its panoply of trade mark rights worldwide). Hence, the rights owner is the party who can most easily furnish this evidence.[65] The imposition of the onus of proof on the trade mark owner is also appropriate when considering the rationales underlying the seizure of goods in transit. On its merits, this extraordinary customs measure offers the rights owner TRIPS-plus protection in the form of preventive action prior to the arrival of the goods at their final destination:

> 'The proprietor of the trade mark, who could block the goods in the country of final destination, is entitled to enforce his right already in the country of transit. This can give him considerable advantages: the block can be easier, because the goods are in fact standing in customs – even if for a short time – and it is possible to avoid their scattering; the holder of the goods can act more easily in the country of transit, if he is a resident thereof or in a country closer to it – from a cultural, economic or legal point of view – than in the country of final destination.'[66]

In copyright cases, the rights owner may have even less difficulty in providing evidence of protection in the country of final destination. As literary and artistic works enjoy protection without registration,[67] the existence of copyright protection in the destination country for an 'article' in the sense of Art. 51, footnote 14 TRIPS will often follow from the very nature of the work concerned. Even though the originality test is not harmonised at the international level, it seems possible to presume – in light of the remarkably low threshold that has become a widespread standard[68] – that creations falling under 'classical' work categories and having sufficient market

---

64. V. Di Cataldo, 'Goods in Transit and Trade Mark Law (and Intellectual Property Law?', 49 IIC [2018] (forthcoming), section 8.
65. *Di Cataldo* (*supra* n. 64), section 8. As to the remaining difficulty of an inquiry into foreign trade mark law in cases where the transit seizure leads to a dispute between the rights owner and the declarant or holder of the goods, see *Heath* (*supra* n. 24), pp. 898–900.
66. *Di Cataldo* (*supra* n. 64), section 9.
67. Art. 5(2) Berne Convention. For a detailed discussion of the scope of the prohibition of formalities, see *S. van Gompel*, Formalities in Copyright Law – An Analysis of their History, Rationales and Possible Future, The Hague/London/New York: Kluwer Law International 2011, pp. 179–193.
68. See the description of the originality test in *P. Goldstein and P.B. Hugenholtz*, International Copyright – Principles, Law, and Practice, 2nd ed., Oxford: Oxford University Press 2010, pp. 189–191; *World Intellectual Property Organization* (WIPO), WIPO Intellectual Property

success to make them a target of piracy – a current hit by a famous pop star, the latest Hollywood movie, a bestselling novel – satisfy the originality test not only in the country of transit but also in the country of destination. In the case of Berne Union or WTO Members, an obligation to offer protection against copying moreover follows from the minimum right granted in Art. 9(1) Berne Convention.[69] Hence, the task of providing evidence does not seem particularly burdensome. Admittedly, this is different in cases involving industrial design. As Art. 2(7) Berne Convention allows each Berne Union country to take an individual decision on the extension of copyright protection to works of applied art, the described presumption in favour of the rights owner can hardly be applied. Countries offering protection under specific industrial design legislation offer the possibility of registration instead.[70] The rights owner can thus resort to a design registration in the country of final destination to provide the evidence necessary for a seizure of goods in transit.

F. CONCLUSION

The new EU trade mark right against goods in transit raises serious concerns about an erosion of the international freedom of transit and a destabilisation of central pillars of the international edifice of IP protection. For this reason, countries in other regions should refrain from following the EU model. The discussion of the flaws of EU legislation, however, yields important guidelines for the establishment of a system that might survive scrutiny in light of Art. V GATT 1994. If a transit seizure system imposes the burden of proving protection in the country of final destination on the rights owner, and if the system is strictly aligned with the TRIPS notion of 'counterfeit trademark and pirated copyright goods',[71] it might be possible to configure the seizure mechanism in a way that avoids unnecessary delays in the sense of Art. V(3) GATT 1994.

However, even in such a case one obstacle remains: under Art. XX(d) GATT 1994, a country introducing IP enforcement measures against goods in transit must explain why these measures are 'necessary' even though the goods, by definition, have no impact on the domestic market.[72] To surmount this hurdle, one may be tempted to argue that preventive protection of trade mark and copyright owners is required because of poor enforcement standards in the country of final destination. This line of reasoning, however, seems patronising, if not pejorative.

Handbook – Policy, Law and Use, 2nd ed., WIPO Publication No. 489(E), Geneva: WIPO 2004, p. 42.
69. For the text of the Berne Convention for the Protection of Literary and Artistic Works (1971), see http://www.wipo.int/treaties/en/ip/berne/ (accessed 9 May 2018).
70. For a detailed analysis of the various approaches to industrial design protection, see the contributions to E. Derclaye (ed.), The Copyright/Design Interface – Past, Present and Future, Cambridge: Cambridge University Press 2018. As to international filing strategies ensuring the acquisition of industrial design registrations, see M. Rieger-Jansen, 'Internationale depotstrategieën in het modellenrecht', 41 BMM Bulletin 83 [2015], pp. 83–89.
71. Art. 51, footnote 14 TRIPS.
72. As Heath (supra n. 24), p. 903, points out, Art. XX GATT 1994 may also require the grant of a right against goods in transit at the national level in order to base the customs measures on a finding of infringement.

It may even be counterproductive. If a small coalition of enforcement champions embarks on world policing on the basis of measures against goods in transit,[73] there seems to remain little incentive for other countries to strengthen their enforcement capabilities. When specialised enforcement hubs take care of the problem of trade mark counterfeiting and copyright piracy, the argument of a pressing need to enhance IP enforcement across all countries and continents loses its power of persuasion. Instead of levelling-out country differences and supporting the evolution of shared standards for a globalised market in knowledge goods,[74] the introduction of measures against goods in transit may impede the realisation of this objective by lessening the need for worldwide counterfeit and piracy control. Therefore, it seems preferable to strive for generally accepted, shared enforcement standards. Attempts to perform the pirouette of seizing goods in transit without impeding the freedom of transit do not seem helpful.

---

73. As to the risk of excessive world policing, see *Große Ruse-Khan/Jäger* (*supra* n. 23), pp. 502–520.
74. *Ullrich* (*supra* n. 57), p. 374.

PART 3

OBSTACLES TO DOMESTIC TRADE

CHAPTER 6
The Green, Green Grass of Evergreening Patents

Roberto Reis and Claudia Chamas

A. INTRODUCTION

Patents, as was acknowledged as early as 1623 in the English Statute of Monopolies, act as a barrier to trade. They are exclusive rights granted by a government to manufacture, use, offer for sale, sell or import products or processes embodying the patented invention. They give the holder the right to prevent third parties from exploiting the patented invention in a given territory for a limited period of time in exchange for the full description of the invention and making it available to the public. As an exclusive right and thus an exception to the principle of free trade and competition, their existence directly influences the possibilities and conditions under which a particular technology can be marketed, whether nationally or internationally. In other words, patents are related to trade and by their exclusionary power can constitute legal (or illegal) barriers. This understanding was consolidated by the Agreement on Trade-Related Aspects of Intellectual Property Rights (TRIPS).

The TRIPS Agreement,[1] administered by the World Trade Organization, established new mechanisms of dispute settlement and enforcement beyond previous agreements such as the Paris Convention for the Protection of Industrial Property[2]

---

1. Agreement on Trade-Related Aspects of Intellectual Property Rights, Annex 1C of the Marrakesh Agreement Establishing the World Trade Organization ('WTO Agreement'), signed on 15 April 1994, 33 I.L.M. 1197 (1994).
2. Paris Convention for the Protection of Industrial Property, adopted in Paris on 20 March 1883, entered into force on 7 July 1884; last revised at the Stockholm Revision Conference, adopted in Stockholm on 14 July 1967 and entered into force 26 April 1970, 828 U.N.T.S. 305.

or the Berne Convention.[3] Although TRIPS comprises flexibilities, initial acceptance to use such flexibilities was not untroubled.

After a short time, especially for developed countries, TRIPS seemed to be enough not to ensure protection and enforcement of intellectual property, so TRIPS-plus clauses were negotiated via free trade agreements. A wide range of 'evergreening' mechanisms is one of the most notable TRIPS plus outcomes pursued in these agreements.

The relationship between patents and trade was further discussed among the WTO Member States leading to the Doha Declaration[4] within the World Health Organization (Resolution WHA 61.21) and the World Intellectual Property Organization (Development Agenda). Although non-binding, these post-TRIPS interpretations are directly related to the application of flexibilities, including the space to manoeuvre to define inventive step criteria and to exercise limitations or exceptions to patentability.

This chapter analyses strategies for extending the duration of patents, aimed at maintaining an innovator's maximum profit by preventing new entrants in the pharmaceutical field, known collectively as 'evergreening' of patents. Evergreening strategies can effectively pose hurdles to legitimate trade – this is the case when they can produce low quality intellectual property that often does not benefit society but rather impose legal barriers to trade and competition.

To allow a more comprehensive view of the evergreening issue, the following contribution is divided into four sections: First, the factors are presented that motivate companies to seek a maximum extension of their rights by employing sometimes questionable mechanisms. Secondly, different evergreening strategies are addressed. Two different groups of strategies are introduced, one based on chemical modifications and another grounded on legal manoeuvres. The third part will address policy mechanisms that have been adopted by some developing nations in order to mitigate the evergreening problem as well as recommendations of international bodies to balance innovation and access to medicines. Finally, in the fourth part, final remarks are made.

It should also be pointed out that since evergreening is understood to be a myriad of strategies aimed at extending the revenue return for intellectual property holders, this chapter does not propose an exhaustive analysis but will seek to provide a general understanding of the subject.

B. THE PHARMACEUTICAL INDUSTRY AND PATENTING STRATEGIES

The fact that chemical and pharmaceutical sectors are highly dependent on patent protection is primarily because it is relatively easy to replicate the involved technology and processes. Through reverse engineering, a competitor can produce a substance in little time and at a fraction of the cost. Thus, unlike other technological fields where copying capacity is limited due to operational or technical challenges, in the

---

3. Berne Convention for the Protection of Literary and Artistic Works (1971) adopted in Paris on 24 July 1971, as amended on 28 September 1979, Stockholm Treaty Doc. No. 99-27 (1986).
4. WTO Ministerial Conference, Declaration on the TRIPS Agreement and Public Health (Doha, 20 November 2001) [WT/MIN(01)/DEC/2].

pharmochemical case, patent protection of intellectual property is a paramount instrument for innovators.

Fields such as pharmaceuticals and chemicals can be easily copied and firms seek patent protection to discourage imitation. This view is aligned with the findings of Mansfield who sought to identify the relevance of technological innovations in different fields and their relationship with patent protection and other forms of appropriation.[5] According to Mansfield, patent protection is especially important for the development and launch of 30% or more of innovations in only two industrial sectors, namely pharmaceuticals and chemicals.[6]

Once a patent essentially grants exclusivity by blocking competition for a particular invention, patent protected inventions that do not have due and expected merit may, in practice, end up acting as major barriers to legitimate trade.[7]

Neither the Paris Convention nor the TRIPS Agreement define the concept of 'invention'. In fact, for an invention to be deemed patentable, it is required to show novelty, inventive step, industrial application/usefulness and sufficient disclosure. The sovereignty of national intellectual property laws to interpret such requirements was cemented in the Paris Convention and preserved under TRIPS. As will be discussed later in the present chapter, countries such as Argentina and India have adopted TRIPS-compliant interpretations of patent requirements that restrict the patentability of inventions, such as second and further medical uses, polymorphs, combination, me-too, solvates and hydrates.

The political leeway to modulate the interpretation of the patentability criteria can be important to avoid a major drift of the patent system away from its intended objective: to reward those who contribute to technological progress by creating new and inventive products and processes for the benefit of society.

In this chapter, we will discuss strategies used particularly by the pharmaceutical industry to ensure maximum extension of their monopolistic rights through administrative, legal and commercial strategies, known collectively as evergreening.

The innovative pharmaceutical industry (in contrast to the generics industry) is highly dependent on the promotion of new drugs and new uses for known molecules. This strategy is based on the fact that in many countries, new molecules or even minor modifications of known drugs are usually covered by the monopoly conferred by patent protection.[8]

With patents on many blockbuster drugs reaching the end of their patent term (known as 'patent cliff'[9]) and multinational companies facing increased competition

---

5. *Mansfield*, 'Patents and Innovation: An Empirical Study', 32(2) Management Science 173 [1986], p. 174.
6. *Ibid.*
7. *Dwivedi, Sharanabasava, and Latha*, 'Evergreening: A Deceptive Device in Patent Rights', 32(4). Technology in Society 324 [2010], p. 329.
8. *Correa*, 'Ownership of Knowledge: The Role of Patents in Pharmaceutical R&D', 84(10), Bulletin of the World Health Organization 784 [2004], p. 785.
9. According to the 2014 IMS Report, from 2014 to 2018, USD 121 billion of revenue will be lost due to generic competition. Up to 2018, global brands such as Nexium, Celebrex, Symbicort, Abilify, Gleevec, Crestor, Zytiga and Cialis will face patent expiration. IMS Institute for Healthcare Informatics. Global Outlook for Medicines Through 2018 [2014]

by generic manufacturers, the pharmaceutical industry may be approaching a new phase of its current business model.[10]

Food and Drug Administration (FDA) data show that requests for approval of new chemical entities are on a downward curve, from 45 new requests in 1996 to 22 in 2016[11] although with a recovery to 46 new molecules in 2017.[12] Despite the dip in 2016, researchers including Munos,[13] and Light and Lexchin[14] envision that the number of new molecules approved is not necessarily falling, but instead has remained relatively stable over the past 50 years, suggesting that the innovative capacity of the 'big pharma' is close to its limit.

Another important challenge faced by the pharmaceutical industry is the increasing costs related to the development of its products. Estimates regarding the expense of covering the entire R&D pipeline vary greatly. Classical studies such as that of Dimasi and colleagues[15] have argued that increasing funds are necessary to successfully develop a new drug, with initial estimates of USD 802 million (as of 2000). More recently, a pharmaceutical industry-supported study of the Tufts Center for the Study of Drug Development claims a total of approximately USD 2.56 billion (as of 2013) to develop a new drug.[16]

On the other hand, there are critical voices that claim that the presented figures show several biases, such as the investment's cost of opportunity, state funding research mostly in early phases, the interest of multinational pharmaceutical companies in inflating their estimates to justify the high cost of new therapies etc.[17]

---

available at http://static.correofarmaceutico.com/docs/2014/12/01/informe_ims.pdf (accessed on 28 January 2018).
10. *Kaitin*, 'Deconstructing the Drug Development Process: The New Face of Innovation', 87(3) Clinical Pharmacology & Therapeutics, 356 [2010], p. 360; *Ringel and Coy*, A new wave of pharma mergers could put innovative drugs in the pipeline [2017], available at https://www.statnews.com/2017/07/24/mergers-pharma-drug-development/ (accessed 31 January 2018); *Scannell et al.*, 'Diagnosing the Decline in Pharmaceutical R&D Efficiency', 11 Nat Rev. Drug Discov. 191 [2012], p. 191.
11. See Food and Drug Administration, Novel Drug Approvals for 2016 [2017] available at https://www.fda.gov/downloads/Drugs/DevelopmentApprovalProcess/DrugInnovation/UCM536693.pdf (accessed on 28 January 2018).
12. See Food and Drug Administration, Novel Drug Approvals for 2017 [2018] available at https://www.fda.gov/Drugs/DevelopmentApprovalProcess/DrugInnovation/ucm537040.htm (accessed on 15 March 2018).
13. *Munos*, 'Lessons from 60 Years of Pharmaceutical Innovation', 8 Nature Reviews Drug Discovery 959 [2009], p. 961.
14. *Light and Lexchin*, 'Pharmaceutical Research and Development: What Do We Get for All that Money?', 344. BMJ 1 [2012], p. 1.
15. *DiMasi, Hansen and Grabowski* The Price of Innovation: New Estimates of Drug Development Costs', 22(2) Journal of Health Economics 151 [2012], p. 166.
16. *DiMasi, Grabowski and Hansen*, 'Innovation in the Pharmaceutical Industry: New Estimates of R&D Costs', 47 Journal of Health Economics 20 [2016], p. 26.
17. *Avorn*, 'The $2.6 Billion Pill – Methodologic and Policy Considerations', 14 The New England Journal of Medicine 1877 [2015], p. 1878.

Institutions such as Doctors Without Borders claim that big pharma figures could be much lower, from USD 50 to 186 million, even when accounting for product failures.[18]

Adding to the challenges faced by the pharmaceutical industry, regulatory demand is constantly increasing for the sake of greater transparency, efficacy and safety of new drugs. National policies are increasingly aimed at optimising public procurements' expenditure, and greater pressure from organised civil societies and local governments are aimed at increasing access to medicines, especially for neglected populations.[19]

While it seems that the current business model of the pharmaceutical industry is based on incremental innovations by minor modifications of well-known drugs, since unlike the radical innovations, the former require less investment and development time, with higher success rates, it is important to differentiate between 'incrementality' and 'triviality' in the patent debate.[20]

The perception is that the relatively low level of new drugs annually marketed leads to intensified development based on molecules already known. Nevertheless, it is important to discuss whether all incremental inventions are relevant or whether some of them could be labelled 'trivial', adding little or nothing to existing therapies, while only increasing health costs.

A radical innovation, something absolutely new, can be extremely costly and difficult to achieve, whereas to modify something known and to call it 'new' (incremental innovation) can be considerably easier and sometimes equally desirable. A small modification can bring significant advantages in the pharmaceutical field, or can be a trivial invention or a product of little value.

A paradigmatic example of an incrementality that has brought great advantage is the development of the paediatric formulation of AZT.[21] Prior to this innovation, there was no treatment available for paediatric AIDS patients.

In contrast, when innovative companies patent 'new inventions', they often seek protection for minor modifications of old medicines, providing little or no advantage to existing therapies. This is a strategy to extend the monopoly of inventions that would otherwise fall into the public domain by the expiration of the original patents.

The exploitation or 'reheating' of old patents that does not lead to improvements of clinical use and merely acts to secure economic advantages to the IPR holder is considered one form of 'evergreening'.

---

18. Medicins Sans Frontieres, R&D Cost Estimates: MSF Response to Tufts CSDD Study on Cost to Develop a New Drug [2014] available at http://www.doctorswithoutborders.org/article/rd-cost-estimates-msf-response-tufts-csdd-study-cost-develop-new-drug (accessed on 28 January 2018).
19. *Kola and Landis*, 'Can the Pharmaceutical Industry Reduce Attrition Rates?', 3(8) Nature Reviews Drug Discovery 711 [2004], p. 711.
20. *Morgan, Ruth and Greyson*, 'Toward a Definition of Pharmaceutical Innovation', 2(1) Open Medicine 4 [2008], p. 5; *Cohen, Cabanila and Sosnov*, 'Role of Follow-on Drugs and Indications on the WHO Essential Drug List', 31 Journal of Clinical Pharmacy and Therapeutics 585 [2006], p. 590.
21. Zidovudine, first antiretroviral developed in 1987. *Vella, Schwartländer, Papa Sow, Eholie and Murphy*, 'The History of Antiretroviral Therapy and of its Implementation in Resource-Limited Areas of the World', 26(10) Aids 1231 [2012], p. 1231.

Although there are many different definitions, evergreening comprises a multitude of strategies used by patent holders to harvest the maximum revenue from their products by extending the exclusivity granted by the privileged position that they enjoy. Evergreening relies on a secondary patent or on legal manoeuvres to extend monopolistic rights without proportionate benefit of any sort.[22] These strategies can be lawful or unlawful, and in any event come very close to competitive abuse.

The present text proposes to divide the issue of pharmaceutical evergreening into two groups. The first is based on chemical modification strategies, in order to obtain extended patent protection. The second is based on legal tactics to the same end.

C. EVERGREENING PRACTICES BASED ON CHEMICAL MODIFICATIONS

The following strategies are mainly used for 'about to expire' patents, by chemically modifying, selecting, combining or finding new uses for these patented products.

I. Selection Patents/'Me-too' Patents

As the name suggests, me-too patents are based on new patents for small chemical modifications of an already known and proprietary structure. It is an extremely common strategy to develop new compounds based on well-established chemical families.

In order to develop a slightly modified structure, a selection of compounds takes place. In practice, the strategy is not new, and the selection is made based on the combination of an invariable molecular core structure associated with variable radicals, chemically known as Markush structure, Markush-type claims or a Markush claim strategy.[23] Figure 1 illustrates how the Markush claim works.

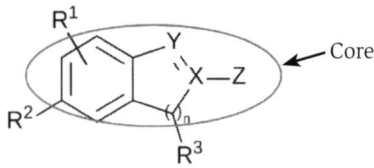

Fig.1. Markush claim

Radicals R1, R2 and R3 are attached to the constant, invariable part of the molecule (core). Depending on the molecule, R1, R2 and R3 may contain several different atoms or even larger molecules. In a hypothetical example where R1, R2 and R3 have 10 possibilities each, the number of possible combinations could reach 1,000 compounds. In some cases, where the number of radicals attached to the molecular

---

22. *Correa*, 'Pharmaceutical Inventions: When is the Granting of a Patent Justified?', 1(1–2) International Journal of Intellectual Property Management 4 [2006], p. 17.
23. Named after the US decision *Ex parte Markush*, 1925 C.D. 126 (Commissioner of Patents 1925). This type of claim is not only discussed in the context of evergreening, but also in the context of unity of the invention: See EPO decision W 3/94 of 15 December 1994, OJ EPO 1994, 775.

core is higher, it could cover hundreds of thousands of possible molecules that all, in theory, are protected by the initial Markush claim.

When the initial patent document is filed, the claims seek to protect the entire Markush structure, even without defining every one of the possible combinations. One or a few selections are required for protection. Evergreening happens when the patent of the initially selected molecule is about to expire and the company selects its 'new' me-too molecule from the same Markush family. If granted, the new me-too molecules could be protected under a new and independent patent, guaranteeing an extension of patent protection.

A well-known example is the drug family based on the inhibition of HMG-CoA reductase, popularly known as statins, which are medicines that inhibit the main enzyme involved in endogenous cholesterol production. Inhibiting that enzyme drastically reduces cholesterol levels, and thereby achieves the desired therapeutic effect. Examples of statins include simvastatin, atorvastatin, lovastatin, pravastatin and rosuvastatin.

Figure 2 shows the chemical structure of simvastatin and lovastatin. The only difference between these molecules is the replacement of a hydrogen by a methyl (CH_3) radical, which is an absolutely trivial modification for a person skilled in the art of organic synthesis.

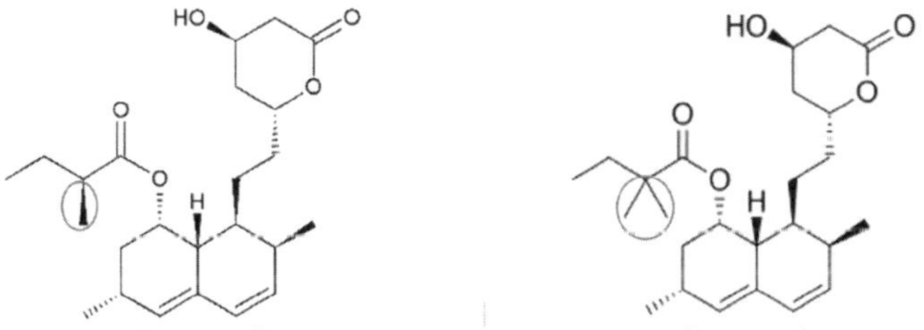

Fig. 2. Structure of simvastatin and lovastatin showing trivial modification (hydrogen to CH_3).

The strategy here is this: the pharmaceutical company that owns the patent for the oldest molecule, aware of its expiration and imminent loss of market exclusivity, seeks to patent a me-too drug. In parallel, the company starts a commercial advertisement strategy aimed at doctors (and patients, in some cases) with the objective of persuading them to replace the old medicine with the new one, which has its own patent and, therefore, a new period of exclusivity, allowing the maintenance of a high commercial value due to the new monopoly. Often, the new molecule does not represent any significant clinical advantage over the old one.

Besides the usual lack of better efficiency under clinical conditions, the new structure may also lack inventive step, an unequivocal requirement for the grant of a patent. If to a technician skilled in the art a 'new' molecule derives from an obvious or evident modification, the criterion of inventive step is not met, and thus the patent should not be granted.

II. New Formulations/New Concentration Patents

Another very common form of evergreening is based on new formulations or new concentration patents. The IPR holder modifies the original concentration of substances already known, whose patents are about to expire, or develops new pharmaceutical formulations, changing the original presentation of the first patented drug.

An example is the anti-HIV drug known as Didanosine. Among other presentations on the market, it is possible to find tablets of 100 mg, gelatin capsules of 400mg capsules and powder for paediatric oral solution of 4g.

Once again, it is not possible to affirm an inventive step for this kind of modification, since the proposed change is obvious and trivial to the technician skilled in the art.

III. Polymorph Patents

Polymorphism[24] is a very common and natural feature of organic molecules. It is characterised by the intrinsic and natural ability of these compounds to present different patterns of their crystalline structure. Although possessing the same chemical formula, they may present different structures which in some cases allows the presentation of different physico-chemical characteristics and even different biological effects. A classical example is carbon, which may exist as graphite, diamond, graphene, fullerene or in amorphous form. Although the composition is absolutely the same (pure carbon), the crystalline lattice arrangements make the final presentation quite different, as shown in Figure 3.

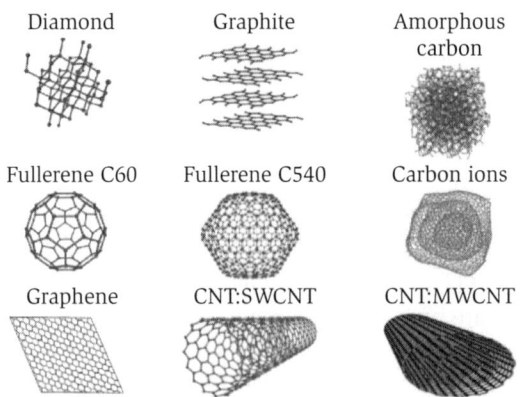

Fig. 3. Carbon polymorphs, graphite and diamond

Source: Săndulescu et al., 2015[25]

---

24. From the Greek (*poly* – several, *morph* – shape).
25. *Săndulescu, Tertis, Cristea and Bodoki* New Materials for the Construction of Electrochemical Biosensors [2015] available at 'https://www.intechopen.com/books/biosensors-micro-and-nanoscale-applications/new-materials-for-the-construction-of-electrochemical-biosensors' accessed on 28 January 2018.

The mechanism of polymorph-based evergreening starts from the moment that an innovative company, when developing a new molecule, investigates the possibility of polymorphism of a given drug, but when filing the first patent for a substance does not request protection for any polymorphic structures other than the one described in the original application. When the first patent protection period comes to an end, a new patent request for another polymorphic structure is made which can guarantee another 20 years of exclusivity for the same substance.

Due to the possibility of presenting unexpected and non-obvious physico-chemical and/or biological effects, polymorphs are eligible for patent protection in most countries. If polymorphs show a clear advantage in clinical use, such as better absorption, fewer side effects, a more comfortable use regimen for the patient, or better clinical results, they could be protected. However, it is quite usual that many of these polymorphs show no advantage whatsoever over the previously known and patented molecules. In that case, they should not be patented in order to avoid evergreening.

A case of patent protection related to polymorphism is currently under discussion in Brazil: patent protection was first applied for rufinamide (Figure 4), used against convulsions, seizures and severe epilepsy, in the European Union in April 1985 and was due to expire in 2005. However, in July 1997, approximately eight years before the patent expiration, the patent holder applied for a second patent related to a polymorph of rufinamide, to be granted for the same clinical indications as the first patent.

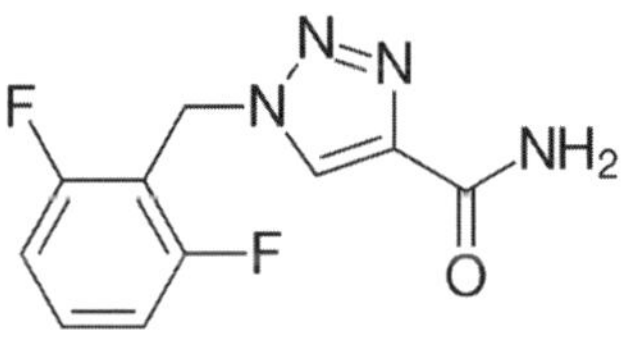

Fig. 4. Rufinamide (anticonvulsant/antiepileptic).

During the examination procedure before the Brazilian Patent Office, the polymorphic patent application[26] was refused for lack of inventive step, as it was considered obvious for a technician skilled in the art to try to synthesise it in the knowledge that organic molecules in most cases have polymorphs. Besides, no clinical advantage was demonstrated.

The patent holder claimed that the new polymorph had never been described and that it was more thermodynamically stable (although a significant instability was never reported to be a problem for that molecule before).

The Brazilian Patent Office did not accept the argument and maintained the rejection. Thus, the company filed an appeal[27] before the Rio Federal Court against the patent office's decision. There has not yet been a court ruling in this case.

---

26. BR9804947-0.
27. 13th Federal Court of Rio de Janeiro, Case 0011226-08.2015.4.02.5101, Novartis AG versus Brazilian Patent Office.

IV.   Enantiomers

Isomers are organic substances that have the same molecular formula but different structural properties and characteristics. Isomers that present optical activity are called enantiomers. They have three main characteristics: their molecule is asymmetrical, they are the mirror image of each other and they are non-superposable, that is, if we place one molecule above the other, they will not be the same, as the arrangement of the binding atoms will be different.

Enantiomers are considered the most important isomers with regard to biochemical reactions. The activity that each enantiomer exerts on an organism may be different. Drugs that have an enantiomeric structure often contain equal amounts of both enantiomers, one deflects polarised light to the left (S-enantiomer) and the other to the right (R-enantiomer). A half-and-half mixture of each enantiomer is called a racemate.

An interesting case involving enantiomers occurred with AstraZeneca's drug Prilosec, chemically known as omeprazole. Omeprazole is a proton pump inhibitor used to decrease the secretion of hydrochloric acid in the stomach, treating cases of dyspepsia, peptic ulcer and gastroesophageal reflux.

The first patent for omeprazole was obtained in the United States (US 6090827) and was valid until 2001. The drug achieved great commercial success as one of the best selling in the pharmaceutical industry with sales of USD 26 billion.[28] Prilosec (omeprazole) is a racemate, but only the S-enantiomer has clinical effects. *In vivo*, the patients metabolise the R-enantiomer and transform it into the biologically active S-form.

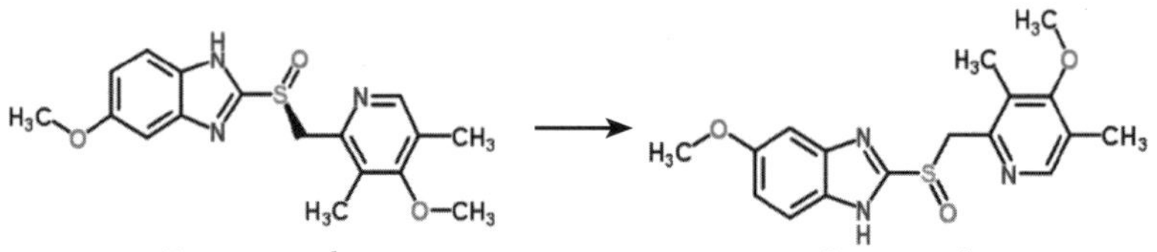

Esomeprazole
Molecular formula: $C_{17}H_{19}N_3O_3S$
Average mass: 345.416 Da
Chemical name: 5-methoxy-2-[(S)-(4-methoxy-3,5-dimethylpyridin-2-yl) methanesulfinyl]-1H-1,3-benzodiazole

Omeprazole
Molecular formula: $C_{17}H_{19}N_3O_3S$
Average mass: 345.416 Da
Chemical name: 6-methoxy-2-[(4-methoxy-3,5-dimethylpyridin-2-yl) methanesulfinyl]-1H-1,3-benzodiazole

Fig.5. Omeprazole and esomeprazole molecules

Source: Goyal Difference between omeprazole and esomeprazole [2015], available at https://drugsdetails.com/difference-between-omeprazole-and-esomeprazole/ (accessed on 28 January 2018).

Prior to the expiration of the Prilosec patent, the patent holder released a new brand drug called Nexium, which was nothing more than the pure S-enantiomer

---

28. *Supra* n. 7, p. 327.

of omeprazole, that is, the active component, which is known commercially as esomeprazole. Figure 5 shows esomeprazole and omeprazole, respectively. As shown, both molecules have the same molecular formula, differing only in their atoms' spatial disposition.

AstraZeneca asserted that esomeprazol would be more efficient against erosive esophagitis when compared to the previous formulation, and the pharmaceutical company commissioned four different studies to compare the efficacy of Nexium against Prilosec in patients with this condition.

The four studies compared 20 mg of Prilosec against a double dose of 40 mg of Nexium. The rationale was that the company planned to seek approval for a 40 mg dose of Nexium against erosive esophagitis for which a 20 mg dose of Prilosec was the established standard regime. Two out of four studies showed that Nexium did not outperform Prilosec, even with this increased dosage. However, two studies found Nexium to perform better than Prilosec. The results of the favourable studies were published while those of the other two studies were not released.

Out of the four, only one study, comparing the same dosages of 20 mg for both Prilosec and Nexium, showed no difference in healing rates during the initial course of treatment and only a marginal (90% against 87%) improved healing rate after eight weeks for Nexium. This result was largely used in advertisements within the medical community to persuade the prescribing doctors that Nexium was indeed better than Prilosec.[29]

According to Dwivedi and collaborators:

'Acting quickly, AstraZeneca got FDA approval for Nexium in February, 2001 – a few months before the patent on Prilosec was to expire. At the same time AstraZeneca exploited the federal provision of pediatric exclusivity in the US which gives a six month extension on existing market exclusivity for conducting tests on effectiveness of a drug on children. This extended the exclusivity of Prilosec fending off the generics for a further six months.

The extra time gained was used to campaign for the drug. AstraZeneca launched one of the most massive marketing campaigns in the history of the USA after it got the FDA approval. The company spent $500 million a year on direct-to-consumer marketing, hospital discounts on the drug, free samples for doctors and media advertising. All this effort resulted in a substantial fraction of the patients transferring to Nexium. In 2001 alone the company transferred 40% of Prilosec users to Nexium and managed a 9% growth in its gastrointestinal franchise.'[30]

Was a selection of one enantiomer of a known substance deemed patentable by showing all three requirements: novelty, inventive step and industrial application, or was that strategy a classic case of evergreening? One could argue that both novelty and inventive step are absent once the molecule is already known and isolation and clinical testing of medically relevant stereoisomers are routine procedures for a technician skilled in the art.[31]

---

29. *Supra* n. 7, p. 327, 328.
30. *Supra* n. 7, p. 328.
31. In Japan, the Supreme Court in a decision of 24 March 2017 (case no. 2016 (Ju) 1242 *DKSH et al. v. Chugai Pharmaceutical*, forthcoming in IIC 2018 – *Maxacalcitol*) affirmed

V. Combination Patents

Combination patents are as straightforward as the name implies. They are represented by the combination of two or more drugs in a viable pharmaceutical composition. The isolated medicines can be under patent protection or not, but the pharmaceutic company will certainly seek patent protection for the combination product.

A good example is Gilead's PrEP[32] drug called Truvada, an antiretroviral drug approved for the treatment of HIV/AIDS that combines two drugs into one tablet: tenofovir desoproxyl fumarate (TDF, 300 mg) and emtricitabine (FTC, 200 mg).

The patentability of Truvada, despite the undeniable efficiency demonstrated in clinical trials, has been the subject of controversy in some countries, such as Argentina, Brazil and India. These three Patent Offices refused the patent on the grounds of lack of inventive step. It was understood that the simple combination of two antiretroviral drugs did not meet the criterion of inventiveness once both drugs were already known and established to treat HIV and a reasonable chance of success due to synergistic effect could be expected.

VI. Hydrates and Solvates

A very common modification in pharmaceutical formulations is the transformation of a known compound into a hydrated or solvated form. The compound is said to be hydrated when the solvent used is water and a solvate for all other possible solvents. In fact, solvents are incorporated into the crystal lattice of the molecule, as shown in Figure 6.

Solvants/hydrates

Molecular *adducts* that incorporate *solvent molecules* in their crystal lattices;

Solvent is water . . . . Hydrates
Solvent is other solvents . . . . . . Solvates

Non-solvated   Solvate

Fig.6. Solvates and hydrates structure

> Source: Gong, Pharmaceutical solid from screening, characterization, and selection [2012] available at https://www.slideshare.net/simoncurtis/pharmaceutical-solid-form (accessed on 28 January 2018)

---

equivalent infringement for the use of a trans-isomer where the cis-isomer had been patented. This would indicate that the court did not consider the trans-isomer to be an inventive modification of the trans-isomer.

32. Pre-exposure prophylaxis.

Hydrates and solvates are of particular relevance in the process of obtaining polymorphic substances. According to the literature, in some cases the solvent can be considered impure, while in other cases it may lead to increased stability of the solvated substance, with a corresponding better applicability in clinical practice.[33]

Again, the question is whether hydration/solvation of a molecule, a well-known process to a technician skilled in the art and a routine experimental activity, should be considered inventive, fulfilling the criterion of inventive step.

Patent protection for such cases where no improvement in efficacy is demonstrated, is most likely deemed as a mere evergreening patent with unjustifiable exclusivity.

VII. Second Medical Use Patents

The second medical use, or the second therapeutic use, is the possibility of patenting the same substance to treat another therapeutic application.[34] Although widely accepted, there are several opinions against granting protection to inventions for second or further medical uses.[35]

Opponents argue that the patenting of new medical uses through a Swiss-type claim[36] inconsistently expands the scope of protection with respect to the novelty requirement, since such claims confer protection for the use of a compound to prepare a medication which will normally comprise the same compound used in the first therapeutic indication.[37] In addition to the lack of novelty, another objection raised against that kind of patent strategy is related to non-industrial applicability, since the element of new medical use is an identified effect and not a product or method of preparation.[38]

An interesting case of a second medical use patent relates to Allergan's blockbuster, called Lumigan. The product is a prostaglandin analogue chemically known as bimatoprost, used to treat glaucoma. After the commercialisation of Lumigan,

---

33. *Griesser*, 'The Importance of Solvates. Polymorphism in the Pharmaceutical Industry', 225 Wiley-VCH 218 [2006] Weinheim, p. 213.
34. *Silva and Antunes*, 'Controvérsias sobre a proteção patentária de segundo uso médico de compostos químicos conhecidos', 33(8) Química Nova 1821 [2010], p. 1823.
35. While the original text of the European Patent Convention only mentioned the first medical indication as patentable subject matter, the Enlarged Board of Appeal in decision G 1/83 (OJ 1985, 60) held that second medical uses were patentable under the Swiss-type claim formula (see *infra*). Second medical uses are now explicitly patentable under Art. 54(4) and (5) of EPC 2000. Particularly the French courts were critical of this interpretation: Paris District Court, *Dosage Regime/Finasteride* 28 September 2010, IIC [2011], p. 474.
36. Swiss-type claims are a juridical manoeuvre to bypass the novelty requirement once the same (previously disclosed) substance is already known. It is written as 'the use of compound X for the preparation of a medicament for the treatment of condition Y'. This formula was mandated by the EPO Boards of Appeal for all second and further medical uses in decision G 1/83. Under the EPC 2000, it is no longer required to formulate second and further medical use patents in this manner. See decision G 2/08 (OJ EPO2010, 456).
37. *Armstrong*, 'The Arguments of Law, Policy and Practice against Swiss-type Patent Claims', 32 Victoria U. Wellington L. Rev. 201 [2001], p. 201.
38. *Supra* n. 37, p. 202.

a curious side effect was reported, namely hirsurtism (growth of hair, in this case eyelashes). The observation led the company to realise an aesthetic potential for the drug and thus a new patent was sought. Latisse, the same product in the same concentration but with a different use was released. Figure 7 shows both first and second medical use patented products.

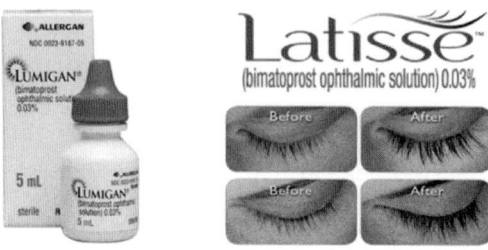

*Fig. 7. Lumigan and Latisse from Allergan Pharmaceutics.
Same product, different uses.*

There is no international consensus concerning the patentability of new therapeutic indications. Some jurisdictions such as the United States and EPC countries have decided to grant patents for new uses. Most developing countries have chosen not to grant such patents because they consider that new use applications do not meet the basic patentability criteria (novelty, inventive step and industrial application), that they are equivalent to methods of treatment, or even mere discoveries related to an already known product, which does not comply with the definition of an invention.[39]

D. EVERGREENING BASED ON LEGAL STRATEGIES

The following strategies are based mainly on creating legal barriers to prevent competition. They can occur in an *erga omnes* fashion (e.g. influencing legislation to modify the law) or *inter partes* by a direct court challenge to competitors.

I. Research Exemption Blockage

Among the different mechanisms that foster competition, one in particular allows the procedure for obtaining a generic marketing authorisation to be initiated close to the expiration date of a reference medicine. That legal mechanism is known in the US as 'bolar exception or bolar provision',[40] which allows a laboratory to use a patented reference medicine, normally close to the final days of patent protection, in order to perform the necessary tests for marketing approval from the drug regulatory agency.

---

39. *Supra* n. 22, p. 16.
40. 'Bolar Exception' derives its name from a leading case in the United States that discussed the possibility of early work before the expiration of the patent (*Roche Products v. Bolar Pharmaceutics*. 733 F. 2d. 858, Fed Cir., cert. Denied 469 US 856, 1984). In other countries, it is also referred to as research exemption.

Allowing bioequivalence tests has a double advantage for the country: in addition to enabling the rapid entry of the generic drug in the market, fostering competition and inevitably reducing the final cost of medicines, it allows a learning process by using information about the invention (learn-by-doing/learn-by-copying).

Under great pressure, some countries are forced not to use research exemption for that purpose,[41] which would in effect extend the length of time necessary for competitors to develop legal copies of expired patents. With the blocking of anticipated work, there would be artificial exclusivity even in the absence of a valid patent. The extra time after patent expiration necessary to carry out the entire pre-grant tests for marketing authorisation would thus amount to time-limited evergreening for the holder of the (expired) patent.

II. Data Exclusivity

Data exclusivity essentially prevents regulatory authorities from relying on data submitted by originator companies in order to register a generic product. By implication, as long as exclusivity lasts, generic producers have to submit their own safety and efficacy data. This would oblige them to repeat clinical and pre-clinical trials, something that takes time and that they usually cannot afford. As a result, the availability of generics will be delayed, even if a patent has already expired.[42]

In brief, the clinical test data begins with research into a new drug. It can be divided in the pre-clinical stage and the clinical stage. The pre-clinical stages take place in the laboratory in order to determine that toxic effects *in vitro* and *in vivo* (studies with animals) do not occur. The clinical stage or human clinical trial is classified in four consecutive phases. Phase I through phase III represent the pharmaceutical development. Phase IV represents the post-marketing pharmaco-surveillance.[43]

A generic producer can request marketing authorisation for a new version of a product already registered (without patent protection) and only needs to demonstrate that the product is therapeutically equivalent to the original. To do that, it is necessary for the applicant to accomplish bioequivalence and bioavailability tests. The drug regulatory agency uses the initial dossier generated by the original producer to establish safety and efficacy and to avoid all the clinical tests being redone.[44]

The data exclusivity prevents the drug regulatory agency from relying on the data supplied by the original innovative company to compare the bioequivalence and

---

41. For a comparative overview and historical perspective, see *Heath*, 'The Patent Exemption for Clinical Trials in the US, Germany and Japan', AIPPI Journal of the Japanese Group 267 [1997] (English edition) 267–295.
42. *Timmermans*, 'Monopolizing Clinical Trial Data: Implications and Trends', 4(2) PLoS Medicine 206 [2007], p. 206, 207.
43. *Pugatch*, 'Intellectual Property and Pharmaceutical Data Exclusivity in the Context of Innovation and Market Access', ICTSD-UNCTAD Dialogue on Ensuring Policy Options for Affordable Access to Essential Medicines 1 [2004], available at <https://www.iprsonline.org/unctadictsd/bellagio/docs/Pugatch_Bellagio3.pdf>, accessed on 25 January 2018, p. 4.
44. If the results prove satisfactory in terms of efficacy and safety, the dossier is presented to the drug regulatory agency and, after review and discussion, marketing authorisation is issued. Alternatively, as has become common, additional studies may be requested.

bioavailability tests results and grant a marketing licence for an equivalent generic version of the same medicine. This in effect provides a de facto monopoly for the original producer. Even when a medicine is not under patent protection in a given country, data exclusivity creates a new monopoly, similar to that of a patent, blocking the registration of a generic medicine in that same country.[45]

The generation of clinical trial data is very labour-intensive, implies high costs and has been the subject of heated discussions in the pharmaceutical intellectual property area.[46]

Protection term (years)

3	5	4–6	6	6–10	8*	10	15
Poland	Australia, Bolivia, Canada, Colombia, Costa Rica, Ecuador, Jordan, Mexico, Egypt, New Zealand, Peru, Singapore, Switzerland, USA	Korea	Austria, China, Czech Rep., Estonia, Japan, Slovak Rep., Slovenia	Hungary, Latvia, Romania	European Community	Panama	Guatemala

Table 1. Countries That Provide Data Exclusivity**

* Data protection in the EU follows the formula 8 + 2 + 1, in that a pharmaceutical product would have eight years of data exclusivity added to two years of market exclusivity and finally one more year of protection for new indications of an existing product.

** Although many countries already have a data exclusivity provision, bilateral trade agreements usually impose even more rigid standards.

Source: Adapted from The International Federation of Pharmaceutical Manufacturers Association, 2011.[47]

Before TRIPS entered into force, countries could autonomously decide whether to protect clinical trial data or not. Developed countries, especially the United States, tried to insert into TRIPS the first international standard on the subject, what is now Art. 39.3.[48] No consensus was reached during the negotiations. TRIPS established broad parameters for national rules, thereby giving WTO Member countries the freedom

---

45. *Correa*, 'Implications of Bilateral Free Trade Agreements on Access to Medicines', 84(5) Bulletin of the World Health Organization 399 [2006], p. 401.
46. *Supra* n. 43, p. 399
47. *International Federation of Pharmaceutical Manufacturers Association*, Data exclusivity: encouraging development of new medicines [2016], available at https://www.ifpma.org/wp-content/uploads/2016/01/IFPMA_2011_Data_Exclusivity__En_Web.pdf. (accessed on 28 January 2018).
48. TRIPS – 'Section 7: Protection of undisclosed information. Art. 39.3.- Members, when requiring, as a condition of approving the marketing of pharmaceutical or of agricultural chemical products which utilize new chemical entities, the submission of undisclosed test or other data, the origination of which involves a considerable effort, shall protect such data against unfair commercial use. In addition, Members shall protect such data

to apply different models for such protection.⁴⁹ Table 1 shows the data exclusivity term for countries that grant such protection.

Test data must be protected if national authorities require its submission. Thus, if a company relies on an approval granted in a foreign country, the obligation does not apply. In addition, Art. 39.3 does not require protection to be given to data that are already publicly available, but only to undisclosed data. Some national authorities (e.g. the FDA), demand the publication of part of the clinical data, for reasons of transparency and making available for possible specialists' comments. By definition, published data would be free from exclusivity.

Furthermore, protection is mandated only for new chemical entities. Members have considerable discretion in defining this concept and can exclude any second medical indications, new formulations or dosage forms.

Art. 39.3 TRIPS also requires countries to protect test data against 'unfair' commercial use. Protection must be conferred against dishonest commercial practices. Practices expressly required or permitted by law (such as abbreviated procedures of marketing approval) may not be considered dishonest. Granting marketing approval to a second entrant, based on the similarity to a previously approved product, is not deemed an 'unfair commercial use' under Art. 39.3.⁵⁰

According to Pugatch:

> 'The underlying logic of data exclusivity suggests that it is an expression of private trade secrets and, as such, should be independent of patents.[...] Compared with patents, the market power of data exclusivity is in theory less restrictive, mainly because it does not legally prevent other companies from generating their own registration data. [...] However, in practice, the vast financial resources and extended time required for gathering and generating pharmaceutical registration data for a new drug create a market barrier that is too high for generic-based companies.'⁵¹

There could be, in practice, a halt to the development of generic products because the interested companies would have to spend enormous amounts of resources to gather these data, along with years of tests and unnecessary repeated clinical trials on humans, increasing the costs of the production chain and blocking access to cheaply priced generics.

Frequently and especially in developing countries such as India and Brazil, data related to the three phases of clinical trials that are mandatorily prescribed by legal documentation are actually data on a previously approved drug, mainly in

---

against disclosure, except where necessary to protect the public, or unless steps are taken to ensure that data are protected against unfair commercial use.'

49. *Roffe and Spennemann*, 'The Impact of FTAs on Public Health Policies and TRIPS Flexibilities', 1 (1–2) Int. Journal of Intellectual Property Management 75 [2006], p. 77, 78.
50. *Correa*, Protecting Test Data for Pharmaceutical and Agrochemical Products under Free Trade Agreements, Paper submitted to the Fourth ICTSD-UNCTAD Bellagio Dialogue on Moving the Pro-development IP Agenda Forward: Preserving Public Goods in Health, Education and Learning, 29 November – 3 December [2004], available at <http://www.iprsonline.org/unctadictsd/bellagio/docs/Correa_Bellagio4.pdf> (accessed on 15 January 2018).
51. *Supra* n. 43, p. 6.

the case of generics. Thus, the repetition of the entire clinical trial is not necessary; thereby, the approval process becomes faster and the time necessary to launch the generic medication on the market is shorter. Besides, there is the obvious factor that it substantially reduces the costs and duration of the tests.[52]

In 2006, the use of previous test results led the powerful US-based Pharmaceutical Research and Manufactures of America (PhRMA), whose members include the major world pharmaceutical companies (such as Pfizer, Novartis, GSK and MSD, among others), to lobby the United States Trade Representative (USTR) in order to push for exclusivity in clinical trial-related data submitted in India, which today is seen as one of the largest producers of generic medications.[53]

In this effort, 1974 US Trade Act (USTA) was invoked because its Section 301 authorises the United States to open investigations and impose punitive measures such as trade sanctions against countries that violate trade agreements. An investigation under Section 301 can lead to negotiations for a bilateral agreement between the United States and the respective country, or even to commercial sanctions if it is not possible to reach an agreement.[54]

According to the PhRMA, the request for protection of clinical trial data was based on Art. 39.3 TRIPS, an allegation that rapidly generated a document at the United Nations Conference on Trade and Development (UNCTAD) that explained that this clause does not constrain any governmental authority to accept results of clinical trials from a company in order to validate drugs that are similar to another, considering this to be a TRIPS-plus demand.[55]

After negotiations to impose data exclusivity got stuck in the multilateral arena, developed countries, especially the United States but also others such as Japan and members of the European Union, focussed their attention on bilateral trade agreements (BTA) with developing countries. Those agreements touch upon several trade areas, and one of the most important ones is related to pharmaceuticals.

In general, those BTAs with developing countries can include several TRIPS-plus demands, for example that regulatory authorities should withhold the marketing authorisation of generic versions of patented drugs (known as linkage), patent term extensions to compensate 'any unjustified delay' to grant a patent, second medical use patents allowing a drug to gain an extra 20 years of monopolistic protection, denial of an abbreviated registration procedure for generics and the protection of clinical trial data independent of the patent status of a drug, with the possibility of surpassing the patent term.[56]

---

52. It is worth emphasising that generic producers do not have access to the originator's previous data, and actually the drug regulatory agency is the only one who can use this data to analyse the subsequent generic request.
53. Acharya, 'Health-India: Campaign to Stop Monopoly of Clinical Trial Data', Inter Press Service News Agency [2007] available at http://www.ipsnews.net/2007/02/health-in-dia-campaign-to-stop-monopoly-of-clinical-trial-data/. (accessed on 12 January 2018).
54. Drahos, 'BITs and BIPs: Bilateralism in Intellectual Property', 4 Journal of World Intellectual Property 791[2004], p. 792.
55. UNCTAD/ICTSD Capacity Building Project on Intellectual Property Rights and Sustainable Development [2002] available at http://www.iprsonline.org/unctadictsd/docs/RB%20 2.7_forIprsonline.pdf (acessed on 10 January 2018), pp. 10, 11.
56. Supra n. 42, p. 206.

The debate about the scope and standard of data exclusivity is quickly reaching developing countries, especially those that have local productive capacity in the pharmaceutical industry, even if based on generic products.[57]

The impact of such data protection can be quite significant if a drug is not patented or registered in a country, and if it is also commercially unavailable. An interested company would be legally prevented from delivering a generic brand, thereby leaving the country without any alternative to obtain the medicine. It could also happen that a non-patented drug benefits from a market exclusivity of five to ten years, depending on the adopted standards. Another possible scenario is the impossibility of a compulsory licence once the data exclusivity provision 'blocks' the regulatory agency from granting a marketing licence even in an emergency situation.

III. Patent Linkage

A pharmaceutical drug can be introduced into the market, either by the originator company or by different generic manufacturers if the reference drug is not protected by a patent. To this end, both the originator and the generic manufacturer have to first obtain marketing approval from the national drug regulating authority. Patent linkage is the practice of linking drug marketing approval to the patent status of the originator's product by not allowing the granting of marketing approval to any third party prior to the expiration of the patent term or its invalidity, unless consented to by the patent owner.[58]

Under the WTO TRIPS Agreement, member countries agree to grant exclusive rights to patent holders for a limited period of time. Art. 28.1(a) TRIPS states that

> 'where the subject matter of a patent is a product, to prevent third parties not having the owner's consent from the acts of: making, using, offering for sale, selling, or importing for these purposes that product.'

When conjugating Art. 28 TRIPS along with Art. 39.3 (protection of undisclosed information), some Member States created a patent linkage structure. The 'patent linkage' demands that the generic manufacturer interested in obtaining marketing approval for a medicine proves to the drug regulatory agency that such product is not patent protected, or the patent is invalid. In so doing, patent linkage prevents a generic producer from obtaining market approval while the original version of that drug is still patented, unless 'by consent or with the acquiescence of the patent owner'.[59]

---

57. See *OECD-Trade Directorate*, Regional Trade Agreements and the Multilateral Trading System (Paris: 20 November 2002), TD/TC(2002)8/FINAL. See also: *Abbott*, The Doha Declaration on the TRIPS Agreement and Public Health and the Contradictory Trend in Bilateral and Regional Free Trade Agreements, Quaker United Nations Office, 14 April 2004.
58. *Galantucci*, 'Data Protection in a US-Malaysia Free Trade Agreement: New Barriers to Market Access for Generic Drug Manufacturers', 17 (4) Fordham Intell. Prop. Media & Ent. LJ 1083 [2006], p. 1097.
59. *Mittal*, 'Patent Linkage in India: Current Scenario and Need for Deliberation', 15 Journal of Intellectual Property Rights 187 [2010], p. 187.

1. Patent Linkage in United States and the Paragraph IV Provision

A clear example of evergreening related to the linkage mechanism can be seen in the Unites States and is known as the Paragraph IV Provision. The FDA is responsible for granting marketing approval for pharmaceuticals. Under the legislation known as the Hatch-Waxman Act (1984),[60] patent linkage is provided statutorily in the US. To this end, the FDA provides a list of pharmaceutical products, their uses and their current patent status. This publication is commonly known as the 'Orange Book'.

When filing for approval of an Abbreviated New Drug Application (ANDA) – the application for approval of a generic drug – the generic company must declare one of the following four grounds:[61]

1. that the drug has not been patented;
2. that the patent has already expired;
3. the date on which the patent will expire, and that the generic drug will not be marketed until the expiry of the patent;
4. that the patent is not infringed or is invalid.

In the first and second cases, the FDA may grant immediate approval. For ground 3, the FDA usually grants marketing approval only after patent expiration. In reference to ground 4, when certifying that the patent is not infringed or invalid, the applicant must notify the patentee of its filing and state the rationale behind these claims. That mechanism triggers what is called 'Paragraph IV provision'. The patentee has 45 days after such notice to file an infringement suit and if an infringement suit is filed, an automatic 30 months stay of marketing approval is placed on the drug. If the patent is determined to be valid by the court and infringement has occurred, the generic drug will not be approved until the patent term expires.

As highlighted by Mittal, the Hatch-Waxman Act allows the faster introduction of generic competition in exchange for limited, but ironclad, periods of data protection, increased rights for innovators to recoup patent terms affected by regulatory delays, and a linkage system conditionally allowing registration of generic equivalents in the absence of patent infringement.[62]

2. Patent Linkage in the European Union

The European Union has not implemented a system of patent linkage. Innovative pharmaceutical companies have tried to implement such a provision, but faced fierce opposition from Member States.[63]

---

60. Hatch-Waxman amended the Federal Food, Drug, and Cosmetic Act. Section. Pub. L. No. 98-417, 98 Stat. 1585 (1984)505(j) of the Act, codified as 21 U.S.C. § 355(j).
61. See *Heer*, 'Patent linkage: Balancing patent protection and generic entry', [2017] available at https://www.drugpatentwatch.com/blog/patent-linkage-resolving-infringement/ (accessed on 28 February 2018).
62. *Supra* n. 59, p. 188.
63. *Ibid.*

Patent linkage was considered contrary to EU regulatory law as it undermines the provision on research for the purposes of obtaining marketing approval (discussed previously in section 4.1).

In a 2015 press release,[64] the European Generic Medicines Association stated that patent linkage was contrary to EU regulatory law as it undermined the Bolar provision which sought to encourage quick access to the post patent market for EU generic medicines.

In a 2009 report on an inquiry into the Pharmaceutical sector,[65] the European Commission clearly stated that

> 'under EU law, it is not allowed to link marketing authorisation to the patent status of the originator reference product. Art. 81 of the Regulation[66] and Art. 126 of the Directive[67] provide that authorisation to market a medicinal product shall not be refused, suspended or revoked except on the grounds set out in the Regulation and the Directive. Since the status of a patent (application) is not included in the grounds set out in the Regulation and in the Directive, it cannot be used as an argument for refusing, suspending or revoking marketing authorisation.'

3. *Patent Linkage in Other Relevant Countries*

The adoption of patent linkage shows that there are discrepancies in its application. For example, whilst Australia, China and Singapore have patent linkage systems that mirror the United States, Argentina, Brazil, India, Indonesia, Malaysia, Thailand and Vietnam do not have that provision.

It is clear that the current lack of international consensus means that sovereign nations are not mandated to conform to the rules of patent linkage, although it is clear that many bilateral or regional trade agreements, mainly between developed and developing countries, force the adoption of TRIPS-plus clauses, such as patent linkage.

---

64. See European Generic Medicines Association, 'The EGA's thoughts on how to improve the legal and regulatory framework for generic and biosimilar medicines', [2015] available at http://www.hup.hr/EasyEdit/UserFiles/Granske_udruge/HUP-UPL/EGA_Vision_2015.pdf (accessed on 25 February 2018).
65. See European Commission, 'Pharmaceutical Sector Inquiry Final Report', [2009] available at http://ec.europa.eu/competition/sectors/pharmaceuticals/inquiry/staff_working_paper_part1.pdf (accessed on 25 February 2018).
66. Regulation (EC) No 726/2004 of the European Parliament and of the Council of 31 March 2004 laying down Community procedures for the authorisation and supervision of medicinal products for human and veterinary use and establishing a European Medicines Agency. Official Journal of the European Union, L 136, 30/04/2004, pp. 1–33.
67. Directive 2004/27/EC of the European Parliament and of the Council of 31 March 2004 amending Directive 2001/83/EC on the Community code relating to medicinal products for human use. Official Journal of the European Union, 30/04/2004 P. 34–57.

IV. Other Strategies

1. Pay-for-Delay

The pay-for-delay strategy is quite straightforward. Innovative pharmaceutical companies can postpone generic competition and price erosion of their products by agreeing to pay a generic competitor to withhold its competing product from the market for a certain period of time. These so-called 'pay-for-delay' agreements have arisen as part of patent litigation settlement agreements between innovators and generic companies. They are 'win-win' agreements as the brand name pharmaceutical prices stay high, and the brand and generic share the benefits of the brand's monopoly profits. The big losers are consumers because they miss out on generic prices that can be as much as 90 percent lower than brand prices. In the US alone, the Federal Trade Commission estimates that from 2009 to 2019, pay-for-delay agreements will cost approximately USD 3.5 billion per year or nearly USD 35 billion over the next ten-year period.[68]

Good examples were reported in the Pharmaceutical Sector Inquiry by the European Commission in 2008. The French pharmaceutical company Servier was fined EUR 330 million for delaying entry of the generic high blood pressure medicine perindopril in the market, and in 2013, American company Johnson & Johnson and Swiss based Novartis were fined EUR 16 million for delaying entry of the generic version of the painkiller fentanyl.[69]

2. Establishment of Generic Units by Innovative Companies

One relatively new field of play for the big pharma giants is to compete against generics in the generic arena by developing or buying generic plants. Innovative companies are showing an ever-increasing interest in setting subsidiary generic units or establishing partnerships with major generic manufacturers in order to build a position in generic drugs before other competitors take a market share. Over the past decade, 'Big Pharma' have acquired small generic units to expand their business models.

There are many examples of this buy-in strategy around the world.[70] For instance, AstraZeneca and the Indian generic manufacturer Torrent Pharmaceuticals signed a contract in 2010 under which Torrent will manufacture and supply generic versions

---

68. See Federal Trade Commission, 'Pay-for-Delay: how drug company pay-offs cost consumers billions', [2010] available at https://www.ftc.gov/sites/default/files/documents/reports/pay-delay-how-drug-company-pay-offs-cost-consumers-billions-federal-trade-commission-staff-study/100112payfordelayrpt.pdf (accessed on 28 February 2018).
69. Kumar and Nanda, 'Ever-greening in Pharmaceuticals: Strategies, Consequences and Provisions for Prevention in USA, EU, India and Other Countries', 6 (185) Pharmaceutical Regulatory Affairs: Open Access1[2017], p. 2.
70. See Federal Trade Commission, 'Authorized Generic Drugs: short-term effects and long-term impact', [2011] available at https://www.ftc.gov/sites/default/files/documents/reports/authorized-generic-drugs-short-term-effects-and-long-term-impact-report-federal-trade-commission/authorized-generic-drugs-short-term-effects-and-long-term-impact-report-federal-trade-commission.pdf (accessed on 28 February 2018).

for AstraZeneca's emerging markets. Novartis established Sandoz as a subsidiary unit for manufacturing generic drugs and Novartis's profit in generics rose to USD 7.5 billion (up to 2009). Novartis further acquired a generic business in oncology which further added to this profit.[71]

3. 'Give away' Patents

One very recent and creative strategy to avoid having its patents attacked was disclosed by Allergan pharmaceutics. In brief, they announced in September 2017 the transfer of their patents on a best-selling eye drug to the Saint Regis Mohawk tribe in upstate New York, US.[72]

Under the deal, which involves the dry-eye blockbuster drug restasis, Allergan committed to pay the natives USD 13.75 million immediately. In exchange, the tribe will claim 'sovereign immunity' as grounds for dismissing a patent challenge through a unit of the United States Patent and Trademark Office. The tribe will lease the patents back to Allergan, and will receive USD 15 million in annual royalties as long as the patents remain valid.

This creative and surprising legal move has caught the attention of the pharmaceutical world, setting off speculation about whether other drug companies would soon follow that strategy in order to protect their patents from challenges through a patent-review process that is highly unpopular with the industry.

The announcement is perhaps the most novel attempt to avoid the US patent-review process that was created in 2011 as a way to streamline patent challenges by allowing them to be decided by an administrative panel, the Patent Trial and Appeal Board (PTAB). Many innovative companies claim that the process is redundant because patents are usually challenged in federal courts.

The Indian company Teva Pharmaceuticals, one of the generic companies that is challenging Restasis patents, stated that the Allegan move could be described as 'a new and unusual way for a company to try to delay access to high-quality and affordable generic alternatives'.[73]

E. DEVELOPING COUNTRIES' INITIATIVES TO MITIGATE EVERGREENING

According to the 2017 IgeaHub,[74] all top ten pharmaceutical companies are based in the developed world (six in the US, two in Switzerland, one in the UK and one

---

71. *Supra* n. 69, p. 2.
72. See *Mullin*, 'Drug Company Hands Patents off to Native American Tribe to Avoid Challenge', [2017] available at https://arstechnica.com/tech-policy/2017/09/how-a-native-american-tribe-ended-up-owning-six-key-patents-on-an-eye-drug/ (accessed on 28 February 2018).
73. See *Rosen*, 'Tribal justice? A Clever New Patent Transfer Strategy Seeks to Avoid Patent Office Scrutiny', [2017] available at http://www.aei.org/publication/tribal-justice-a-clever-new-patent-transfer-strategy-seeks-to-avoid-patent-office-scrutiny/ (accessed on 28 February 2018).
74. IgeaHub Pharmaceutical Club, 'Top 10 Pharmaceutical Companies', 2017 [2018] available at https://igeahub.com/2017/03/14/top-10-pharmaceutical-companies-2017/ (accessed

in France). Pressured by 'Big Pharma', many developed countries have pursued higher levels of intellectual property protection against developing countries, mainly TRIPS-plus clauses such as data protection, blockage of research exception, linkage, limitations to compulsory licence, etc. The pressure is exerted in different forums, especially in bilateral or regional trade agreements.

As a countermeasure, some developing countries have started to discuss and implement legislation to avoid granting trivial patents and/or evergreening practices. India and Argentina are the best examples of such movement. In 2005, India passed the Patent Amendment Act,[75] which explicitly targets secondary trivial patents. Section 3(d) states that secondary patents are not subject to protection unless they show increased efficacy.[76]

> '3(d) the mere discovery of a new form of a known substance which does not result in the enhancement of the known efficacy of that substance or the mere discovery of any new property or new use for a known substance or of the mere use of a known process, machine or apparatus unless such known process results in a new product or employs at least one new reactant.'

For the purposes of this clause, salts, esters, ethers, polymorphs, metabolites, pure form, particle size, isomers, mixtures of isomers, complexes, combinations and other derivatives of known substance shall be considered to be the same substance, unless they differ significantly in properties with regard to efficacy.[77] Argentina followed India's example and approved new guidelines for pharmaceutical patents.[78] Accordingly, it was defined that secondary use patents should not be granted. For example, polymorphs are considered a natural occurrence and for that reason they are 'discovered', not invented, and thus are not patentable.

Many other secondary methods of exploitation are excluded from patentability, such as pharmaceutical compositions, selection inventions, me-too and new formulation patents, second medical use patents, etc. Argentina's guidelines on pharmaceutical patentability are even more restrictive when compared to India's resolution in that even if a secondary method of exploitation shows increased efficacy, it is excluded from patentability.

A debate on the patentability of second medical uses, polymorphism and others also took place in Brazil. In 2008, the Brazilian Interministerial Group of Intellectual

---

on 5 March 2018).
75. India's Ministry of Law and Justice, The Patents (Amendment) Act, 2005 [2005] available at http://www.wipo.int/edocs/lexdocs/laws/en/in/in018en.pdf (accessed on 28 February 2018).
76. However, the term 'increased efficiency' is not well defined.
77. This provision was held to be in compliance with India's international obligations under TRIPS by the Madras High Court in *Novartis v. Union of India*, MANU/TN/1263/2007. The decision is commented on by R. Parthasarathy and H. Goddar, 'Patentability of Pharmaceutical Products in India The Novartis Case', 38 IIC 38 (2009); see also S. Shadowen, K. Leiffer and J. Lukens, 'Bringing Market Discipline to Pharmaceutical Product Reformulations', 40 IIC 698, 712 (2011).
78. Argentina's Ministerio de Industria, Ministerio de Salud e Instituto Nacional de la Propiedad Industrial, Resolución Conjunta 118/2012, 546/2012 y 107/2012 [2012] available at http://www.wipo.int/wipolex/en/text.jsp?file_id=288443 (accessed on 28 February 2018).

Property, created in 2001, debated the international scenario and technical issues for developing a Brazilian position, taking into account the views of different government agencies. Since then, there have been some legislative initiatives in Congress both to restrict and to relax patentability criteria, yet no law has been agreed upon. The current guidelines[79] allow secondary patents when they meet the three patentability criteria. As an example, secondary medical use is accepted only if the metabolic route is clearly characterised and differs from that of the first application, or me-too drugs are patentable only when they show non-obvious or unforeseen advantages.

In the multilateral arena, efforts have focused on the balance between innovation protection and access to medicines. The United Nations Development Programme, led by Professor Carlos Correa from Buenos Aires University, published a Guideline for the Examination of Patent Applications relating to Pharmaceuticals.[80] The report aimed at providing guidance for countries to enhance the functioning and transparency of the patent system for the timely and affordable access to lifesaving treatment. The publication examined initiatives in countries such as Argentina, Ecuador, India and the Philippines, and recognised the key role patent offices and patent examiners play in safeguarding the appropriate balance between protecting the rights of inventors and incentivising innovation, and helping to promote accessibility and the affordability of treatments.

Moving away from the guideline perspective, other relevant documents[81] were produced in the past years related to patents and access to medicines. The common ground among those is the need to balance incentives, innovation and access.

In 2001, prompted by serious public health problems afflicting many developing and least-developed countries, especially those resulting from HIV/AIDS, tuberculosis, malaria and other epidemics, the Doha WTO Ministerial Declaration on the TRIPS Agreement and Public Health[82] sought to address the important question of access to medicines, especially those protected by patents.

The Doha Declaration stressed the need for the TRIPS Agreement to be part of the wider national and international action towards resolving these problems. It

---

79. Instituto Naciona da Propriedade Industrial, Aspectos relacionados ao exame de pedidos de patente na área de química [2017] available at http://www.inpi.gov.br/menu-servicos/DIRETRIZESEXAMEREAQUMICA17032017.pdf (accessed on 15 January 2018) (Portuguese only).
80. *Correa*, 'Guidelines for Pharmaceutical Patent Examination: Examining Pharmaceutical Patents from a Public Health Perspective', [2016] available at http://www.undp.org/content/undp/en/home/librarypage/hiv-aids/guidelines-for-the-examination-of-patent-applications-relating-t.html (accessed on 15 January 2018).
81. CEWG, 'WHO Research and Development to Meet Health Needs in Developing Countries: Strengthening Global Financing and Coordination', [2012] available at http://www.who.int/phi/CEWG_Report_5_April_2012.pdf. (accessed on 14 March 2018); Commission on Intellectual Property Rights, Innovation and Public Health, WHO Public health, innovation and intellectual property rights [2006] available at < http://www.who.int/intellectualproperty/report/en/ > (accessed on 14 March 2018); World Health Assembly, WHA Global strategy and plan of action on public health, innovation and intellectual property (WHA61.21) [2008] available at http://www.wpro.who.int/health_research/policy_documents/global_strategy_may2008.pdf. (accessed on 14 March 2018)
82. World Trade Organization [2001] available at https://www.wto.org/english/thewto_e/minist_e/min01_e/mindecl_trips_e.htm (accessed on 15 March 2018).

was recognised that intellectual property protection is a relevant incentive for the development of new medicines but at the same time raises concerns in relation to high prices. The Declaration made it clear that the TRIPS Agreement does not and should not prevent members from taking measures to protect public health and should be interpreted and implemented in a manner supportive of WTO members' rights to protect public health and, in particular, to promote access to medicines for all. The Declaration reinforced the right of WTO members to use, to the full, the provisions in the TRIPS Agreement, which provide flexibility for this purpose.

Seven years after the Doha Declaration, Members States adopted the Global Strategy and Plan of Action on Public Health, Innovation and Intellectual Property[83] (Resolution WHA61.21) (GSPOA, 2008). GSPOA addressed the needs of developing countries while aiming to foster innovation.

> 'The global strategy proposed that WHO should play a strategic and central role in the relationship between public health and innovation and intellectual property within its mandate. Member States endorsed by consensus a strategy designed to promote new thinking in innovation and access to medicines, which would encourage needs-driven research rather than purely market-driven research to target diseases which disproportionately affect people in developing countries.'[84]

One of GSPOA's most important points concerns the use of TRIPS flexibilities. The message is clear regarding policy freedom for the definition of criteria for patentability, according to the objectives of each country:

> 'There is a crucial need to strengthen innovation capacity as well as capacity to manage and apply intellectual property in developing countries, including, in particular, the use to the full of the provisions in the TRIPS Agreement and instruments related to that agreement, which provide flexibilities to take measures to protect public health.'[85]

In addition to the aforementioned initiatives, there are several movements at the international level, such as the Development Agenda negotiated at WIPO. The texts negotiated or under negotiation are a good reflection of the tensions between developed and developing countries concerning the internalisation of the TRIPS Agreement.

F.   FINAL REMARKS

The patent system was designed to reward innovation, and for that purpose, it should be maintained and improved. The intellectual property system undeniably

---

83. World Health Organization, 'The Global Strategy and Plan of Action on Public Health, Innovation and Intellectual Property', [2008] available at http://www.who.int/phi/implementation/phi_globstat_action/en/ (accessed on 10 March 2018).
84. World Health Organization, 'Global Strategy and Plan of Action on Public Health, Innovation and Intellectual Property', [2011] available at http://www.who.int/phi/implementation/phi_globstat_action/en/ (accessed on 10 March 2018)
85. World Health Organization, 'Global Strategy and Plan of Action on Public Health, Innovation and Intellectual Property', [2011] p. 15, available at http://apps.who.int/medicinedocs/documents/s21429en/s21429en.pdf (accessed on 10 March 2018).

plays a fundamental role to that end. It is, nonetheless, very important to avoid a misuse of this system by granting artificial monopolies to inventions that do not meet minimum standards.

Legitimate trade is paramount for the generation of revenues and for keeping the wheels of the economy turning. IPRs are directly related to the ability to trade, once patent owners have a temporary legal right to make, sell, use and especially block third parties from exploiting the protected invention. A system that is too weak does not bring enough incentives to new inventions; a protection regime that creates unjustified artificial monopolies is also unwanted, as it will provoke elevated transactional costs, hampering access to innovations for the people most in need. In such a system, unjustified monopolies amount to barriers to legitimate trade. Trivial patents in any area could have deleterious effects on society. This is particularly so in the pharmaceutical field where they can have the potential to affect access to medicines by delaying market entry of generic products.

The pharmaceutical area is especially susceptible to abuse where patents are paramount for the business model and society demand is inelastic, therefore is it important that countries promote intellectual property rights that reward innovators but at the same time avoid abuses of a dominant position.

CHAPTER 7
Exhaustion and Second-Hand Digital Goods/Contents

Matthias Leistner and Lucie Antoine

Rules on the domestic exhaustion of copyrighted goods serve the freedom of commerce and do not allow the copyright owner to control the second-hand market of such goods. This established balance may considerably shift in favour of copyright owners and platform providers should the exhaustion principle not apply to digital products.

Since the Court of Justice of the EU (CJEU) in its landmark decision *UsedSoft* decided that the exhaustion principle is applicable at least to the online distribution of software, the practical and scientific debate partially shifted to the question of whether this ruling can be extended to other digital goods. In view of the fact that exhaustion aims at balancing the copyright owner's right with the freedom of commerce, by not allowing the copyright holder to control a potential resale, at first glance it seems to be essential to apply the exhaustion principle to all kinds of digital goods to safeguard legitimate trade in the digital era. However, there are also valid reasons – both in a doctrinal and practical sense – which throw considerable doubt on extending the *UsedSoft* doctrine to other digital goods.

A. THE STARTING POINT IN EUROPEAN LAW: *USEDSOFT* AND ITS APPLICATION IN THE MEMBER STATES

The lively debate concerning the resale of used software and the application of the exhaustion principle[1] has peaked – for the time being – in the CJEU's *UsedSoft* decision rendered in 2012.[2] The decision was based upon a reference from the German

---
1. See e.g. *Schneider/Spindler*, 'Der Kampf um die gebrauchte Software – Revolution im Urheberrecht?', Computer und Recht (CR) 489 [2012].
2. Case C-128/11 *UsedSoft v. Oracle* [2012] ECLI:EU:C:2012:407.

Federal Court of Justice (BGH) regarding the interpretation of Arts. 4(2) and 5(1) of Directive 2009/24[3] (hereinafter Software Directive).[4]

I. The Facts

Oracle allowed its customers – instead of transferring a material medium – to directly download a copy of the offered client server software to their computers after agreeing to Oracle's licence agreement. The licence agreement granted 'the right to store a copy of the program permanently on a server and to allow a certain number of users to access it'.[5] An additional maintenance agreement allowed downloading updates and patches from Oracle's website. Oracle offered group licences for the database software in question for a minimum of 25 users each. UsedSoft bought such 'used licences' from first acquirers and re-sold them to second acquirers. The latter directly downloaded the software from Oracle's website in an updated version as UsedSoft referred to the existing maintenance agreement. Subsequently, Oracle brought an action in order to terminate UsedSoft's resale practices, claiming copyright infringement.

II. The Ruling

1. *Introduction*

As to the German Federal Court's reference, the CJEU had to decide the question of whether the condition of a first sale in the sense of Art. 4(2) Software Directive resulting in the exhaustion of the distribution right was fulfilled in cases where customers download the program from the internet with the copyright holder's consent, instead of obtaining a material medium.[6] Furthermore, it had to interpret the conditions and the extent of the lawful acquirer's rights set forth in Art. 5(1) Software Directive, especially the question as to whether the second acquirer – as a 'lawful acquirer' – could rely on those use rights as well.

In sum, the European Court held that granting a use right for an unlimited period of time in return for paying a fee amounts to a 'sale' according to Art. 4(2) Software Directive. This in turn makes the second acquirer a lawful user in the sense of Art. 5(1) Software Directive. The exhaustion principle is therefore applicable and guarded by Art. 5(1) Software Directive with regard to its practical implementation in the person of the second acquirer. Thus, the decision practically leads to an equal treatment of downloaded software and software on a material medium if certain requirements are fulfilled. However, splitting a licence package in cases of client-server

---

3. Directive 2009/24/EC of the European Parliament and of the Council of 23 April 2009 on the legal protection of computer programs.
4. German Federal Court (BGH) Case I ZR 129/08 *UsedSoft I* (3 Feb 2011), Gewerblicher Rechtsschutz und Urheberrecht (GRUR) 418 [2011].
5. *UsedSoft* (*supra* n. 2), para. 21.
6. The Court decided to answer the questions in an order which differed from the German Federal Court's reference, see para. 34 of the decision. Further *Schneider/Spindler* (*supra* n. 1) CR 489, 491 [2012]; *Schneider/Spindler*, 'Der Erschöpfungsgrundsatz bei "gebrauchter" Software im Praxistext', CR 213 [2014].

software is not possible as this might lead to additional acts of reproduction and cuts the link between the copy of the software and the use rights.[7]

2. Conditions of Online Exhaustion

As a result of the CJEU's decision, three main conditions can be derived for online exhaustion and hence a lawful resale of used/second-hand software.

a. Appropriate Remuneration

In the digital context, a 'first sale' pursuant to Art. 4(2) Software Directive requires that the customer obtains a permanent use right for the software in return for the payment of a fee.[8] Thus, the first condition is a 'fee intended to enable [...] [the right holder] to obtain a remuneration corresponding to the economic value of the copy'.[9] The Court bases this requirement on grounds of the specific subject matter of copyright protection and thus in a concept of primary European law: the exhaustion principle aims at limiting restrictions of the distribution to what is necessary to safeguard the specific subject matter of the relevant intellectual property right in order to avoid the partitioning of markets.[10] Allowing a copyright holder to control the resale of downloaded copies and demanding further remuneration although the first sale establishes a sufficient chance to obtain an appropriate remuneration would, however, go beyond what is necessary to safeguard the relevant subject matter of copyright.[11] As the CJEU already took a similar approach[12] in earlier decisions such as *Murphy*,[13] this can be seen as a general, primary law-based concept that the specific subject matter of the economic exploitation rights consists in enabling the copyright holder to obtain an appropriate remuneration – thus not going beyond what is necessary to protect this objective.[14] Recently, the Court once more declared

---

7. *UsedSoft* (*supra* n. 2) paras. 69 et seqq., 86. In cases of separately sold licences (workplace licences) by contrast this would be possible, see German Federal Court (BGH) Case I ZR 8/13 *Used Soft III* (11 Dec 2014), GRUR 772 [2015].
8. *UsedSoft* (*supra* n. 2) para. 45.
9. *UsedSoft* (*supra* n. 2) paras. 63, 72.
10. *UsedSoft* (*supra* n. 2) para. 62.
11. *UsedSoft* (*supra* n. 2) para. 63.
12. CJEU Case C-403, 429/08 *Football Association Premier League v. Murphy* [2011] ECLI:EU:C:2011:631, para. 107 et seqq.; *Malevanny*, 'Die UsedSoft-Kontroverse: Auslegung und Auswirkungen des EuGH-Urteils', CR 422, 425 [2013]; *Leistner*, 'Das Murphy-Urteil des EuGH: Viel Lärm um nichts oder Anfang vom Ende des Territorialitätsgrundsatzes im Urheberrecht?', Juristenzeitung (JZ) 1140, 1141 [2011]; *Senftleben*, 'Die Fortschreibung des urheberrechtlichen Erschöpfungsgrundsatzes im digitalen Umfeld', Neue Juristische Wochenschrift (NJW) 2924, 2926 [2012].
13. C-403, 429/08 *Football Association Premier League v. Murphy*. The decision concerned the pan-European licensing of satellite broadcasting rights.
14. See *Leistner* (*supra* n. 12) JZ 1140, 1141 [2011]; *Vinje/Marsland/Gärtner*, 'Software Licensing After Oracle v. UsedSoft', Computer Law Review International (CRi) 97, 101 [2012]; *Leistner*, 'Europe's Copyright Law Decade: Recent Case Law of the European Court of Justice and Policy Perspectives', 51 Common Market Law Review (CMLR) 559, 575 [2014].

the InfoSoc Directive's[15] principal objective to be the chance to obtain an appropriate remuneration.[16]

b.   Unlimited Use Right

Secondly, in return for paying such a fee, the right to use the copy must be granted for an unlimited period of time.[17] The Court assumes a so-called indivisible whole of concluding a user licence agreement and downloading a copy of the program from the internet. Granting an unlimited use right in this context corresponds to a transfer of the right of ownership of the copy in question, thereby fulfilling the definition of a 'sale'.[18]

On the other hand, Oracle and the Commission asserted that offering a download would constitute a 'making available to the public' pursuant to Art. 3(1) InfoSoc Directive, resulting in the inapplicability of the exhaustion principle.[19] The CJEU rejected this finding, arguing that, first, the Software Directive constitutes a *lex specialis* in relation to the InfoSoc Directive and, secondly, 'the existence of a transfer of ownership changes an "act of communication to the public" [...] into an act of distribution referred to in Article 4 of the [Software] directive'.[20] Based on this reasoning, the Court furthermore rejected the argument that Recital 29 of the InfoSoc Directive would put an obstacle to online exhaustion for computer programs.[21]

Consequently, the condition of a 'first sale' in the sense of Art. 4(2) Software Directive is fulfilled if the computer program is downloaded from the internet.

c.   Making Copy Unusable

Thirdly, the first acquirer is obliged to make all of his other copies unusable at the time of the copies' resale.[22] This additional requirement is due to the non-rivalry of intangible goods, which unlike tangible goods may be used by several persons at the same time.

---

15. Directive 2001/29/EC of the European Parliament and of the Council of 22 May 2001 on the harmonization of certain aspects of copyright and related rights in the information society (hereinafter InfoSoc Directive).
16. Case C-610/15 *Stichting Brein/Ziggo [The Pirate Bay]* [2017] ECLI:EU:C:2017:456, para. 22: 'In that regard, it should be borne in mind that it follows from recitals 9 and 10 of Directive 2001/29 that the latter's principal objective is to establish a high level of protection for authors, allowing them to obtain an appropriate reward for the use of their works [...]'.
17. *Ibid.*, paras. 45, 72.
18. *Ibid.*, paras. 42, 45 et seq.
19. *Ibid.*, para. 50.
20. *Ibid.*, paras. 51 et seq.
21. *Ibid.*, paras. 53 et seqq.; see with regard to Recital 29 further infra section B.I.3.
22. *Ibid.*, paras. 70 et seqq.

III. Remaining Problems and Practical Difficulties of Implementation in the Member States

Although these three conditions seem quite clear and easy to handle at the high level of European law, the practical legal construction of applying the exhaustion principle to the online distribution of software under national law is more difficult and results in practical problems.

1. Sale

The CJEU bases its reasoning for affirming a 'sale' on the inseparable unity of the downloaded copy and the conclusion of a licence agreement because downloading a copy would be pointless if it could not be used by its possessor.[23] However, this is a debatable doctrinal construction due to various reasons, particularly as it interlinks very different concepts.[24] By alleging a 'transfer of ownership' that results from such a 'sale', the Court for instance implicitly refers not only to copyright, but to 'property'.[25] Yet, the concept of property and which 'goods' can be subject thereto widely differs among the Member States.[26] In addition, the right holder retains all rights to the computer program, but solely grants certain rights, which is not in line with the understanding of a 'sale'.[27]

2. Scope of the Second Acquirer's Rights of Use

Furthermore, practical problems arise with regard to the scope of the second acquirer's rights of use. As a result of assuming a 'sale', the CJEU construes the second acquirer's rights of use by applying Art. 5(1) Software Directive, since the 'buyer' is a lawful acquirer due to the exhaustion of the resold copy.[28] Still, the scope of the rights of use which are granted by this provision remains unclear: does the general statutory scope of Art. 5(1) Software Directive apply, or does the specific scope agreed upon by the first acquirer under the licence prevail? This question gains importance especially in the context of user-specific licences (e.g. for students). The German Federal Court of Justice laudably tried to provide some clarification in this regard: it held that beyond certain minimum acts set forth in the German equivalent of Art. 5(1) Software Directive, the scope of the rights of use is defined by the terms

---

23. *Ibid.*, para. 44.
24. *Schneider/Spindler* (*supra* n. 1) CR 489, 498 [2012]; *Spindler*, 'Privatrechtsdogmatik und Herausforderungen der "IT-Revolution"' in *Auer* et. al (eds.), Privatrechtrechtsdogmatik im 21. Jahrhundert, Festschrift für Wilhelm Canaris, Berlin/Boston 2017, p. 709, 734 et seq.; *Ohly*, 'Privatrechtsdogmatik und geistiges Eigentum', in *ibid.*, p. 988, 996 et seq.; *Leistner* (*supra* n. 14) CMLR 559, 583 [2014].
25. *Spindler* (*supra* n. 24), p. 735.
26. *Moon*, 'Revisiting UsedSoft v. Oracle: Is Software Property and Can It Be Sold?', CRi 113, 117 [2017]; *Heydn*, 'Remarks to *UsedSoft*', Multimedia und Recht (MMR) 591 [2012].
27. *Hilty/Köklü/Hafenbrädl*, 'Software Agreements: Stocktaking and Outlook – Lessons from the UsedSoft v. Oracle Case from a Comparative Law Perspective', 44 International Review of Intellectual Property and Competition Law (IIC) 263, 276 [2013].
28. *UsedSoft* (*supra* n. 2) paras. 73 et seqq.

of the original licence.[29] As a result, a copy of the original licence has to be handed over to the second acquirer in order to properly inform him about the granted rights. Likewise, the German Federal Court established a further due diligence obligation for lawfully reselling a software copy.[30]

However, even substantively defining the rights of use on the basis of the original licence terms does not allow 'bringing home' restrictions to certain user groups of second acquirers because the basic use of the program is subject to the mandatory minimum rights of use set forth in Art. 5(1) Software Directive, which cannot be over-ridden by contract.[31] Consequently, in the German market, such user-specific licences no longer broadly exist in their traditional form. Rather, they were substituted for instance by contracts or licensing agreements with universities. Nevertheless, one useful possibility of price discrimination thereby no longer exists.[32] Moreover, 'moving' licences, as the German Federal Court of Justice assumes, lead to considerable practical difficulties in implementing, documenting and, ultimately, providing evidence for the fulfilment of the resulting additional implementation requirements in court.[33] This aggravates the practical difficulties in implementing the requirements of the CJEU's *UsedSoft* decision, which are considerable.

3. Making the Copy Unusable

Proving the destruction of the first acquirer's copy and disclosing the whole licensing chain results in immense practical difficulties. While the German Federal Court applies very strict standards of proof arising from the national rules of civil procedure,[34] the CJEU seems to require that software producers themselves are responsible for establishing the necessary technical protection measures (such as product keys) to verify whether the first acquirer's copy was indeed made unusable.[35] The main

---

29. German Federal Court (BGH) Case I ZR 129/08 *Used Soft II* (17 Jul 2013) GRUR 264, 266 [2014], paras. 28 et seqq.; German Federal Court (BGH) *Used Soft III* (*supra* n. 7) GRUR 772 [2015].
30. BGH *Used Soft III* (*supra* n. 7) GRUR 772, 778 [2015], paras. 64 et seq.
31. Hoeren, 'Der Erschöpfungsgrundsatz bei Software – Körperliche Übertragung und Folgeprobleme', GRUR 665, 667 [2010]; *Schneider/Spindler* (*supra* n. 6) CR 213, 215 [2014].
32. Cf. *Marly*, 'Der Handel mit so genannter "Gebrauchtsoftware"', Europäische Zeitschrift für Wirtschaftsrecht (EuZW) 654, 655 [2012]; cf. *Vianello*, 'Handel mit gebrauchter Software für Schüler, Studenten und Lehrkräfte – Die aktuelle Rechtsprechung des BGH', MMR 139, 139 [2012]; see also in another context *Vinje/Marsland/Gärtner* (*supra* n. 14) CRi 97, 101 [2012]. See with regard to further problems of licences for universities or corporations *Schneider*, 'Software als handelbares verkehrsfähiges Gut – "Volumen-Lizenzen" nach BGH', CR 413, 419 [2015].
33. See further *Leistner*, 'Segelanweisungen und Beweislastklippen: eine problemorientierte Stellungnahme zum BGH-Urteil UsedSoft II', Wettbewerb in Recht und Praxis (WRP), 995, 1000 et seq. [2014].
34. BGH *Used Soft II* (*supra* n. 29) GRUR 264 [2014] and *Used Soft III* (*supra* n. 7) GRUR 772 [2015], assuming that notary affidavits are not sufficient. According to these rulings, testimony by the responsible employees could suffice, yet this contradicts the ratio of CJEU's decision. See further *Leistner* (*supra* n. 33) WRP 995, 997 [2014].
35. *UsedSoft* (*supra* n. 2) para. 79. Regarding the time in which the copy has to be destroyed, the CJEU referred to the time of the resale (*UsedSoft* para. 70) while the German Federal

problem in this context is that the differences at the interface of autonomous European copyright and national general civil law as well as civil procedural law lead to considerably different standards regarding the application of the *UsedSoft* doctrine throughout the Member States.

According to the CJEU's decision, implementing technical protection measures is only justified in order to control the destruction of the first copy.[36] Technical protection measures that go beyond this objective, such as trying to control the resale, are consequently unlawful.[37] The same seems to apply to the distribution in the form of individual online accounts, which are accompanied by contract provisions prohibiting the transfer of a personal ID to third persons, as this ultimately aims at impeding the resale of the downloaded software.[38]

Moreover, the lack of a material copy which could serve as a certain minimum means of proof of originality and lawfulness in trade further complicates the practical feasibility of trade in second-hand software.[39] Certainly, the use of certificates,[40] audit rights[41] and – in the future – even information technology itself can arguably provide remedies, as for instance block chain technology is undoubtedly suitable in principle to prove a complete licensing chain.[42]

Court specified in this regard that the copy has to be made unusable no later than when the second acquirer activates his copy by downloading it from the right holder's website (cf. German Federal Court (BGH) Case I ZR 4/14 *Green IT* (19 Mar 2015) GRUR 1108 [2015], paras. 48 et seqq.).

36. *UsedSoft* (*supra* n. 2) para. 79. For coherence problems resulting from the different standard for technical protection measures concerning computer games, see infra section B.I.2.
37. *Haberstumpf*, 'Der Handel mit gebrauchter Software im harmonisierten Urheberrecht', CR 561, 570 [2012]; *Schneider* (*supra* n. 35) CR 413, 422 [2015].
38. *Lee*, 'UsedSoft GmbH v. Oracle International Corp (Case C-128/11) – Sales of "Used" Software and the Principle of Exhaustion', 43 IIC 846, 853 [2012]; *Senftleben* (*supra* n. 12) NJW 2924, 2927 [2012]; *Schneider* (*supra* n. 32) CR 413, 421 [2015]. The German Federal Court held for video games that such online accounts with a monitoring function would be permissible, German Federal Court (BGH) Case I ZR 178/08 *Half Life 2* (11 Feb 2010), GRUR 822 [2010]. However, at least with regard to software in the strict sense this standard cannot be applied any more, *Leistner* (*supra* n. 33) WRP 995, 1002 et seq [2014]; with regard to more complex services, such as participation in a continuously changing online gaming environment, the situation is less clear.
39. *Spindler*, 'Der Handel mit Gebrauchtsoftware – Erschöpfungsgrundsatz quo vadis?', CR 69, 72, 74 [2008]; *Schneider/Spindler* (*supra* n. 1) CR 489, 493 [2012]; *Bräutigam*, 'Second-Hand Software in Europe', CRi 1, 8 [2012]; *Leistner*, 'Gebrauchtsoftware auf dem Weg nach Luxemburg', CR 209, 213 [2011].
40. *Leistner* (*supra* n. 39) CR 209, 213 [2011].
41. *Schneider/Spindler* (*supra* n. 6) CR 213, 220 [2014].
42. See *Rosati*, Digital copies, exhaustion, and blockchains: lack of legal clarity to be offset by technological advancement and evolving consumption patterns?, [2017] available at: http://ipkitten.blogspot.de/2017/05/digital-copies-exhaustion-and.html (accessed 9 March 2018); *Blocher/Hoppen/Hoppen*, Softwarelizenzen auf der Blockchain, CR 337 [2017]; see already *Ulmer/Hoppen*, 'Was ist das Werkstück des Software-Objektcodes?', CR 681, 685 [2008].

4. Unlimited Period of Time

Additionally, the requirement of an 'unlimited period of time' is not further defined at the European level. For instance, the German Federal Court ruled that the requirement of an unlimited period of use can also be met if the program is only temporarily functional and automatically deactivated after the service time has elapsed.[43] As the right to use the copy is granted for the entire duration of its operability, this would in fact amount to an 'unlimited period'. Yet, such an understanding is hardly compatible with the term 'first sale' according to Art. 4(2) Software Directive, as it was specified in *UsedSoft*.

5. Maintenance Agreement

The CJEU extends the 'sale' and therefore the exhaustion principle not only to the original copy the first acquirer downloaded, but – fictitiously – to the updated copy if the first sale was accompanied by the conclusion of a maintenance agreement.[44] According to the Court, all functionalities that were corrected, altered or added form an integral part of the originally downloaded (so-called) copy and can be used by the first acquirer for an unlimited period of time.[45] As a result, the latest version of the software downloaded directly by the second acquirer is covered by the original sale and thus subject to exhaustion as well. But enabling the second acquirer to get all future updates and patches, and even being able to use the program properly, would require transferring the maintenance agreements separately since – contrary to the licence agreement – these do not pass automatically.[46] This entails further contractual agreements and therefore further uncertainties and problems.

6. Excluded Objects of Exhaustion

Contrary to the broad understanding as to the updated versions, the CJEU meanwhile made clear in a later decision what is not suitable as an object to online exhaustion. The first acquirer cannot transfer a (material) back-up copy made under Art. 5(2) Software Directive to a second acquirer on the grounds that he has damaged, destroyed or lost the original medium sold to him.[47] The argumentation is based on the assumption that a back-up copy may be made and used only to meet the sole needs of the person having the right to use the respective program, not in order to resell that program to a third party.[48]

At the same time, according to the CJEU, a lawful acquirer is entitled to download a copy from the right holder's website if the material medium originally sold to him is destroyed, since this would constitute a necessary reproduction in the

---

43. BGH *Green IT* (*supra* n. 35) GRUR 1108 [2015].
44. *UsedSoft* (*supra* n. 2) paras. 64 et seqq.
45. *UsedSoft* (*supra* n. 2) para. 67.
46. *Schneider/Spindler* (*supra* n. 1) CR 489, 498 [2012]; *Leistner* (*supra* n. 33) WRP 995, 999, 1001 [2014].
47. Case C-166/15 *Ranks* [2016] ECLI:EU:C:2016:762, para. 44.
48. Case C-166/15, para. 43.

sense of Art. 5(1) Software Directive.[49] Although exhaustion concerning the originally sold material medium (CD-ROM, DVD) would no longer be possible, the downloaded copy could still be resold (as far as the first acquirer proves the destruction of his copy) due to the exhaustion of the 'virtual copy'.[50] The exhaustion principle, however, originally aims at guaranteeing the free movement of 'goods' in the sense of a material medium.[51] With this line of argumentation, the Court further strengthens the focus on a 'virtual copy' (already rooted in *UsedSoft* where the concept of the inseparable unity of the so-called copy and the licence agreement was also purely fictitious) as the relevant subject matter to anchor the exhaustion principle, whereby the limits of exhaustion become increasingly blurred.[52]

Additionally, the CJEU interprets Art. 5(1) of the Software Directive broadly, qualifying the second acquirer as a 'lawful acquirer' pursuant to this provision, while it applies a very strict standard to Art. 5(2) Software Directive.[53] Anyhow, making back-up copies is one of the mandatory minimum rights explicitly granted by Art. 5(2) Software Directive. Thus, it does not seem convincing to limit the circulation of the copy and thereby diminishing the economic essence of this exception for the lawful user according to Art. 5 Software Directive.

a.   *Consequences in Practice*

In fact, the numerous difficulties in implementing the *UsedSoft* doctrine, which are partly due to certain contradictions and vague concepts in the judgment itself and partly the result of (overly strict) standards with regard to the application of the *UsedSoft* requirements by the national courts, from these authors' viewpoint have led to a situation where the second-hand software market in Europe is either grey and uncertain or controlled by the incumbents in the software market such as Microsoft, Oracle and the like. As regards a possible generalisation of the *UsedSoft* doctrine, the aftermath of *UsedSoft* does not provide for a particularly encouraging panorama.

---

49. Case C-166/15, para. 54; however, this seems to be rather an *obiter dictum* as this statement does not appear in the final ruling, *Wiebe*, 'Von der Erschöpfung der ‚virtuellen Kopie' zur Erschöpfung der Lizenz?', Zeitschrift für Urheber- und Medienrecht (ZUM) 44, 47 [2017].
50. *Hauck*, 'Der Erschöpfungsgrundsatz im Patent- und Urheberrecht', EuZW 648 [2017]; *Wiebe* (*supra* n. 49) ZUM 44, 45 et seq. [2017].
51. *Wiebe*, 'The Principle of Exhaustion in European Copyright Law and the Distinction Between Digital Goods and Digital Services', GRUR Int. 114 [2009]; *Wiebe* (*supra* n. 49) ZUM 44, 45 [2017].
52. *Wiebe* (*supra* n. 49) ZUM 44, 45 et seq. [2017]; cf. *Leistner* (*supra* n. 33) WRP 995, 995 [2014]; cf. *Dreier/Leistner*, 'Urheberrecht im Internet, die Forschungsherausforderungen', GRUR 881, 888 [2013]. Also skeptical but with regard to the German Federal Court's *UsedSoft III* decision, *Sattler*, Remarks to *UsedSoft III*, GRUR 779, 779 et seqq. [2015].
53. *Hauck* (*supra* n. 50) EuZW 648 [2017]; *Heydn*, Remarks on *Ranks*, MMR 19, 23 et seq. [2017].

B. EXTENSION OF THE *USEDSOFT* DOCTRINE TO OTHER SECOND-HAND DIGITAL GOODS

Despite these difficulties, the basic economic considerations behind *UsedSoft* led to the follow-up question as to whether the exhaustion doctrine for digital software could and should also be applied to other digital goods such as e-books, audiobooks or video games. As the CJEU tried to strike a balance between exclusive copyright protection and the needs of legitimate trade for the digital era[54] within the European Union, the same approach could be fruitful beyond software.

However, although the CJEU set forth certain requirements and standards for online exhaustion of computer programs which may indeed be applied to a digital context in general, many further problems arise – all the more with regard to other digital goods. Arguing from an economic perspective that focusses on safeguarding legitimate trade or a policy approach based on the coherence of European copyright law, it may nonetheless seem convincing to generalise the online exhaustion beyond computer programs. Consequently, beyond the fundamental question as to whether – with hindsight – *UsedSoft* was a helpful judgment, the key question is whether there are reasonable grounds that justify a distinction between computer programs, hybrid works and other digital goods.

I. Legal Framework and Status Quo

1. *UsedSoft* Judgment

The *UsedSoft* decision itself contains no clear statement concerning the extension of online exhaustion to other kinds of digital goods.[55] On the one hand, the CJEU relies on an economic point of view stating that the sale of a computer program on CD-ROM or DVD and the sale of a program by downloading it from the internet are similar.[56] Furthermore, it refers to the fundamental freedoms in general ('in order to avoid partitioning of markets') to define the objective of exhaustion without differentiating between 'goods' and 'services'.[57] Such interpretation may speak in favour of extending the *UsedSoft* doctrine to other digital goods. On the other hand, the CJEU explicitly states that the Software Directive constitutes a *lex specialis* in relation to the InfoSoc Directive, thereby pointing in the opposite direction.[58] Offering the download of a computer program would constitute a first sale within the Software Directive's meaning even if it might be covered at the same time by the concept of 'communication to the public' pursuant to Art. 3(1) of the InfoSoc Directive – which is not contained in the Software Directive.[59] The CJEU furthermore stresses that the

---

54. *Leistner* (*supra* n. 14) CMLR 559, 574 [2014].
55. *Leistner* (*supra* n. 33) WRP 995, 1003 [2014]; *Ohly*, Urheberrecht in der digitalen Welt, Munich 2014, p. F51 et seq.; *Stieper*, 'Remarks to UsedSoft', ZUM 668, 670 [2012]; *Ganzhorn*, 'Ist ein E-Book ein Buch?', CR 492, 494 [2014].
56. *UsedSoft* (*supra* n. 2) paras. 61 et seq.
57. Cf. *ibid.*, para. 62.
58. *Ibid.*, para. 51.
59. *Ibid.*, para. 51.

intention of the European Union legislature was to assimilate tangible and intangible copies of computer programs for the purposes of the protection laid down by the Software Directive.[60] Arguing from this perspective, a different treatment of software and other digital goods seems to be inherent.

2. Further European Case Law

a. Attempts at Generalising Usedsoft Beyond Software

In contrast to the *UsedSoft* decision itself, Advocate General Szpunar in the case *VOB/Leenrecht* proposed that the InfoSoc Directive ('copies of the work') as well as the Directive on rental and lending rights[61] essentially use the same terminology as the Software Directive ('copy of a program').[62] Due to the principle of terminological consistency[63] and coherence of European copyright, the term 'copy' used in both the InfoSoc Directive and the Directive on rental and lending right, ought to be understood as including digital copies without a physical medium – corresponding to the definition and conditions set forth in *UsedSoft*.[64] The CJEU did not follow the Advocate General's reasoning but at least ruled – without clarifying the question of digital exhaustion itself – that e-lending would be covered by the Directive on rental and lending right.[65] In the context of answering the second referred question, the Court held that e-books could be subject to Art. 4 InfoSoc Directive, from which a certain tendency may be deduced to treat the second sale of digital goods consistently with the *UsedSoft* decision.[66] At the same time, the judgment shows a cautious approach as ultimately the Court exclusively relied on an interpretation of the Directive on rental and lending right.

Even before this decision, Advocate General Kokott had proposed a general exhaustion principle for e-books, e-music and other digital goods in the widely noted *Murphy* case.[67] But the CJEU did not follow the Advocate General's opinion, either.[68]

In fact, the more recent *Allposters* decision[69] rather seems to point in the opposite direction as it rejects exhaustion for cases where a reproduction of a protected work

---

60. Cf. *ibid.*, para. 58.
61. Directive 2006/115.
62. Case C-174/15 *VOB v. Leenrecht* [2016] Opinion of Advocate General *Szpunar* 16 June 2016, ECLI:EU:C:2016:459, paras. 50 et seqq. See *Malevanny* (supra n. 12) CR 422, 426 [2013].
63. This principle was even developed by the CJEU itself, Case C-403, 429/08 *Football Association Premier League v. Murphy* [2011] ECLI:EU:C:2011:631; *Hansen/Wolff-Rojczyk*, Remarks to UsedSoft, GRUR 908, 909 [2012].
64. *VOB v. Leenrecht* [2016] Opinion of Advocate General *Szpunar* 16 June 2016, ECLI:EU:C: 2016:459, para. 52.
65. Case C-174/15 *VOB v. Leenrecht* [2016], ECLI:EU:C:2016:856, paras. 27 et seqq.
66. *Marly/Wirz*, 'Die Weiterverbreitung digitaler Güter', EuZW 16, 19 [2017].
67. Case C-403, 429/08 *Football Association Premier League v. Murphy* [2011] Opinion of Advocate General *Kokott*, 3 February 2011, ECLI:EU:C:2011:43, paras. 187 et seq.
68. Applying the exhaustion principle to the *Murphy* case would not have worked, however, as a different subject was at issue.
69. Case C-419/13 *Allposters v. Pictoright* [2015], ECLI:EU:C:2015:27.

has undergone an alteration of its medium and is placed on the market again in its new form.[70]

While the picture with regard to the question of a fundamental extension of online exhaustion to all copyright protected subject matter is so far incoherent, clarification might be underway. In 2017, the Court of The Hague decided to submit a reference to the CJEU and recently (March 2018) finalised the questions on the generalisation of online exhaustion to be referred to the CJEU. A decision on this can therefore be expected in 2019.[71]

b. *Nintendo: Inconsistencies in the Legal Framework for Complex Software Products*

In fact, consideration of online exhaustion beyond computer programs are not only of a general nature with regard to entirely different products such as e-books or e-music, but also point to certain specific 'inner' inconsistencies with regard to complex software products as such.

When looking at mixed or hybrid complex works, such as computer programs, specific overlap problems appear as unitary products consist of various categories of works governed by different rules. Video games as the epitome of mixed works for instance contain computer programs but furthermore consist of many different work elements, such as *inter alia* the story, virtual worlds or audio-visuals.[72] In respect of inner consistency with regard to such unitary products, it has to be asked whether all computer programs – regardless of being contained in a hybrid work – can be treated alike at all. The CJEU in its *Nintendo* decision ruled that as far as parts of a video game, such as the story, graphics etc., form part of its originality, they are protected together with the entire work by copyright in the context of the system established by the InfoSoc Directive.[73] By contrast, naturally, the code as such can be protected under the Software Directive. The decision's wording makes clear, however, that the entire work is not covered by the Software Directive, and would

---

70. Referring to this decision also *Dreier* in *Dreier/Schulze* (eds.), Urheberrechtsgesetz, Munich 2015, 5th edition, § 69c para. 24a. *Rosati*, 'New CJEU reference ... asking whether InfoSoc Directive envisages digital exhaustion', [2017] at: http://ipkitten.blogspot.de/2017/07/new-cjeu-reference-asking-whether.html (accessed 8 March 2018).
71. Rechtbank Den Haag, Case C/09/492558/HA ZA 15-827, 12-07-2017, available in Dutch at: https://uitspraken.rechtspraak.nl/inziendocument?id = ECLI:NL:RBDHA:2017:7543 (accessed 16 March 2018); see for an English translation *Rosati* (*supra* n. 70). See finalised questions in Rechtbank Den Haag, Case C/09/492558/HAZA15-827, 28-03-2018, available in Dutch at: https://uitspraken.rechtspraak.nl/inziendocument?id = ECLI:NL:RB-DHA:2018:3455 and for an English translation *Rosati*, Does the InfoSoc Directive envisage digital exhaustion? Questions in the Tom Kabinet CJEU reference finalized (at last) [2018] available at: http://ipkitten.blogspot.de/2018/03/does-infosoc-directive-envisage-digital.html (both accessed 22 April 2018).
72. Case C-355/12 *Nintendo v. PC Box* [2014] ECLI:EU:C:2014:25, para. 23.
73. Case C-355/12 (*supra* n. 72), para. 23. In this regard, the question appears as to whether all parts have to be treated separately or whether the video game as a whole is protected under both directive regimes.

thus (under the InfoSoc Directive) not be a suitable object of online exhaustion.[74] Obviously, this leads to the application of different protection standards – on the one hand the Software Directive for computer programs and on the other hand the InfoSoc Directive for other categories of works – with regard to one and the same unitary product.

Looking for instance at the legal treatment of technical protection measures, such different results become perfectly apparent and practically relevant. While technical protection measures regarding computer programs are only justified in order to control the disabling of the first acquirer's copy in the context of exhaustion,[75] technical protection measures with regard to other work categories according to Art. 6 of the InfoSoc Directive have to pass a general proportionality test.[76] For online-distributed video games, this raises the issue that only rights in the computer programs included in a video game as such would be exhausted whilst rights in other work categories that equally form part of this unitary game would not, thereby hindering a resale and thus development of any second-hand market. Practically, the overlap results in the following paradox: computer programs in the strict sense must not contain technical protection measures that impede resale, yet hybrid works such as video games can contain such measures as far as they are proportionate in the sense of Art. 6 InfoSoc Directive.[77] Consequently, some scholars promote extending the online exhaustion at least to such hybrid works, as otherwise the overlap effectively undermines the effectiveness of the *UsedSoft* doctrine, since most software products are 'mixed', anyway.[78] From the present authors' viewpoint, these considerations are indeed justified. However, this does not solve the fundamental problem as to whether and on what concepts to generalise the *UsedSoft* doctrine beyond the area of computer software.

3. European Primary and Secondary Law

As the existing case law of the CJEU hitherto contains no clear guidance with regard to a possible further generalisation of *UsedSoft*, in the following part, European primary and secondary law will be interpreted in order to develop a correct solution for the online exhaustion issue for other subject matter on the basis of existing legislation.

Contrary to the Software Directive, the InfoSoc Directive does not distinguish between tangible or intangible forms of a copy.[79] Recital 29 states that '[t]he question of exhaustion does not arise in the case of services and on-line services in particular' which applies explicitly 'with regard to a material copy [...] made by a user of such

---

74. Such understanding is promoted by the German Federal Court (BGH) Case I ZR 25/15 *World of Warcraft I* (6 Oct 2016) GRUR 266 [2017], para. 66.
75. *UsedSoft* (*supra* n. 2) paras. 79, 87.
76. Case C-355/12 (*supra* n. 72), para. 30; see also *Schneider/Spindler* (*supra* n. 6) CR 213, 222 [2014].
77. *Schneider/Spindler* (*supra* n. 6) CR 213, 222 [2014]. Regarding the proportionality of technical protection measures for video games, see further *Conraths*, 'Verhältnismäßigkeit technischer Schutzmaßnahmen für Videospiele', CR 170 [2018].
78. *Schneider/Spindler* (*supra* n. 6) CR 213, 222 [2014].
79. *UsedSoft* (*supra* n. 2) para. 55.

a service with the consent of the right holder'.[80] Although recitals in general are not legally binding,[81] they have to be considered for the Directive's interpretation. Hence, within the scope of the InfoSoc Directive, applying the *UsedSoft* doctrine to other digital goods seems to be clearly inappropriate, especially as material copies are explicitly mentioned.[82]

However, it has to be borne in mind that Recital 29 goes back to the *Coditel I* decision,[83] in which the CJEU rejected applying the exhaustion principle to the right of public communication with regard to public performances of a film.[84] The ruling thus concerned the specific case of film screening where a single fee cannot economically satisfy the right holder's interest in obtaining an appropriate remuneration.[85] This might have been the reason why the CJEU held the situation in question to be different from placing a tangible form of the work at the disposal of the public.[86] Notwithstanding these qualifications and conditions, the ruling was – perhaps prematurely – generalised in Recital 29 of the InfoSoc Directive.[87] Recital 29 of the InfoSoc Directive hence explicitly lays down that offering a download is not to be treated as a 'sale', but constitutes a service.[88]

---

80. Recital 29 reads: 'The question of exhaustion does not arise in the case of services and on-line services in particular. This also applies with regard to a material copy of a work or other subject matter made by a user of such a service with the consent of the right holder. Therefore, the same applies to rental and lending of the original and copies of works or other subject matter which are services by nature. Unlike CD-ROM or CD-I, where the intellectual property is incorporated in a material medium, namely an item of goods, every on-line service is in fact an act which should be subject to authorization where the copyright or related right so provides.'
81. *Ganzhorn* (*supra* n. 55) CR 492, 494 [2014]; *Hartmann*, 'Weiterverkauf und "Verleih" online vertriebener Inhalte – Zugleich Anmerkung zu EuGH, Urteil vom 3. Juli 2012, Rs. C-128/11 – UsedSoft ./. Oracle', GRUR Int. 980, 982 [2012]; *Kubach*, 'Musik aus zweiter Hand – ein neuer digitaler Trödelmarkt?', CR 279, 282 [2013].
82. *Senftleben* (*supra* n. 12) NJW 2924, 2925 [2012]; *Leistner* (*supra* n. 12) JZ 1140, 1142 [2011]; *Leistner* (*supra* n. 39) CR 209, 213 f. [2011]; *Wiebe* (*supra* n. 51) GRUR Int. 114, 116 et seqq. [2009]. Contra: *Hoeren/Jakopp*, 'Der Erschöpfungsgrundsatz im digitalen Umfeld – Notwendigkeit eines binnenmarktkonformen Verständnisses', MMR 646, 649 [2014]; *Rigamonti*, 'Der Handel mit Gebrauchtsoftware nach schweizerischem Urheberrecht', GRUR Int. 14, 23 [2009]; *Hartmann* (*supra* n. 81) GRUR-Int. 980, 983 et seq. [2012]; *Ganzhorn* (*supra* n. 55) CR 492, 494 [2014].
83. Case 62/79 *CODITEL v. Ciné Vog Films* [1980], ECR 881.
84. *Leistner* (*supra* n. 12) JZ 1140, 1141 [2011]; *Leistner*, 'The German second-hand software controversy', in *Drexl* et. al (eds.), Technology and Competition, Contributions in Honour of Hanns Ullrich, p. 205, 226; cf. *Schneider/Spindler* (*supra* n. 6) CR 213, 223 [2014]; *Redeker*, 'Das Konzept der digitalen Erschöpfung – Urheberrecht für die digitale Welt', CR 73, 76 [2014].
85. *Leistner* (*supra* n. 12) JZ 1140, 1141 [2011]; *Leistner* (*supra* n. 39) CR 209, 212 et seq. [2011]
86. Case 62/79 *CODITEL v. Ciné Vog Films* [1980], ECR 881, paras. 12 et seq.; *Wiebe* (*supra* n. 51) GRUR Int. 114, 114 et seq. [2009]; *Leistner* (*supra* n. 39) CR 209, 212 [2011].
87. *Leistner* (*supra* n. 12) JZ 1140, 1141 [2011]; *Leistner* (*supra* n. 39) CR 209, 212 et seq. [2011]; *Leistner* (*supra* n. 14) CMLR 559, 575 [2014].
88. *Bäcker/Höfinger*, 'Online-Vertrieb digitaler Inhalte: Erstvertrieb, nachgelagerte Nutzungen und nachgelagerte Märkte', ZUM 623, 637 [2013]. Recital 33 of the Database Directive (Directive 96/9/EC) explicitly excludes online databases from exhaustion in the same

Given the historical background, one might thus argue that Recital 29 only concerns the specific situations of public performances that are similar to 'a service' and where a one-time payment does not provide the right holder with an appropriate remuneration for the use of his work. In *Coditel I*, it was decisive that the public performance could be repeated without limits and that the right holder could only get an appropriate remuneration by further controlling these performances.[89] Yet according to the economic assumptions behind *UsedSoft* where an unlimited right of use was granted, a download amounts to a 'sale', equalling the right holder's interests in these cases with those of right holders selling a material medium, where a one-time payment would be appropriate. One might therefore argue that in comparable situations of 'sale' of other work categories, Recital 29, read in light of its historical background, does not prevent the development of a principle of online exhaustion. Effectively, this would amount to a teleological limitation of Recital 29.

The question as to whether such a narrow construction of Recital 29 of the InfoSoc Directive would be in line with European primary law is not easy to answer. European primary law distinguishes between goods and services with regard to the fundamental freedoms (Art. 28 et seqq. TFEU – Art. 56 TFEU).[90] It might be in line with that fundamental distinction to qualify only tangible goods as suitable objects of exhaustion.[91] Ultimately, the question comes down to an economically reasonable definition of the concepts of goods and services. If 'sale' of digital goods – under a teleological single market-oriented perspective – were found to be closer to the concept of free movement of goods than to the free movement of services,[92] primary law would not prevent but even support the development of a general principle of online exhaustion in spite of Recital 29 of the InfoSoc Directive.

Referring to the CJEU's statement that 'the existence of a transfer of ownership changes an "act of communication to the public" provided for [in Art. 3 InfoSoc Directive] into an act of distribution referred to' in Art. 4 of the Software Directive,[93]

---

manner. The CJEU confirmed this in its decision *BHB v. Hill*, Case C-203/02 (2004), ECLI:EU:C:2004:695, para. 59. See further *Wiebe* (*supra* n. 51) GRUR Int. 114, 114 et seq., 116 et seqq. [2009]. However, it is to be considered in this regard that the Database Directive – comparable to the Software Directive – grants necessary use rights in its Art. 6(1).

89. Case 62/79 *CODITEL v. Ciné Vog Films* [1980], ECR 881, paras. 12 et seq. The Commission's first draft of the InfoSoc Directive relies on the same reasoning in order to consider online distribution as a service, see *Wiebe* (*supra* n. 51) GRUR Int. 114, 114 et seq. [2009].

90. *Wiebe* (*supra* n. 51) GRUR Int. 114, 114 et seq. [2009]; *Leistner* (*supra* n. 39) CR 209, 212 [2011]; *Bäcker/Höfinger* (*supra* n. 88) ZUM 623, 637 [2013]. Cf. also *Senftleben* (*supra* n. 12) NJW 2924, 2926 [2012] who assumes that excluding digital exhaustion in the InfoSoc and the Database Directive constitute the real exception of a general principle. Since in *UsedSoft*, the CJEU refers to the *Murphy* decision (see paras. 62 et seq.) in which the freedom of service (Art. 56 TFEU) was decisive, it is argued that this distinction would become blurred, *Vinje/Marsland/Gärtner* (*supra* n. 14) CRi 97, 101 [2012]; *Dreier/Leistner* (*supra* n. 52) GRUR 881, 888 [2013].

91. *Wiebe* (*supra* n. 51) GRUR Int. 114, 114 et seq. [2009]; *Leistner* (*supra* n. 39) CR 209, 212 [2011]; *Bäcker/Höfinger* (*supra* n. 88) ZUM 623, 637 [2013]; *Senftleben* (*supra* n. 12) NJW 2924, 2926 [2012].

92. CJEU Case C-403, 429/08 (*supra* n. 12).

93. *UsedSoft* (*supra* n. 2) para. 51.

it can therefore be argued that Recital 29 of the InfoSoc Directive does not contradict the application of online exhaustion to other digital goods.[94]

4. Member States

At the level of the Member States, the courts of first and second instance were not uniform in extending the exhaustion principle to other digital goods such as e-books or audio books. German Courts, for instance, consistently refused to apply online exhaustion to e-books,[95] audio books[96] and computer games.[97] In contrast, the Dutch Courts found that online exhaustion in general is possible and specifically confirmed such reasoning for e-books.[98] It was in the course of these proceedings that the Court of The Hague decided to submit the above-mentioned reference to the CJEU.[99] Accordingly, there is no uniform trend throughout the Member States as to whether or not to apply online exhaustion to digital goods beyond computer programs.

II. Main Problems with Regard to Other Digital Goods

In sum, the actual status quo does not lead to a clear answer as to whether digital exhaustion should be extended to all categories of copyrighted works. Even though some of the above-mentioned arguments weigh heavily in favour of a general principle of online exhaustion in cases of first sale, considerable doubts remain with regard to the 'technical' legal construction of online exhaustion. These problems are even more prominent with regard to general copyright than in the specific area of software, as will be presently shown. In addition, the immense practical problems of implementing the *UsedSoft* ruling even in the relatively coherent software markets[100] will no doubt resurface in the context of other digital goods.

---

94. *Dreier* (*supra* n. 70) § 69c para. 24a.
95. Court of Appeal (OLG) Hamburg Case 10 U 5/1 (14 Dec 2014), Gewerblicher Rechtsschutz und Urheberrecht Rechtsprechungs-Report (GRUR-RR) 361 [2015].
96. Court of Appeal (OLG) Hamm Case 22 U 60/13 *Hörbuch-AGB* (15 May 2014), GRUR 853 [2014] and Court of Appeal (OLG) Stuttgart Case 2 U 49/11 (3 Nov 2011), GRUR-RR 243 [2012].
97. District Court (LG) Berlin Case 16 O 73/13 (11 Mar 2014) *Seriennummer* GRUR-RR 490 [2014] and District Court (LG) Berlin Case 15 O 56/13 (21 Jan 2014), Zeitschrift für Urheber- und Medienrecht – Rechtsprechungsdienst (ZUM-RD) 504 [2014]. With regard to mixed works see further *supra* section B.I.2.
98. See for an overview in the English language *Rosati* (*supra* n. 70); *Apel*, 'Keine Anwendung der "UsedSoft"-Rechtsprechung des EuGH jenseits von Computerprogrammen – Eine Bestandsaufnahme zur Erschöpfung bei "gebrauchten" digitalen Gütern', ZUM 640, 643 [2015]. After an preliminary injunction (District Court of Amsterdam Case C/13/567567/ KG ZA 14-795 SP/MV, *Nederlands Uitgeversverbond and Groep Algemene Uitgevers v. Tom Kabinet* (2014), see for the decision in English CRi 47 [2015]) equally the Court of Appeal held that exhaustion is generally possible for e-books (Case 200.154.572/01 SKG, 20-01-2015, available in Dutch at: https://uitspraken.rechtspraak.nl/inziendocument?id=E-CLI:NL:GHAMS:2015:66 (accessed 16 March 2018).
99. See *supra* section B.I.2.a.
100. See *supra* section B.I.

1. Construction of the Second Acquirer's Rights of Use

The main problem with regard to general copyright is how to construct the second acquirer's necessary rights of use for transferring and using – especially reproducing – digital goods under the InfoSoc Directive. This is because the InfoSoc Directive does not contain a provision similar to Art. 5 Software Directive which grants rights of use to the lawful acquirer.[101] Lacking a comparable provision, an acquirer may solely rely on rights granted by the underlying licensing agreement.[102] Accordingly, a second acquirer could derive his rights of use only from a lawfully transferred copy and the rights vested therein.[103] This ultimately comes down to the key question as to whether a lawful resale requires the right holder's consent and whether contractual clauses which prohibit a transfer are valid or void.[104] Hence, the missing mandatory exception in the InfoSoc Directive seems to argue in favour of a search for market-oriented solutions to the problem in contract law.

One possible way out might be a presumption of the seller's implied consent to grant necessary rights of use to the second acquirer if all requirements developed in *UsedSoft* are met.[105] In that regard it could be argued that the first sale doctrine allowing the resale would be 'pointless' if the second acquirer was not allowed to use the acquired goods.[106] Thus, the first acquirer's rights of use would have to be transferable to the second acquirer.[107]

Another approach would be a primary law oriented interpretation of the InfoSoc Directive in light of the CJEU's *Evora* judgment.[108] In the decision, the Court used Art. 36 TFEU (former Art. 30 ECT) for extending the exhaustion principle in order to justify that 'besides being free to resell [...] [trade marked] goods, [the acquirer] is free to make use of the trade mark in order to bring to the public's attention the further

---

101. *Bäcker/Höfinger* (supra n. 88) ZUM 623, 638 [2013]; *Leistner* (supra n. 14) CMLR 559, 584 et seq. [2014]; *Ohly* (supra n. 55), p. F52. Similarly, Art. 6 Database Directive provides certain minimum use rights.
102. *Bäcker/Höfinger* (supra n. 88) ZUM 623, 638 [2013]; *Haberstumpf* (supra n. 37) CR 561, 567 [2012].
103. *Haberstumpf* (supra n. 37) CR 561, 567 [2012]; cf. *Leistner* (supra n. 33) WRP 995, 1000 [2014].
104. *Leistner* (supra n. 39) CR 209, 215 [2011]; *Hilty*, '"Exhaustion" in the Digital Age', Max Planck Institute for Innovation and Competition Research Paper No. 15-09, available at: http://ssrn.com/abstract=2689518 (accessed 16 March 2018), p. 11; *Haberstumpf* (supra n. 37) CR 561, 566 [2012].
105. *Hilty/Köklü/Hafenbrädl* (supra n. 27) 44 IIC 263, 285, 288 [2013]; *Hilty* (supra n. 104), p. 4 et seq., 16 et seqq.; *Naylor/Parris*, 'After ReDigi: contrasting the EU and US approaches to the re-sale of second-hand digital assets', 35 European Intellectual Property Review (EIPR) 487, 490 [2013].
106. *Hilty/Köklü/Hafenbrädl* (supra n. 27) 44 IIC 263, 285, 288 [2013]; *Hilty* (supra n. 104), p. 12, 19.
107. *Hilty/Köklü/Hafenbrädl* (supra n. 27) 44 IIC 263, 285, 288 [2013]; *Hilty* (supra n. 104), p. 12, 19.
108. Case C-337/95 *Dior v. Evora* [1997], ECLI:EU:C:1997:517; *Leistner*, Urheberrecht in der digitalen Welt, JZ 846, 851 [2014]; *Dreier* (supra n. 70) § 69c para. 25; *Leistner* (supra n. 14) CMLR 559, 584 [2014].

commercialization of those goods.'[109] However, in light of the decisions discussed above,[110] it seems that the CJEU is hesitant to take such a step.[111]

Alternatively, rights of non-commercial use by private parties could at most be construed under the private copying exception (Art. 5(2)(b) InfoSoc Directive).[112] However, the InfoSoc Directive is not mandatory in this regard and resulted in different approaches amongst the Member States.[113] But even if applicable, this would solely provide a remedy for private users and at the same time result in further questions regarding the private copying exception's relation to further-reaching restrictions in end-user licensing contracts.[114]

2. Economic Considerations

The CJEU states that 'from an economic point of view, the sale of a computer program on CD-ROM or DVD and the sale of a program by downloading from the internet are similar.'[115] From this perspective, it may seem persuasive to generalise the concept of online exhaustion beyond computer programs.[116] But even in an economic context, two important additional aspects have to be taken into account. First, unlike a physical medium, digital goods can be used by more than one person (non-rivalry) and are not subject to relevant degradation.[117] This is different for computer programs that without regular updating become outdated and suffer a reduction in value.[118] In sum, an economic comparability cannot be apodictically presumed, as certain differences and various aspects of the works in question have to be considered.[119]

---

109. Case C-337/95 *Dior v. Evora* [1997], ECLI:EU:C:1997:517, para. 38.
110. See section B.I.2.
111. Cf. also *Rosati* (*supra* n. 70).
112. *Malevanny* (*supra* n. 12) CR 422, 426 [2013]; *Stieper* (*supra* n. 55) ZUM 668, 670 [2012]; *Bäcker/Höfinger* (*supra* n. 88) ZUM 623, 638 [2013]; *Ohly* (*supra* n. 55) p. F53.
113. *Malevanny* (*supra* n. 12) CR 422, 426 [2013].
114. *Leistner* (*supra* n. 14) CMLR 559, 584 [2014].
115. *UsedSoft* (*supra* n. 2) para. 61.
116. *Leistner* (*supra* n. 12) JZ 1140, 1141 [2011]. See e.g. *Druschel*, 'Die Regelung digitaler Inhalte im Gemeinsamen Europäischen Kaufrecht (GEKR)', GRUR Int. 125, 131 [2015]; *Redeker* (*supra* n. 84) CR 73, 74 [2014].
117. *Zech*, 'Vom Buch zur Cloud. Die Verkehrsfähigkeit digitaler Güter, Zeitschrift für Geistiges Eigentum', ZGE, 368, 393 et seq. [2013]. Skeptical in this regard *Hilty* (*supra* n. 104), p. 15.
118. *Zech* (*supra* n. 117) ZGE 368, 394 [2013].
119. *Ohly* (*supra* n. 55), p. F52; *Vinje/Marsland/Gärtner* (*supra* n. 14) CRi 97, 101 [2012]; *Haberstumpf* (*supra* n. 37) CR 561, 569 et seq. [2012]; *Leistner* (*supra* n. 12) JZ 1140, 1141 [2011]; cf. *Hansen/Wolff-Rojczyk* (*supra* n. 63) GRUR 904, 909 [2012]. See also for an economic in-depth analysis *Kerber*, 'Exhaustion of Digital Goods: An Economic Perspective', ZGE 149 [2016] who even comes to the conclusion that from an economic perspective 'despite the important benefits of exhaustion it is very questionable whether it can be recommended to support the emergence of entirely free secondary markets for copyright-protected digital copies' stating 'that the non-application of exhaustion might be recommended as the general rule and exhaustion only should be applied under more or less narrowly defined conditions', p. 166.

Secondly, even when assuming an economic comparability and extending online exhaustion to works of music, literature etc., this might ultimately result in even further strengthening and consolidating of the market position of dominant software producers and service providers, in particular platforms and infrastructure providers such as Google, Oracle, Microsoft or Amazon. This is mainly due to practical problems in implementing new second-hand markets with regard to digital goods. As for traditional exhaustion, the physical copy of the work (even a DVD with holograms etc.) is a valid token of authenticity, lawful ownership and transferability in trade; as for digitally distributed works, a comparable token of lawfulness does not exist and will have to be replaced by different mechanisms, such as (costly and complicated) evidence, (often insufficient) certificates, or TPMs. The use of such measures, in particular TPMs, might lead to new risks for free competition in second-hand markets and might make the establishment of second-hand trade business models by new entrants too complicated and costly and thus even erect new market entry barriers. Therefore, only at a first glance, new service providers entering the second hand digital goods market could rearrange the existing structures of market power.[120] On a more thorough analysis, it seems more likely that leading firms will adapt to the new situation by changing their licence terms, providing access- or use-based models[121] or even offering second-hand sales themselves.[122] Establishing rental models for instance will probably not result in lower prices but merely reduce the market for second-hand software causing at the same time increased administrative costs in comparison with the single payment of a fee.[123] Further, unlike 'global players', smaller businesses or start-ups may not be able to offer a resale system which complies with the difficult standards of the *UsedSoft* decision and prove such compliance in court.

Looking at the objective of the exhaustion principle, that is, not to allow the right holder to control the resale of copyrighted works, this might amount to adverse and undesired consequences for the digital goods markets. Particularly, it has to be considered how right holders would adapt and design their future licence agreements and which conditions they would impose on their costumers – possibly leaving them in a less favourable situation than before.[124]

III. Conclusion

The existing framework of European copyright law is inconclusive regarding the question as to whether the *UsedSoft* online exhaustion principle should be extended beyond the specific area of computer programs. For certain hybrid works which are close to computer programs as such, an extension of online exhaustion should be considered. With regard to the more fundamental question as to whether the principle should be generalised for all categories of works, various reasons may justify a different treatment of software and other digital goods. A major obstacle consists

---

120. *Mezei*, 'Digital First Sale Doctrine Ante Portas', Journal of Intellectual Property, Information Technology and E-Commerce Law (JIPITEC) 23, 55 [2015], para. 186.
121. See *infra* section C.
122. *Mezei* (*supra* n. 120) JIPITEC 23, 55 [2015], para. 186.
123. *Vinje/Marsland/Gärtner* (*supra* n. 14) CRi 97, 100 [2012].
124. See in the same direction *Vinje/Marsland/Gärtner* (*supra* n. 14) CRi 97, 101 [2012].

in the fact that the InfoSoc Directive lacks a provision similar to Art. 5 Software Directive which grants necessary rights of use to the lawful acquirer. Accordingly, the CJEU seems reluctant to extend the online exhaustion to all digital goods under the existing provisions.

Against this inconclusive background, the practical and technical problems stemming from the *UsedSoft* decision with regard to the resale of software weigh substantially against any premature generalisation. Indeed, under an economic and policy perspective, it seems questionable if such extension would result in a coherent framework for digital resale markets.[125]

C. FUTURE PERSPECTIVE: ALTERNATIVE MECHANISMS IN EUROPEAN LAW TO GUARANTEE THE FREE MOVEMENT OF COPYRIGHT-RELATED GOODS & SERVICES

As to guaranteeing the free movement of copyright-related goods and services in the digital age, extending the online exhaustion to all digital goods represents one (and perhaps not even the most preferable) remedy.

Indeed, many of the above-mentioned questions will disappear as cloud services (e.g. SAAS) and other access- or use-based models become prevalent – both for software and other digital goods.[126] As they are classified as rental models and do not constitute 'sales' in the sense of the *UsedSoft* doctrine, the exhaustion principle is not applicable in the first place.[127] This development reflects the general trend from transferring ownership in a copy towards providing a service ('from property to access'), which holds true for all kinds of digital goods.[128] By changing their licence terms, software producers and service providers will try to circumvent a possible exhaustion and thereby hinder an evolving second-hand market through the backdoor. In the end, the *UsedSoft* decision thus primarily should have major effects on contract law and indeed the main question should be whether mandatory contract law rules are needed in the specific area of end-user licence contracts with regard to the different kinds of copyrighted works.

Consequently, the present authors take the view that ultimately all comes down to a review of the underlying contract and licensing terms – with regard to the relevant type of contract ('sale/rental/licence'?), the validity of terms excluding the transfer of

---

125. For a comprehensive overview over the opinion of German scholars see *Specht*, 'Beschränkung der Verkehrsfähigkeit digitaler Güter durch technische Schutzmaßnahmen', ZGE 289, 290, Fn. 5 [2016].
126. *Rosati* (*supra* n. 42); *Hilty* (*supra* n. 104), p. 3, 22; *Zech*, 'Lizenzen für die Benutzung von Musik, Film und E-Books in der Cloud', ZUM 3 [2014]; *Becker*, 'Ein modernes Urheberrecht. Von der Nutzungshandlung zum digitalen Lebensbereich', ZGE 239, 246 et seq. [2016]; *Senftleben* (*supra* n. 12) NJW 2924, 2927 [2012]; *Leistner* (*supra* n. 39) CR 209, 215 [2011]; *Wiebe* (*supra* n. 51) GRUR Int. 114, 118 [2009].
127. *Becker* (*supra* n. 126) ZGE 239, 246 [2016]; *Witzel*, 'Remarks to the UsedSoft decision', CRi 116, 123 [2012]; *Leistner* (*supra* n. 33) WRP 995, 1002 [2014].
128. *Ohly* (*supra* n. 55), p. F50; *Vinje/Marsland/Gärtner* (*supra* n. 14) CRi 97, 100 [2012]; *Arnerstål*, Licensing digital content in a sale of goods context, GRUR Int. 882, 883 [2015]; *Becker* (*supra* n. 126) ZGE 239, 243 et seqq. [2016]; *Hofmann*, E-Lending – Elektronisches Vermieten und elektronisches Verleihen aus urheberrechtlicher Sicht, ZUM 107, 108 [2018].

the copy/licence/personal ID/product key to third persons, the validity of technical protection measures etc. – instead of looking solely at statutory constructions.[129] For instance, a contractual provision in standard terms which prohibits the acquirer from reselling the respective software, although online exhaustion applies according to the *UsedSoft* doctrine, is void.[130]

Furthermore, the underlying contractual framework of rental models such as the characteristic obligations or standard terms are to be assessed as they may impose new obstacles to legitimate trade or the freedom of service resulting in even worse conditions for end users.[131] On a European level, guidelines, for instance best practices or standard contract terms as they already exist in other fields (e.g. data protection law), should hence be developed.[132]

Looking at the bigger picture, the new challenge in the digital era consists of construing copyright and general civil law in the light of constitutional law.[133] Developing a substantive concept of materialised contractual freedom with regard to the use of copyright protected subject matter could provide a remedy.[134] After assessing the existing use contracts, such an approach should take into account the fundamental rights and freedoms as well as a behavioural economic analysis of law.[135] Moreover, existing civil law rules for certain types of contracts – where such typological rules exist – for sales, rental etc. should be considered further. Thereby, certain core principles within the legal framework could be identified and developed which should ultimately serve the control of end-user licensing contracts, in particular with regard to the legal control of standard terms in such contracts. On this basis, new contract law rules for contracts between service providers and users ('tertiary

---

129. *Ohly* (*supra* n. 55), p. F55; *Zech* (*supra* n. 117) ZGE 368, 383 et seqq. [2013]; *Schneider/Spindler* (*supra* n. 6) CR 213 [2014]. See for exemplary licence terms of Netflix or Spotify in *Arnerstål* (*supra* n. 128) GRUR Int. 882, 883 [2015].
130. *Ohly* (*supra* n. 24), p. 999; *Leistner* (*supra* n. 33) WRP 995, 1002 [2014].
131. *Zech* (*supra* n. 126) ZUM 3 [2014].
132. *Ohly* (*supra* n. 24), p. 995 who at the same time refers to the difficulties due to the differences of the Member States. *Arnerstål* (*supra* n. 129) GRUR Int. 882, 884 et seqq. [2015] suggests harmonising the licensing of digital content in context of a general contract law.
133. *Leistner* (*supra* n. 39) CR 209, 215 [2011]; cf. *Ohly* (*supra* n. 24), p. 994 et seqq.
134. *Leistner* (*supra* n. 39) CR 209, 215 [2011]; cf. *Ohly* (*supra* n. 24), p. 994 et seq. See further *Leistner,* Richtiger Vertrag und lauterer Wettbewerb, Tübingen 2007; *Elkin-Koren*, 'Copyright Policy and the Limits of Freedom of Contract', 12 Berkeley Tech. L.J. 93 (1997), available at: http://scholarship.law.berkeley.edu/btlj/vol12/iss1/4 (accessed 14 March); *Elkin-Koren*, 'Copyright in a Digital Ecosystem', in *Okediji* (ed.), Copyright Law in an Age of Limitations and Exceptions, New York 2017, pp. 132–168; *Fisher III*, 'Property and Contract on the Internet', 73 Chi.-Kent. L. Rev. 1203 (1998), available at: http://scholarship.kentlaw.iit.edu/cklawreview/vol73/iss4/11 (accessed 14 March 2018). For a study from 2010 commissioned by the *Strategic Advisory Board for Intellectual Property Policy*, see Research Report The Relationship Between Copyright and Contract Law, available at: http://eprints.bournemouth.ac.uk/16091/1/_contractlaw-report.pdf (accessed 28 March 2018).
135. Concerning e.g. price discrimination, incentives etc. See further *Elikin-Koren/Salzberger*, The Law and Economics of Intellectual Property in the Digital Age, Oxon 2013.

copyright contract law'[136] or even different mechanisms like private ordering[137]) should be developed. In that regard, the consumers' reasonable expectations and their protection against certain asymmetries are to be considered.[138] Ultimately, this should result in a framework of non-mandatory and possibly certain mandatory contract law rules for standard and individual end-user licensing contracts.[139]

---

136. *Ohly* (*supra* n. 24), p. 994.
137. *Elikin-Koren/Salzberger* (*supra* n. 135), p. 150 et seqq.
138. *Ohly* (*supra* n. 24), p. 998.
139. The proposal for a Directive on certain aspects concerning contracts for the supply of digital content (Doc. COM(2015) 634 final – 2015/0287 (COD)) is insufficient in that regard and in particular unaware of the essential problems such as the online exhaustion or the resulting implications for contract law (see further *Zoll*, 'The Remedies in the Proposals of the Online Sales Directive and the Directive on the Supply of Digital Content, Journal of European Consumer and Market Law', EuCML 250 [2016]). It rather focuses on minimising the potential contractual risks for consumers to be supplied with non-conforming digital content. This is due to the fact that it merely tries to put together the shambles of the originally planned general EU contract law.

CHAPTER 8
Unjustified Threats and the Repression of Unfair Competition

Anselm Kamperman Sanders

A. INTRODUCTION

I. Information and Disparagement

In an open and competitive economy, information may never be 'perfect' as in a game theory setting, but the law nevertheless addresses the issue that in fair competition, information should be as accurate as practically possible. The Paris Convention[1] of 1883 recognises this principle in the sense that all its Member States should ensure that the competitive market is protected from acts of unfair competition. The Paris Convention lists acts that are calculated to injure the reputation of another's business or goods. These acts are not designed to benefit from the goodwill by creating confusion between one's own products and those of a competitor, but by injuring another's goodwill. The threat of litigation supported by an alleged intellectual property infringement may, in some circumstances, be calculated to do just that; discredit a competitor in the eyes of its consumers, suppliers, intermediaries, distributors, exporters, retailers, or even private individuals or the general public. When the threat of litigation turns out not to be genuine, the question arises as to whether such an unwarranted threat constitutes an act of unfair competition that is restrictive of free trade.

II. Threats and Warning Letters (Definitions)

Warning letters serve a legitimate function if they are used to notify a potential infringer that infringement proceedings may be initiated unless the alleged infringing

---

1. Paris Convention for the Protection of Industrial Property of 20 March 1883, last revised at Stockholm on 14 July 1967, 828 U.N.T.S. 305, and as amended on 28 September 1979.

activities stop. From the perspective of dispute resolution, the warning letter may lead to de-escalation of the conflict, or is conversely the precursor to a trial. The warning enables the alleged infringer to make an assessment as to whether he wishes to test the validity of the right or the non-infringing freedom to operate in court. This is especially true if the communication is addressed to a primary infringer (e.g. a manufacturer or importer) who knows the field of technology or trade. A primary infringer will typically be engaged in acts of manufacture, distribution, storage or offer for sale of infringing items. In relation to industrial property rights, these can be typically classified as follows:

Primary Acts of Infringement[2]		
Patents	For a Product	Making for disposal
		Importing for disposal
	For a Process	Using a process
Trade Marks	Applying a sign to goods or packaging	
	Causing another person to apply a sign to goods or their packaging	
	Importing for disposal, goods to which, or to the packaging of which a sign has been applied	
	Supplying services under a sign	
Designs	Making a product/article for disposal	
	Importing a product/article for disposal	

The term 'secondary infringer' is typically employed to denote those involved in the downstream distribution of items (e.g. distributors, retailers, exporters, etc.), or in the upstream value chain (i.e. component part manufacturers and suppliers). Liability can then arise if a party knowingly induces another person to infringe, or if a party knowingly contributes to the primary infringement. In both cases a communication threatening infringement action is material in ensuring that the secondary infringer is put on notice and thus has knowledge of the fact that, for example, the supply of items to the primary infringer concerns components designed for[3] a combination that is patented and infringing. Ignoring such a warning may then lead to liability for wilful contributory infringement for upstream and downstream actors. The threat of litigation may therefore be very well justified to address activities that directly infringe, or to impute knowledge in case someone contributes to a direct infringement. The threat to alleged secondary infringers may also serve the purpose of locating the primary infringer who directly infringes on account of acts of importation or

---

2. UK IPO, The Intellectual Property (Unjustified Threats) Act 2017 Business Guidance (2017, IPO) at 5, available at: https://www.gov.uk/government/publications/ip-unjustified-threats-act (accessed 16 June 2018).
3. Suppliers of staple or common goods (non-essential elements) that have multiple non-infringing uses do not typically have to worry about liability for contributory patent infringement. See for example the US Supreme Court in *Aro Mfg. Co. v. Convertible Top Replacement Co.* 377 U.S. 476 (1964), or the UPC Agreement Art. 26(2).

manufacture.[4] For this reason, there is no mandatory order in which primary or secondary infringers can or should be sued.

Communication addressed to the public at large clearly has another objective. Communications of this type merely serve the purpose of discrediting the potential infringer acting in a commercial capacity, resulting potentially in loss of sales as customers may shy away from further transactions. Threatening a primary infringer does not lead to harm to the reputation of the alleged infringer, unless this threat is made public. Threats to actors in the upward or downstream distribution chain also have a direct impact on the reputation of the primary infringer and may result in fewer sales, or the drying up of delivery of component parts.

If the threat later turns out to be unjustified because the activities turn out to be non-infringing, or if the patent, design or even trade mark right is invalidated, the damage resulting from such threats may be considerable. Actions for unjustified threats therefore serve to stop disparagement leading to damage and should in principle place the burden on plaintiff and primary infringer for the resolution of disputes on IP validity and infringement.

III. Threats and Obstacles to Legitimate Trade

The notion that intellectual property rights should not become obstacles to legitimate trade is enshrined in the World Trade Organization (WTO) Trade Related Aspects of Intellectual Property (TRIPS) Agreement.[5] Unjustified threats of IP litigation clearly reduce the freedom of trade and may cause harm to legitimate business. Read in combination, Arts. 7 and 8 TRIPS indicate that 'the protection and enforcement of intellectual property should contribute to the promotion of technological innovation [...]',[6] while such measures and procedures to enforce intellectual property rights should not 'themselves become barriers to legitimate trade'.[7]

Interpreted narrowly, one could say that the WTO TRIPS Agreement deals with international trade only, as Art. 8(2) TRIPS speaks of abuse of intellectual property and combatting anti-competitive practices that unreasonably restrain trade or adversely affect the international transfer of technology. However, the TRIPS Agreement also sets minimum standards for domestic enforcement of intellectual property, and through Art. 2 TRIPS imports Arts. 1 through 12 and Art. 19 Paris Convention (1967).

B. THE PARIS CONVENTION

According to the Paris Convention, 'any acts of competition contrary to honest practices in industrial or commercial matters' are to be considered acts of unfair

---

4. See Art. 8 Directive 2004/48/EC of the European Parliament and of the Council of 29 April 2004 on the enforcement of intellectual property rights (OJ L 157 of 30 April 2004).
5. Agreement on Trade-Related Aspects of Intellectual Property Rights, Annex 1C of the Marrakesh Agreement Establishing the World Trade Organization, signed on 15 April 1994, 33 I.L.M. 1197 (1994).
6. Art. 7 TRIPS continued: '[...] and to the transfer and dissemination of technology, to the mutual advantage of producers and users of technological knowledge and in a manner conducive to social and economic welfare, and to a balance of rights and obligations.'
7. First Preamble TRIPS Agreement.

competition. In this sense, the Paris Convention establishes a customary standard in order to establish a level playing field for market participants.

Paragraph 3 of Art. 10*bis* Paris Convention lists a number of acts that are prohibited, where subparagraph 2 is specific in relation to the injurious acts that may give rise to unjustified threats: 'false allegations, in the course of trade, which are of such a nature as to discredit the establishment, the goods or the industrial or commercial activities of a competitor.' The provision, included after the 1934 Hague Conference, addresses allegations directed to the business of a competitor, not to the competitor acting as a private individual. Still, a person's commercial reputation is relevant for the competitor's business and is to be considered as part of the overall goodwill of a business.[8] While the allegations need to be false to be actionable, even the truth may purposively be overstated so as to inflict disproportionate damage.[9] In this light one can also see how the threat of legal action can be qualified as unjustified, or unfair. Intent to harm, or any subjective element is therefore not necessary for the detrimental effect to occur. Knowledge or constructive knowledge of the untruthfulness of the allegation may in some jurisdictions be necessary. For the allegation to take effect, the addressee of the allegation must likely change his or her economic behaviour.[10] The impression that the message about the competitor, his products or services has made on the addressee need, therefore, not be false. Rather, it is enough for the actions resulting from the allegation to have a misleading effect.[11]

Applied in the context of groundless threats not addressed to the alleged infringer himself, the effect may be that private consumers may stop purchasing allegedly infringing products, retailers may stop supplying customers, distributors may cease delivery, suppliers of components may stop supplying an alleged infringer, and intermediaries may stop handling allegedly infringing products. In short, the entire supply chain surrounding an allegedly infringing product and business of a market participant may be affected without the merits or even the accuracy of the allegation being tested in court. This means that if later it turns out that there was no infringement at all, or if a patent, or other IP right, is invalidated, persons may have acted based on a meritless threat and therefore on wrong or misleading information.

---

8. S. *Ladas*, Patents Trade Marks and Related Rights – National and International Protection, 1975, Harvard University Press, at 1725–1727.
9. *Ladas* (*supra* n. 8) at 1726 cites the decision of the German Federal Court 28 November 1952, *GRUR* (1953), 130, and makes reference at 1726–1727 to French practice of qualifying as unnecessarily harmful publications of court decisions: '[L]ong after the judgment has been rendered, for the purpose of vindictiveness, or accompanied by any commentary which is unfair or inaccurate'. One should, however, be clear about the distinction: Information that is correct, in whatever form and context, is not actionable under Art. 10*bis* (3) subparagraph 2, but only to the extent that it can be regarded as misleading, e.g. where a court decision is published that dates 50 years back, while it gives the impression as if it was rendered recently.
10. See *WIPO*, Introduction to Intellectual Property Theory and Practice, 1997, Kluwer Law International, at 265–268; and *T. Cottier and P. Véron*, Concise International and European IP Law, 3rd ed., 2014, Kluwer Law International, on Art. 10*bis* (3)(2) Paris Convention.
11. Note, however, that third example of 'misleading', Art. 10*bis* (3)(2) Paris Convention, was added by the 1958 Lisbon Revision Conference and concerns false or deceptive statements about one's own product.

It is also of importance to realise that the Paris Convention deals with industrial property, meaning that primary and secondary infringers acting in commerce may indeed infringe, but the public at large, or indeed private consumers do generally not infringe as their acts will be those of private use. A threat directed or addressing at this latter category of non-infringers is particularly unjustified in such case, as it may mislead them into thinking that they are liable when they cannot be.

One would expect for the TRIPS Agreement to have expanded on Art. 10*bis* Paris Convention in the context of its enforcement chapter. This is, however, not the case. Although the Paris Convention provision is incorporated in TRIPS by reference,[12] Art. 41(1) TRIPS merely states that Member States should apply enforcement procedures 'in such a manner as to avoid the creation of barriers to legitimate trade and to provide for safeguards against their abuse'. The term 'legitimate' has been defined by the WTO panel in *Canada – Patent Protection of Pharmaceutical Products* as 'a normative claim calling for the protection of interests that are "justifiable" in the sense that they are supported by relevant policies and other social norms'.[13] Applied in this context, enforcement measures must not be used to unfairly hinder another competitor in order not to become barriers to legitimate trade.

C. THREATENING PRACTICES IN HISTORICAL PERSPECTIVE

I. A UK Case of 1881

A trader's business reputation can be encapsulated through the use of a trade mark. Actions against the tarnishment, denegration, or dilution of a trade mark[14] have become the mainstay of European trade mark law, even if controversially so.[15] It is therefore easy to forget that a more encompassing concept of damage to the goodwill of an undertaking extends to other forms of unjustifiable interference with the reputation of all those involved in economic activity. It is this wider concept that is addressed by Art. 10*bis*(3)(2) Paris Convention. Goodwill has been defined as 'the power that attracts custom', 'the benefit of a business having a good reputation under its name and regular patronage', or even 'the primary intangible asset of a company, generally comprised of reputation, contact networks, intellectual property and branding'. In Common Law jurisdictions, the concept of goodwill is at the heart of the tort of passing off.[16] The wider reputational concept can also be applied to unjustified treats that are not so much directed to infringers, but to others in the supply chain, such as suppliers, intermediaries, retailers, and customers. These threats may be classified as unfair competition by misrepresentation. The 1881 UK case of *Halsey*

---

12. Art. 2(1) TRIPS.
13. WT/DS114/13 *Canada – Patent Protection of Pharmaceutical Products* paras. 7.68–69.
14. See A. Kamperman Sanders, 'Odol: The Introduction of a Watery Concept with Steeled Resilience', in Ch. Heath and A. Kamperman Sanders (eds.), Landmark IP Cases and Their Legacy, 2011, Kluwer Law International, pp. 51–62.
15. CJEU Case C-487/07, *l'Oréal v. Bellure*, 18 June 2009, ECLI:EU:C:2009:378.
16. House of Lords, *Erven Warnink B.V. v. J. Townend & Sons (Hull) Ltd.*, [1979] AC 731, [1980] R.P.C. 31; and *Reckitt & Colman Products Ltd v. Borden Inc.*, [1990] 1 All E.R. 873.

v. Brotherhood[17] provides an early example of an effective use of threats. Both parties were involved in the production of steam engines. Mr Brotherhood systematically threatened to sue Mr Halsey's customers for patent infringement, but he never actually sued. The threats alone were sufficient in stopping the recipients from buying Mr Halsey's engines. Mr Halsey sought an injunction against Mr Brotherhood to stop threatening his customers. The courts, however, held that unless it was shown that Mr Brotherhood acted with malice, common law did not provide protection. The case prompted a legislative response in 1883[18] in the form of a statutory remedy covering groundless threats of patent litigation. In time, the UK extended this remedy to cover groundless threats provisions to trade marks, registered and unregistered design rights, European patents, Community trade marks and Community design rights. The UK's Intellectual Property (Unjustified Threats) Act 2017, which received Royal Assent on 27 April 2017, and came into effect in October 2017, furthermore includes threats based on pending industrial property applications, and Unified Patent Court actions.[19]

II. Threats in Practice

Threats to sue can take various forms. The most common will be warning letters, but also other communications or advertisements can be considered, as long as they may be construed or perceived by the recipient as a threat of infringement proceedings. Sending such communications may allow a person aggrieved by the threat to take action. This means that sending threats of litigation is not without risk. In relation to the IP right on which the threat was made, the obvious reaction would be to ask the court for a declaration of non-infringement, or to join pending oppositions or appeal proceedings.[20] Savvy aggrieved parties in the EU would even use the threat as a springboard to bring declaration of non-infringement cases in 'slow fora', where inefficiency, lack of expertise, or backlog would result in a stay of proceedings in other jurisdictions.[21] This 'Italian' or 'Belgian' torpedo practice has been largely neutralised by a recast of the Brussels Regulation[22] that prevents such abuses of the *lis pendens*

---

17. Chancery Division, *Halsey v. Brotherhood* (1881–82) LR 19 Ch 386.
18. T. Cook and C. Atton, 'The Responses in the United Kingdom and United States to Groundless Threats of Patent Infringement Proceedings', 5(2) Queen Mary Journal of Intellectual Property, 2015, pp. 206–213.
19. *UK Law Commission*, Patents, Trade Marks and Designs: Unjustified Threats, Law Com No 360 (2015, HMSO), available at: www.gov.uk/government/publications (accessed on 16 June 2018).
20. See in this context Art. 105 EPC that allows recipients of threats to join proceedings before the EPO.
21. M. Franzosi, 'Worldwide Patent Litigation and the Italian Torpedo', 19 European Intellectual Property Review, 1997, 382.
22. Regulation (EU) 1215/2012 of the European Parliament and of the Council of 12 December 2012 on jurisdiction and the recognition and enforcement of judgments in civil and commercial matters (OJ L 351 of 20.12.2012) (Recast Brussels Regulation). In particular, Art. 31(2) on *lis alibi pendens*: 'Without prejudice to Art. 26, where a court of a Member State on which an agreement as referred to in Art. 25 confers exclusive jurisdiction is seised, any court of another Member State shall stay the proceedings until such time as the court seised on the basis of the agreement declares that it has no jurisdiction under the agreement'.

rule.[23] This allows courts to make sensible[24] decisions in denying jurisdiction over validity and non-infringement claims in respect of foreign parts of European patents or other national rights.[25] Threats based on a European patent also offer the possibility of intervening in ongoing opposition or appeal proceedings before the EPO, Art. 105 European Patent Convention.

Some jurisdictions, like the UK, offer a remedy in direct response to the unjustified threat itself, like an injunction to cease and desist making threats, damages for loss caused by the threat, or a declaration that the threats were unjustified. This statutory action is not available, however, to threats in respect of an allegedly infringing primary

---

23. Art. 27 Brussels I Regulation (EC 44/2001): 'Where proceedings involving the same cause of action and between the same parties are brought in the courts of different Member States, any court other than the court first seised shall of its own motion stay its proceedings until such time as the jurisdiction of the court first seised is established'; and 'Where related actions are pending in the courts of different Member States, any court other than the court first seised may stay its proceedings.' Arts. 33 and 34 of the Recast Regulation provide that the member state court still has discretion to stay proceedings where the same or related matters have already been raised before a non-EU court. This is, however, subject to certain limitations: the foreign judgment must be capable of being recognised and enforced in the member state and the member state court must be satisfied that staying proceedings is necessary for the proper administration of justice.
24. See Italian Supreme Court, 10 June 2013, *The General Hospital Corporation and Palomar Medical Technologies Inc. v. Asclepion Laser Technologies GmbH*, 45 IIC, 2014, pp. 822–824 that revived the 'Italian torpedo' in contrast to the subsequent decisions by the District Court Milan, rejecting jurisdiction in relation to non-infringement claims in respect of Spanish and German parts of a European patent, as well as a German utility model, respectively. District Court Milan, *Schindler v. Otis*, 27 January 2014, Giurisprudenza annotata di diritto industriale 2014, p. 741; and District Court Milan, *BASF v. Bayer*, 14 December 2016, Sentenza, n.13625/2016, RG n.52005/2016; Rivista di diritto industriale, 2017, p. 309, declining jurisdiction over non-infringement of foreign portions of European Patents in light of the Recast Regulation: '[A]rt. 5. 3° comma Reg.n. 44/2001 (ora sostituito dal n. 2015 [sic] del 2012), non implica affatto il mutamento di conclusione assunto dalla Cassazione quanto alla sussistenza della giurisdizione in caso di accertamneto della contraffazione (o non conraffazione) di porzioni non italiane di brevetti europei: invero la richiesta di accertare che una certa condotta non costituisce contraffazione di una privativa implica, comunque, l'efficacia di detta privativa, che ha un perimetro territorialmente limitato allo spazio di vigenza dell'ordinamento giuridico cui fa riferimento; al di fuori di quel perimetro di efficacia, non si potrebbe parlare nè di un fatto di contraffazione né di un fatto di non contraffazione di quella privativa, e, quindi non si potrebbe neppure prospettare un "evento dannoso"'. See similarly for a rejection of jurisdiction in a torpedo case District Court of Genova *Agilent Technologies v. Oerlikon Leybold Vacuum*, 23 April 2014, in relation to invalidity arguments in support of non-infringement claims concerning the German part of a European Patent and a German utility model.
25. See conversely the far less sensible District Court Rome, *Anki v. Stadlbauer*, 5 February 2018, decision no. 2608/2015, holding with simple reference to the 2013 *Asclepion* case that: 'Italian courts have jurisdiction [...] for the French, German, Austrian and UK parts of the patent, on the basis of Art. 5.3, EU Council Regulation 44/2001 of 22 December 2000, whereby the courts for the place where the harmful event occurred or may occur have jurisdiction, and on the basis of Art. 27 of the Regulation, concerning jurisdiction for related actions.' The fact that the Recast Brussels Regulation 1215/2012 of 12 December 2012 supersedes and alters matters seems to have passed this court by. Tipico.

act. It is also important to realise that remedies potentially available for unjustified threats cannot be collated in the total damages resulting from an infringement action. The relief sought can only be awarded if the claim for unjustified threats is made.[26] In other jurisdictions, the dividing line between primary and secondary infringement threats of litigation is not always so clear. Ultimately it boils down to the question as to whether in a jurisdiction the action for unjustified threats is perceived as a useful instrument to ensure that the most natural counterparty of the plaintiff is addressed, and their dispute is settled or taken to trial. In this scenario, validity and (non-) infringement of the IP right can be fully assessed, implying also that the alleged primary infringer is the most natural counterparty. Threatening a secondary infringer may be justified for reasons of information gathering but may unnecessarily harm the reputation and business of a primary infringer. Whether the practice of sending out warning letters to parties other than the primary infringer is also dependent on the, sometimes perverse, incentives present in a legal system. The German Federal Court of Justice differentiates as follows:

> 'Giving out-of-court warning, even to a number of buyers, entails relatively little effort and is thus a common practice. On the other hand, experience shows that a proprietor of IP rights does not easily resolve to initiate proceedings against a buyer, much less against several customers of his competitor.'[27]

Due to the fact that in Germany the costs of pre-litigation warning letters are recoverable once the addressee has agreed to cease the alleged infringement, some German lawyers have made a business of simply sending threatening letters, alleging IP infringement. These communications are often directed to secondary infringers and consumers who have neither the will or the capabilities have the matter decided in court.[28] In the following section, a number of jurisdictions will be compared, starting with those where the issue of a warning letter is most common, and ending with those where the action for unjustified threats is most regulated.

D. COMPARISON

I. The United States

In the US, warning letters form the necessary starting point for litigation and damages. The alleged infringer should be put on notice. The contents of the notice is, however, prescribed in the sense that the communication must be of a nature that 'the recipient

---

26. UK High Court *Carflow Products (UK) Ltd v. Linwood Securities (Birmingham) Ltd and Others*, 7 March 1996, [1996] FSR 424. In this case the plaintiff had shown a prototype of a car steering lock to a company buyer without an express obligation of confidentiality. Threats based on breach of confidence were therefore unfounded, but they were not (automatically) considered in the subsequent infringement case, where the court merely established that the display caused the product to be in the public domain.
27. German Supreme Court, *Warning Letter*,15 July 2005, 37 IIC 94, 97.
28. C. Heath, 'Wrongful Patent Enforcement – Threats and Post- Infringement Invalidity in Comparative Perspective', International Review of Intellectual Property and Competition Law 2008, pp. 307–322.

is informed of the identity of the patent and the activity that is believed to be an infringement, accompanied by a proposal to abate the infringement, whether by license or otherwise.'[29] In case of trade mark infringement, a cease and desist letter can be much more aggressive in view of the interest of avoiding confusion in trade. A recipient may bring claims based on false allegations if the recipient can show, by clear and convincing evidence, that the allegations in the letter were objectively false and that the patent owner made those false allegations in bad faith, knowing them to be false. This is a rather high threshold.

US law is somewhat stricter on the acceptability of warning letters sent to third parties other than the alleged infringer. Such communications may result in an action in unfair competition or tortious interference with business relations. In order to be successful with such a claim, one has to show that false information has intentionally been communicated.[30] In fact, the United States Court of Appeals for the Federal Circuit explained that these state tort claims against a patentee wishing to enforce its rights are pre-empted by federal patent law, unless the patent holder acted in bad faith.[31] This means that state tort law can only be used in the most egregious cases of falsehood. In all other situations, federal patent law prevails in the understanding that the patentee has every right to assert his claims by means of pre-trial notification. In the above-mentioned case, the alleged infringer claimed that the patentee Targus knew that its patents were invalid in view of prior art and had sold the invention more than one year before filing the patent application. The Court of Appeals found, however, that Targus had waited for the USPTO to re-examine the application prior to enforcing the patent and rightfully believed that its sale constituted a form of experimental use that did not destroy novelty. Infringement notices sent to Adept customers were therefore held not to be sent in bad faith and an earlier tortious interference damage award was reversed.

II. Germany

In Germany, warning letters and patent threats are not covered by statutory provisions.[32] Courts have developed liability for unjustified threats to include those in respect of alleged primary infringement.[33] This is because interference with an established and active commercial or industrial enterprise amounting to an obstruction or a demand to restrict the enterprise or bring about its closure is actionable under Section 823(1) of the German Civil Code. Stricter criteria are applied when

---

29. United States Court of Appeals for the Federal Circuit, *SRI Int'l, Inc. v. Advanced Tech. Labs., Inc.*, 23 October 1997, 127 F.3d 1462, 44 USPQ2d 1422.
30. Section 772 of the Restatement (Second) of Torts, '[o]ne who intentionally causes a third person not to perform a contract or not to enter into a prospective contractual relation with another does not interfere improperly with the other's contractual relation, by giving the third person [...] truthful information.'
31. United States Court of Appeals for the Federal Circuit, *800 Adept, Inc. v. Murex Securities, Inc.*, 29 August 2008, 505 F. Supp. 2d 1327 (M.D. Fla. 2007).
32. H-P. *Brack*, 'Patent Infringement Warnings in a Common Law versus a Civil Law Jurisdiction – An Actionable Threat?', International Review of Intellectual Property and Competition Law 2006, pp. 1–31, at pp. 15–28.
33. *Heath* (*supra* n. 28), at pp. 311–312.

threats are communicated to alleged secondary infringers,[34] especially in relation to unexamined rights like utility models.[35]

A warning letter must contain a minimum number of elements for it to be considered a warning, namely: 1) a clear demand for a specific person to stop a specific activity, and 2) a statement to the alleged infringer that proceedings will be initiated if the warning is ignored.[36] This results in the requirement of the presence of an explicit threat. For a threat to be actionable for damages, the warning party must have acted negligently or with intent, resulting in either a lack of justification (the information is misleading, incomplete etc.), or a deficiency (invalidity, revocation, lawful activities, etc.) in the substantive right that is the basis for the warning. The former is interesting, because this also covers situations where there is a failure to mention that appeals or invalidity proceedings are still open or pending. Furthermore, misleading statements, such as a communication directed to consumers warning them against purchasing goods because their delivery would be infringing are actionable under Sections 3 and 4 of the Act Against Unfair Competition.

It is also considered misleading if the person who issues a warning bundles a number of patents and/or other rights if only a few are actually infringed. The recipient should also be enabled to clarify whether a right is infringed and what needs to be done to avoid being sued.

III.   France

In France, recipients of warning letters accused of acts of primary IP infringement, do not have a cause of action against these threats.[37] Actions for denigration based on the general tort clause of Sec. 1382 Civil Code are the basis for action by secondary infringers against unjustified threats. In order to make secondary infringers liable for alleged acts of IP infringement, it is necessary to send them a letter to put them on notice.[38] If neutrally worded, these letters are not actionable.[39]

However, cease and desist letters are actionable if they have been sent to customers or distributors of the primary infringer where: 1) the letter has been sent

---

34. See for example German Federal Supreme Court 17 July 2005, Gewerblicher Rechtsschutz und Urheberrecht (2005), 882 (Unberechtigte Schutzrechtsverwarnung) in which the court held that a manufacturer was unfairly obstructed by an unjustified threat made to one of its retailers. See also R. Sack, 'Der Beschluss des Großen Zivilsenats des BGH vom 15.7.2005 zur Haftung für unbegründete Schutzrechtsverwarnungen – Ende der Diskussion?', Der Betriebsberater (2005), pp. 2368–2373; and V. Deutsch, 'Der BGH-Beschluss zur unberechtigten Schutzrechtsverwarnung und seine Folgen für die Praxis', GRUR 2006, pp. 374–379.
35. German Federal Supreme Court, 17 April 1997, Gewerblicher Rechtsschutz und Urheberrecht (1997), 741 (Chinaherde).
36. Under German law, it is customary and recommendable to send a warning letter prior to initiating court proceedings, as otherwise an immediate acceptance of the claim by the defendant in court will result in an adverse decision on costs against the plaintiff.
37. French Supreme Court, 13 May 1964, Annales 1964, 266.
38. Sec. L615-1 3 French IP Code.
39. Tribunal de Grande Instance Paris, 17 September 2010, 3rd Ch, 3rd Sect., *Ateliers de la Haute Garonne et al v. Brotje Automation*.

widely to the customers of the primary infringer, demonstrating an intent to undermine the latter's reputation;[40] or 2) the letter does not provide an objective report of the legal and procedural position – for example, suggesting that the product is held to be infringing by a court when no such decision on infringement has in fact been issued,[41] or 3) where the judgment is subject to an appeal but this is not disclosed.[42]

IV.   The Netherlands

In the Netherlands, the general tort clause of Book 6, section 162 Civil Code forms the basis for liability, and ill-founded threats may be actionable. Unnecessarily offensive or public threats are considered unlawful, even if justified *per se*.[43] Pending opposition or validity suits are, however, not considered actionable grounds if a patentee continues to threaten potential customers of the alleged infringer.[44]

Making threats without being the IP owner of the rights asserted is also unlawful.[45] In the case of *Vita v. Invoclar*,[46] the issue of unjustified threats is dealt with in the context of section 1019h Dutch Code of Civil Procedure, which implements Art. 6 Enforcement Directive. In the case, Vita sought the nullification of the Dutch part of Ivoclar's European patent for lithium silicate materials, which Ivoclar decided not to defend, a fact that had been noted on the Dutch registry after the commencement of the case. An infringement case based on the German part before the Landgericht Düsseldorf in Germany was still pending when the Dutch case was decided. The case then focussed on the summation that was sent to the German lawyer of Vita, reading: 'Due to Vita's unwillingness to accept the licence terms we proposed, and its ongoing infringements of Ivoclar's patents, we have decided to immediately begin asserting our legal rights against Vita in any country that we deem appropriate'. Ivoclar asserted that it had never threatened Vita with infringement action for the Dutch part of its European patent, but the court considered that this wording 'any country' also amounted to a threat of enforcement in the Netherlands. It also accepted Vita's assertion that its decision to initiate nullity proceedings in the Netherlands was directly related to Ivoclar's decision to start proceedings in Germany, where Vita's product that was at the heart of the dispute in Germany was also available in the Netherlands. In actions claiming nullity of a patent, it is customary to award a modest statutory fee, rather than the full legal costs available when counterclaiming in response to an infringement action. However, in view of the cross-border effect the unjustified threat had in the Netherlands, Ivoclar was ordered to pay the full costs of the procedure.

---

40. Appeal Court Paris, 19 December 2014, *Newmat v. Clipso Productions*, RG no. 12/13999.
41. French Supreme Court, 12 May 2004, case 02-16623, Bulletin 2004 IV, N° 87.
42. French Supreme Court, 7 April 1998, Dossiers Brevets 1998, IV, N° 6.
43. Dutch Supreme Court, 27 January 1989, *Meijn v. Stork*, ECLI:NL:PHR:1989:AD0607; Dutch Supreme Court 29 March 2002, *Van Bentum v. Kool*, ECLI:NL:PHR:2002:AD8184.
44. Dutch Supreme Court, 29 September 2006, *CFS Bakel v. Stork Titan*, ECLI:NL:HR:2006:AU6098.
45. District Court Amsterdam, 13 April 2011, *Handelsmaatschappij Steffex v. W.*, nr. 369026 HA ZA 07-1262, which dealt with a copyright claim.
46. District Court The Hague, 4 April 2018, *Vita Zahnfabrik H. Rauter GMBH & Co.KG v. Invoclar Vivadent AG*, ECLI:NL:RBDHA:2018:3857.

The case *Acteon v. Dürr Dental*, [47] dealt with a similar set of facts as in *Vita v. Ivoclar*. Dürr Dental had initiated infringement proceedings before the Landgericht Mannheim in Germany when Acteon did not sign a declaration attached to the letter threatening litigation undertaking to cease offering the allegedly infringing device (a PSPIX-scanner that was stated to be within the scope of protection of the European Patent '*im Geltungsbereich des Europäischen Patents EP371*'. Although the declaration requested the destruction of the devices located in Germany only, it requested Acteon to submit sales records related to all countries where the patent was in force. In the Netherlands, Acteon initiated nullity proceedings before the District Court of The Hague, only to find that Dürr Dental was not willing to defend the Dutch part of its European patent. The court held that Dürr Dental's communication and actions in Germany constituted a threat of enforcement in the Netherlands and allowed for a bifurcation of the award for costs, meaning the full costs related to the proceedings on the threats were awarded.

V.   Canada

In Canada, the Unfair Competition Act of 1932 introduced the concept of liability for false or misleading statements that discredit the business, goods or services of a competitor, or more generally act or adopt business practices contrary to honest industrial or commercial usage in Canada. Although the Unfair Competition Act has since been superseded by section 7 Trade Marks Act 1985, it applies to all intellectual property rights.[48] The leading case is *S&S Industries v. Rowell.* which was decided by the Supreme Court of Canada.[49] S&S alleged infringement of a patent related to the construction of frames of flat wire to be used in the manufacture of brassières but did not sue the alleged primary infringer Rowell. Instead, S&S sued two of Rowell's customers[50] and advertised the fact in trade papers. The settlements arrived at with the customers were that they agreed not to sell Rowell's product or challenge the validity of S&S's patent. They were also allowed to dispose of their inventories that contained Rowell's wires. Neither of the customers were asked to pay damages or royalties to S&S. The result was highly effective for S&S, as Rowell lost its business

---

47. See similarly District Court The Hague, 11 April 2018, *Acteon Germany GMBH v. Dürr Dental AG,* ECLI:NL:RBDHA:2018:4591.
48. See *MacDonald v. Vapor Canada Ltd* (1977) DLR (3d) 1, but the provision has never been tested for application in copyright; *Canadian Copyright Licensing Agency v. Business Depot Ltd* [2008] FC 737, 330 FTR 133
49. Supreme Court of Canada, 7 March 1966, *S&S Industries v. Rowell* [1966] 48 SCR 193.
50. Supreme Court of Canada, *S&S Industries v. Rowell*, at p. 431, citing a letter sent by S&S to one of Rowell's clients, Exquisite Form Brassière Canada Ltd., of Toronto:
   'We have been informed by our Attorneys that retailers who sell garments containing Flat Wire that do not emanate from us, or any of our licensees, may be subjected to suit. Our point to Mr. Reiner was that in order that we may best protect our interests, we would be forced to go to the stores and involve them in law suits. This brings with it the extreme loss of time on the part of all executives in the store who become involved in lengthy pre-trial examinations as well as expense involved. It is evident that such stores would be reluctant to handle a line which can implicate them in these circumstances.'

in Canada and the American market without S&S exposing its patent to any test of validity.

Upon Rowell's claim for unjustified threats and nullity, the patent was declared invalid by the trial judge. Citing *Halsey v. Brotherhood*,[51] the Supreme Court of Canada defined the elements of the action contained in sections 7(a) and 52 of the Trade Marks Act as: 1) A false or misleading statement; 2) Tending to discredit the business, wares or services of a competitor; and 3) Resulting damage. It also considered:

> 'There is no express requirement that the false or misleading statements be made with knowledge of their falsity, or that they be made maliciously. To interpret these provisions as though such elements were implied would be to construe them as merely restating rules of law which already existed. I do not think this approach is a proper one. The Unfair Competition Act was a statutory code to provide for fair dealing in trade. Section 11 was based upon Article 10 bis of the International Convention for the Protection of Industrial Property, made at the Hague, November 6, 1925, to which Canada was a party.'[52]

According to the majority of judges, the presence or absence of malice would only have been relevant in relation to the assessment of damages.

In spite of this decision, case law is not yet settled. In several cases where a patentee threatened customers of the alleged primary infringer and where the patent was later found to be invalid, claims in damages for unjustified threats have been rejected on the basis that the patent would have been infringed if it had been valid, and the principle that a patent is *prima facie* valid once granted and the patent holder has the right to act on that basis.[53] This was also the position of S&S Industries, but it was rejected.[54] Contrary to the *S&S Industries v. Rowell* case, in subsequent cases the threats to customers were followed by an infringement action against the alleged primary infringer. It is therefore difficult to distinguish any damage caused by the threat from the damage caused by the infringement action. The fact that the patentee has engaged direct action against the alleged primary infringer also implies that the patentee has been willing to test whether the patent was valid and infringed. This is, however, not reflected in the case *M&I Door Systems v. Indoro Industrial Door Co Ltd*,[55] where the judge held that patent is *prima facie* valid and 'the patentee has the right to act on that basis' and that the communication, while false, was 'more informative than threatening', and therefore not actionable.[56]

---

51. *Supra* n. 18.
52. Supreme Court of Canada, *S&S Industries v. Rowell*, at pp. 424-425, *per* Martland J. delivering the majority opinion.
53. Federal Court of Canada (Trial Division), *Sulco Industries Ltd v. Jim Scharf Holdings Ltd* (1996), 69 CPR (3d) 316 (FCTD, prothonotary).
54. Supreme Court of Canada, *S&S Industries v. Rowell*, at p. 428.
55. *M&I Door Systems v. Indoro Industrial Door Co Ltd* (1989) 25 CPR (3d) 477 (FCTD), at p. 523.
56. See A. Kelly Gill, 'Balancing Necessary Monopolies and Free Competition: Threats of Patent Infringement and Trade Libel', 14(2) Revue Canadienne de Propriété Intellectuelle, 1998, p. 125, at 132 arguing that Cullen J's holding in *M&I Door Systems v. Indoro Industrial Door Co Ltd.* is '[s]eemingly in direct contradiction to the Supreme Court's pronouncement in S. & S. Industries'.

In *Excalibre Oil Tools Ltd v. Advantage Products Inc.*,[57] a distinction is also made between cease and desist letters that are threatening and those that are merely informative. The case involved three patents related to downhole pumps. The court found one patent valid, but not infringed, one invalid for reasons of obviousness, and the third invalid in part and not infringed in relation to the remaining claims. The patentee was therefore held to have made misleading statements. These statements were communicated in a letter sent by the patentee's lawyer to a number of customers and former customers of companies distributing so-called torque anchors (a.k.a anti-rotation devices or 'no-turn' tools) produced by Excalibre, the so-called CTA Torque Anchor that is used in oil pumps. The letters stated:

> 'API holds three Canadian patents for anti-rotation tools implementing one jaw';
> 'API holds the first patent position in the world for single jaw anti-rotation tools which utilize a pivoting jaw for engaging the casing, jamming the tool against the casing and preventing rotation of the tool and equipment secured thereto';
> and that API is the 'sole authorized source [in Canada] of single jaw torque anchors utilizing a single jaw projecting from the tool's circumference'.

Further, the lawyer alleged that should such customers purchase CTA Torque Anchors produced by Excalibre, they would be infringing API's patent rights.[58] Other letters sent to these customers read as follows:

> 'API demands Husky immediately cease sourcing the CTA torque anchor. Husky is encouraged to review the attached SOC and assess their own liability in this infringement of API's exclusive rights. [...] Should Husky choose to continue along their current path, API will be compelled to amend their litigation to include Husky.'; or 'The Canadian Patent Act also provides API with similar right [sic] of enforcement against purchasers and as against users of patented torque anchors which are not obtained from authorized sources, including Bronco Energy. [...] Unless Bronco Energy advises this office, by May 23rd, of their immediate cessation of the above infringing activities, API will amend their litigation to include Bronco Energy.'[59]

The result was that many customers stopped using or purchasing CTA Torque Anchors. Not because they believed that they were in fact infringing, but because they simply were risk-averse, or 'loathe to spend the company's money on a legal opinion'. The statements that Excalibre's CTA Torque Anchors infringe the API patents was never tested in court and was therefore held to be misleading, threatening (rather than informative) and discrediting Excalibre's CTA Torque Anchors. The fact that the customers by their purchasing decisions demonstrated their changed behaviour was deemed sufficient to prove causation and damage. This allowed the court to bifurcate damages arising from the threats from those arising from the infringement action.

---

57. Federal Court of Canada, 17 November 2016, *Excalibre Oil Tools Ltd v. Advantage Products inc.*, (2016) fc 1279; available at: https://decisions.fct-cf.gc.ca/fc-cf/decisions/en/item/212585/index.do#_Toc466964589 (accessed 16 June 2018).
58. *Ibid.*, at para. 29.
59. *Ibid.*, at para. 284.

VI. Australia

In Australia, the law on unjustified threats also has its origins in the English case of *Halsey v. Brotherhood*.[60] Currently sections 128 to 132 of the Australian Patents Act 1990 provide that a person or company that has been unjustifiably threatened with patent infringement proceedings may seek an injunction to prevent the threats from continuing, and the recovery of any damages sustained as a result of the threats. An application for relief from unjustified threats will be successful in any case in which it ultimately turns out that a patent is invalid or not infringed, regardless of how objectively reasonable the patentee's original belief may have been. In essence, there is no bar on alleged primary infringers to initiate an unjustified threats action.

The problem of allowing unjustified threats actions to be brought by alleged primary infringers lies in the fact that the patentee will most likely threaten on the basis of the belief that the patent is valid and infringed. An action for unjustified threats by the addressee will immediately force the patentee to cross-claim for infringement, leading to a counterclaim for invalidity. Similarly, if infringement proceedings are initiated, the defendant can still claim that the original threats were unjustified, and in addition counterclaim that the patent is declared invalid.

The groundless threat action thus not only becomes part of the overall litigation strategy, irrespective of the question whether the threats or intimidation were groundless, but it also triggers an almost inevitable path to full trial that can take years to resolve. This is visible in the case of *Australian Mud Company v. Coretell*.[61] The innovation (short-term, 'petty') patent in question related to core sampling, and Australian Mud Company's (AMC) lawyers sent out letters alleging infringement to parties alleged of manufacture and sale of core sampling orientation tools. The unjustified threats action was initiated in 2010 in parallel with a claim for invalidity of the patent. The primary judge held in successive cases that AMC's patent was not infringed, and damages in the order of AUD 1.5 million were ultimately awarded in 2016 against the Australian Mud Company (AMC) for making unjustified threats of patent infringement against Coretell. Then this award was overturned upon appeal in 2017.[62] The appellate court pointed out that causation between the threats and the damage sustained as a result thereof is required, and that this is separate from the damage resulting from the infringement proceedings to which the threats relate.

Similarly, *Mizzi Family Holdings v. Morellini*[63] is an interesting case in which the threat of litigation over alleged infringement of an innovation patent concerning a cane billet planter was communicated by a notice of the patent application alongside an article in a publication called *'Canegrowers Magazine'* in 2010. The article stated: 'We know of farmers who are manufacturing their own version of the new invention whilst the patenting process is operating' and went on to suggest that the

---

60. *Supra* n. 17.
61. Federal Court of Australia, 19 August 2016, *Australian Mud Company Pty Ltd v. Coretell Pty Ltd (No 7)* [2016] FCA 991.
62. Federal Court of Australia (Full Court), 17 March 2017, *Australian Mud Company Pty Ltd v. Coretell Pty Ltd* [2017] FCAFC 44.
63. Federal Court of Australia, 24 December 2013, *Mizzi Family Holdings Pty Ltd v. Morellini* [2013] FCA 1435.

patentee may exercise his rights once the patent is granted leading to fines 'or even loss of the infringing machine plus claims for loss of income'. The article has been authored by a representative of an IP consultancy, a firm that had assisted the patent attorney to draft the Mizzi patent. Although a threat of litigation was not explicitly addressed to Mr. Morellini, the Australian Federal Court held that the juxtaposition of the advertisement and the article did constitute the communication of a threat. Mr. Morellini claimed that the patent was invalid and for 'unjustified threats'. Although invalidity was not established, Mizzi failed to prove infringement, which meant the threat of infringement proceedings would have been unjustified. Subsequently, when another cane grower Mr Girgenti used Morellini's planter, and Mizzi made a verbal allegation of infringement and demanded the payment of a royalty, a second unjustified threat was made. One would therefore think that the consequences for Mizzi would be negative.

However, questions on costs and declaratory relief in relation to the unjustified threats,[64] as well as on damages related to the threats turned out to be more problematic to resolve.[65] In 2017 the court found that:

> 'There is no direct evidence that anybody declined to deal with Mr Morellini as a result of the threats. It seems that even before the newspaper article on 5 April 2010, there was a degree of reluctance concerning any such dealings. That reluctance cannot have been attributable to the threats. Mr Morellini has not demonstrated that any adverse effect resulted from either of the threats. The newspaper article may well have been widely read within the sugar industry, but there is no reason to believe that the incident involving Mr Girgenti was a matter of common knowledge. Some people in the industry may have heard of it. In either case such knowledge may have reinforced previous perceptions, but that is largely speculative.'[66]

The two cases present an important limitation to the unjustified threats action in Australia, but also highlight the difficulty of separating the type of nefarious threat the action is supposed to stop from the general strategy of alleged infringers to use the action as means to introduce (counter)claims for invalidity. It is for this reason that the United Kingdom introduced a primary act exception to the action for unjustified threats in 2004, but at the time only for threats related to patent rights.

VII. The United Kingdom

In the United Kingdom, the 1881 case of *Halsey v. Brotherhood*[67] exposed the shortcoming in the law of torts at the time, meaning that unjustified threats required

---

64. Federal Court of Australia, 1 August 2014, *Mizzi Family Holdings Pty Ltd v. Morellini (No 2)* [2014] FCA 807.
65. Federal Court of Australia (Full Court), 16 February 2016, *Morellini v. Mizzi Family Holdings Pty Ltd* [2016] FCAFC 13.
66. Federal Court of Australia, 1 August 2017, *Mizzi Family Holdings Pty Ltd v. Morellini (No 3)* [2017] FCA 870, at 20.
67. *Supra* n. 17.

the plaintiff to show that the defendant had acted with malice.[68] This resulted in unjustified threats legislation to be enacted in 1883. The original provisions addressed groundless threats in patent disputes, but these have over time been extended to trade marks, designs, Community rights and European patents designated to enter the UK national phase. It is therefore the jurisdiction with the longest tradition on providing redress for groundless threats. The latest version of the legislation, the Intellectual Property (Unjustified Threats) Act 2017, is the result of a reform process that was initiated in 2012. The aim of the reform was to address a number of 'defects' in the law and to harmonise the principles over the various branches of intellectual property. The defects addressed were the lack of clear guidance on permissible communications, the so-called 'Cavity Trays problem' and professional adviser liability for threats. These are addressed below.

Since its inception, the unjustified threats legislation has resulted in decisions that clarified that a threat of legal proceedings must be for the infringement of a patent, trade mark or design right, but that such a right need not be expressly mentioned and can be implicit.[69] The test is whether an 'ordinary recipient in the position of the claimant' would understand the communication to contain a threat. In the case *L'Oreal (UK) v. Johnson & Johnson*,[70] Johnson & Johnson held a trade mark in the UK and Ireland. It initiated proceedings for trade mark infringement against L'Oréal in Ireland and then wrote to L'Oréal in England, which had requested a statement that Johnson & Johnson would not start litigation in respect of the equivalent UK registrations. In its reply, Johnson & Johnson confirmed that proceedings had been commenced in Ireland, stated that the UK management of Johnson & Johnson considered that L'Oréal was also infringing the equivalent UK trade mark, and indicated that third parties that used the mark had heeded to Johnson & Johnson's requests to cease and desist. The letter furthermore indicated that Johnson & Johnson continued their investigations into all relevant facts and law, and would rely on the full six-year limitation period in which to decide as to whether or not to issue proceedings. The letter concluded that Johnson & Johnson would therefore not give the confirmation requested by L'Oréal. According to justice Lightman, the letter that was said to contain the unjustified threat

> 'is the work of a master of Delphic utterances who uses all his skills to say everything and nothing and to convey an enigmatic message which has the same effect on the recipient as a threat or adverse claim while disclaiming to be either.'[71]

Any person aggrieved can seek relief, meaning that one does not have to be the recipient of the threat to initiate legal action, but one has to demonstrate damage

---

68. As continued to be the case for trade libel, which is defined as a malicious attempt to cause damage. See High Court of England and Wales, 20 February 1890, *Colley v. Hart* (1890) 7 RPC 101; and UK House of Lords, 17 December 1900, *The Royal Baking Powder Co. v. Wright, Crossley & Co.* [1901] 18 RPC 95.
69. Scottish Court of Session Outer House, 23 March 1972, *Speedcranes Ltd v. Thomson* 1972 SC 324, [1978] RPC 221.
70. High Court of England and Wales, 7 March 2000, *L'Oreal (UK) Ltd v. Johnson & Johnson* [2000] FSR 686.
71. *Ibid.,* [2000] FSR 686 at para. 12.

which is not minimal, in that his commercial interests 'are or are likely to be adversely affected in a real as opposed to a fanciful or minimal way', although the court should equally not be 'astute to find that a complainant has not been affected in his commercial activities where it is clear that the purpose of the threat was to do so'.[72]

English law also covers two aspects not addressed in the jurisdictions covered above. One of such issues relates to infringement proceedings that could have been brought in different jurisdictions as well as UK courts, such as in EU trade mark cases.[73] Under the Intellectual Property (Unjustified Threats) Act 2017, Community, as well as Unitary, patents are expressly covered under the unjustified threats framework.

Another aspect covers the common practice that parties may be both primary and secondary actors, from manufacturer or importer, down the distribution chain to distributor or seller. A communication can thus cover both primary and secondary acts of infringement, and when combined, the threat related to a secondary act would be actionable for unjustified threats according to the case of *Cavity Trays v. RMC Panel Products*.[74] For patents, the 2004 reform provided that communication to a primary infringer is always permitted, irrespective of whether acts of secondary infringement are also included in the communication. In short, the threats for secondary infringement are not actionable for unjustified threats that are combined with a threat for primary infringement. For trade marks and designs, however, only communications that are limited to primary acts were exempted from liability. The Intellectual Property (Unjustified Threats) Act 2017 provides a full alignment over all the subject matter covered, so that communications to a primary actor may contain threats in respect of both primary and secondary acts of infringement, irrespective of whether they relate to patent, trade mark or design rights.

For communications with secondary infringers, the Intellectual Property (Unjustified Threats) Act 2017 furthermore creates a 'safe harbour' that further limits an aggrieved person to bring a threats action.[75] In such a case the threat must be contained within a 'permitted communication': 1) which does not contain an express threat; and where 2) the part of the communication which contains information that relates to the threat was made for a permitted purpose; and where 3) all of the

---

72. High Court of England and Wales, 9 May 1997, *Brain v. Ingledew Brown Benson and Garret (No 3)* [1997] FSR 51, per Laddie J., who furthermore held that: 'the meaning and impact of the letters in issue has to be decided in accordance with how they would be understood by an ordinary reader. [...] What is particularly important is the initial impression which the letters would have on a reasonable addressee. During court proceedings, it is inevitable that the lawyers, parties and judge will read and re-read the offending passages with ever closer attention. Such meticulous analysis is not what would happen in the real world and the court must guard against being led down a path of forensic analysis to a meaning which is narrower or broader than would occur to the ordinary recipient reading the letter [...] in the normal course of business'.
73. Court of Appeal of England and Wales, 24 May 2011, *Best Buy Co Inc v. Worldwide Sales Corp España SL* [2011] EWCA Civ 618, [2011] FSR 30.
74. Court of Appeal of England and Wales, 6 February 1996, *Cavity Trays Ltd v. RMC Panel Products Ltd* [1996] RPC 361.
75. Intellectual Property (Unjustified Threats) Act 2017, amending the Patents Act 1977, Section 70A(5); amending the Trade Marks Act 1994, section 21A(6); amending the Registered Designs Act 1949, section 26A(5).

information that relates to the threat is information that: is necessary for that purpose, and which the person making the communication reasonably believes to be true. The respective patent, trade mark and design provisions provide for a non-exclusive list of examples of permitted purposes, which amount to: 1) giving notice that a patent, trade mark or design right exists; 2) discovering the identity of a primary actor or whether primary acts of infringement have taken place; or 3) making a person aware of an IP right, where it is relevant to any proceedings that the person is aware of the right.[76] Communications do not have a permitted purpose if they request the person to cease and desist, deliver up or destroy goods, or give an undertaking in relation to the right in question. Finally, a secondary infringer can be justifiably threatened if reasonable steps have been taken to identify a primary actor, but this actor cannot be found. If, for example an overseas manufacturer cannot be located, and no importer can be identified, a supplier may be threatened.[77]

Professional conduct has also been addressed in a number of cases. In *Antec International v. South Western Chicks*,[78] the trade mark agents of Antec alleged that their client's registered trade mark ANTEC FARM FLUID was infringed by the defendant's use of the mark SUPER FARM FLUID. The letter that asserted infringement did not contain the number of the registration, and the agents later found that the words FARM FLUID were the subject of a disclaimer. The agents did, however, not retract the allegation of infringement, nor did they inform the defendants of the registration number. Although the defendant in the case never claimed for unjustified threats, Laddie J. stated in an obiter that:

> 'it is not acceptable for those who have the status of expert professional men in the trade-mark field to use the weight of their professional qualifications to make clearly unsupportable allegations of trade-mark infringement against a trader.'

As was made clear in *Brain v. Ingledew Brown Benson and Garret No. 3*,[79] legal advisors can also be sued either as an individual or as a firm for making groundless threats. In *Reckitt Benckiser v. Home Pairfum*,[80] both Reckitt Benckiser and their legal advisor were sued for unjustified threats of design infringement. Reckitt had sued Home Pairfum over the design of the containers for air fresheners and subsequently faced a counterclaim for unjustified threats that also joined Reckitt's solicitors as defendants to the counterclaim. Laddie J. rejected Home Pairfum's request on the grounds that 'the only real purpose of the application was to retaliate and to make the relationship between the solicitors and their clients uncomfortable.' The Intellectual Property

---

76. Intellectual Property (Unjustified Threats) Act 2017, amending the Patents Act 1977, Section 70B; amending the Trade Marks Act 1994, section 21B; amending the Registered Designs Act 1949, section 26B.
77. Intellectual Property (Unjustified Threats) Act 2017, amending the Patents Act 1977, Section 70C(4); amending the Trade Marks Act 1994, section 21C(3); amending the Registered Designs Act 1949, section 26C(3).
78. High Court of England and Wales, 6 November 1996, *Antec International Ltd v. South Western Chicks (Warren) Ltd* [1997] FSR 278.
79. See *Brain v. Ingledew Brown Benson and Garret (No 3)*, supra n. 73, where Laddie J. held a firm of solicitors liable for unjustified threats.
80. High Court of England and Wales, 13 February 2004, *Reckitt Benckiser UK v. Home Pairfum Ltd* [2004] EWHC 302.

(Unjustified Threats) Act 2017 completely removes professional adviser liability for threats,[81] meaning that lawyers, or registered patent or trade mark attorneys, whether based in the UK or elsewhere, no longer face liability for making threats where they act in their professional capacity or on client's instructions. The reason given is that the risk of liability can be used to 'gain access to a 'deep pocket' in cases involving an impecunious threatener'.[82] This means that the reasoning given in *Reckitt Benckiser v. Home Pairfum* has been generalised to the benefit of professional advisors. This is most curious, as the judge both in *Reckitt Benckiser v. Home Pairfum* and *Brain v. Ingledew Brown Benson and Garret No. 3* was one and the same, and clearly able to distinguish between actionable and unjustified applications for groundless threat actions. It is also noteworthy that one of the members of the working group for legal reform, Professor Sir Robin Jacob,[83] did not support the recommendation to lift professional liability as it is 'a healthy restraint on cowboy (and other) legal advisers – of whom there are lots out there'.[84] His comment on the Bill has also been included in the Law Commission report:

> 'I consider [the Bill] extraordinarily elaborate and complicated. It is not the right solution and in its present form should be dropped. I remain of the opinion that something much simpler – along the nature of "abusive communication" would be enough. Tinkering with this will serve no useful purpose. There is no hurry – threats of IP infringement proceedings are far from top of the problems in the IP world. I am saying this now so no one ever thinks I thought it was a good idea.'[85]

The Intellectual Property (Unjustified Threats) Act 2017, however, passed despite these comments resulting in any change in position. As a result, the UK now has the most elaborate legislation on unjustified threats. Whether it is still capable of doing justice to the general idea contained in the Paris Convention of preventing abusive and misleading communications remains to be seen, as the Intellectual Property (Unjustified Threats) Act 2017 neuters the action in many ways by focusing on the addressee, rather than on the accuracy or unnecessarily damaging effects of the message contained in the communication.

E.   ANALYSIS

What becomes apparent from the comparison above is that the epithet 'unjustified threats' is used to cover divergent standards of liability. These differences may be attributed to the basis for liability, namely whether the liability and remedies for an

---

81. Intellectual Property (Unjustified Threats) Act 2017, amending the Patents Act 1977, section 70D; amending the Trade Marks Act 1994, section 21D; amending the Registered Designs Act 1949, section 26D.
82. *UK Law Commission*, Patents, Trade Marks and Designs: Unjustified Threats, Law Com No 360 (2015, HMSO), para. 1.58, p. 14.
83. The full consultation response can be found at: https://www.lawcom.gov.uk/project/patents-trade-marks-and-designs-unjustified-threats/ (accessed 16 June 2018).
84. *UK Law Commission* (*supra* n. 83), para. 1.45, p. 11.
85. *UK Law Commission* (*supra* n. 83), para. 1.46, p. 12.

action for unjustified threats is to be found in the general balance of interests inherent in the IP system itself,[86] or in the law against unfair competition. Both perspectives are contained in TRIPS and are therefore supposed to be mutually supportive, rather than exclusive. Art. 7 TRIPS expresses the need for the protection and enforcement of intellectual property rights to be 'to the mutual advantage of producers and users of technological knowledge and in a manner conducive to social and economic welfare, and to a balance of rights and obligations'. Most jurisdictions would, on a balance of convenience, start from a position that the IP right holder is entitled to enforce his rights, including provisional remedies, injunctive relief and damages,[87] based on the assumption that the IP right allegedly infringed is valid. It is the duty of every diligent economic operator to assess his freedom to operate, heeding in particular the rights of IP owners. Threats of litigation are thus meant to support this position and are justified as long as they are factually correct.

When they turn out not to be, the balance of rights and obligations shifts, and the IP right holder becomes liable for unjustified threats. This is an *ex post* analysis that is typical of a liability rule[88] rooted in tortious negligence. After all, without the action for unjustified threats, the issue of infringement and validity is not determined, whereas the competitor's reputation and market may have been destroyed on the basis of the threat alone.

Art. 10*bis* Paris Convention, as incorporated by reference in TRIPS, contains an alternative scenario in presenting an action of unjustified threats as one against unfair competition. It veers more towards a property rule,[89] by *ex ante* establishing which type of threats are unjustified, or -as is the case in the UK- establishing which parties can initiate an action for unjustified threats and which parties are shielded from such a claim. As was found in relation to France, even factually correct, but unnecessarily disparaging communications are actionable. Ultimately though, it is the avoidance of testing in court whether the IP right is valid and infringed while communicating threatening and incorrect information that presents the true problem. In all instances, it is clear that this problem is exacerbated if the communication is addressed to secondary infringers and customers of a primary infringer.

Communications to anyone other than a primary infringer are then *prima facie* to be approached with extreme caution by the right holder. Threatening to sue a primary infringer without following through while still 'informing' secondary infringers or customers of this intention (thereby indirectly threatening them, too) is harmful to competition as the validity and infringement is not established. Market transparency is after all deliberately suppressed. Moreover, intentionally not following through on a threat of litigation in this case is misleading in itself. The purpose of the threat to a secondary infringer can only be justified if the primary infringer cannot (yet) be

---

86. See *C. Heath* (*supra* n. 28), who makes a distinction between the 'IP Approach' and the 'Unfair Competition' approach.
87. See also Section 3 of TRIPS.
88. *G. Calabresi and D. Melamed*, 'Property Rules, Liability Rules, and Inalienability: One View of the Cathedral', 85(6) Harvard Law Review, 1972, 1089–1128. When applied to intellectual property, the optimum for regulating entitlements by means of a property versus a liability rule is, however, not easy to establish, resulting in mixed solutions.
89. *G. Calabresi and D. Melamed* (*supra* n. 88).

found or is out of reach. The IP right holder should then be able to demonstrate that the secondary infringer is liable as a material contributory infringer, which again would require a willingness of the right holder to test validity and infringement in court. As with threatening customers, the only other purpose of a threat is to harm the reputation or business of a competitor. This amounts to an unjustifiable attack on another's goodwill that *a priori* entitles the recipient to an action for unjustified threats. Viewed in a narrow sense, the action will force the IP owner before a court and this may result in an injunction to cease making threats or an award of damages. As a bonus, validity and infringement may then also be clarified.

From the perspective of the action for an unjustified threat, we can then observe the following: 1) An alleged primary infringer who is offered his day in court will be able to address issues of validity and non-infringement. He is able to recover the costs of proceedings and damages and should therefore not have recourse to an action for unjustified threats. This only becomes different if the threat of litigation has also been communicated to third parties (secondary infringers, customers, or the public at large) and remains merely a threat while still discrediting the business and goodwill of the alleged primary infringer. In this *Halsey v. Brotherhood* scenario, the alleged primary infringer should be able to have recourse to the action for unjustified threats to get his case heard. Should the threat turn out to be unjustified, an injunction and damages for injury to the reputation should be available in an ex-post analysis where damage to reputation has to be quantified; 2) Alleged secondary infringers should only be threatened for the purpose of disclosure of the location of the primary infringer. If the alleged primary infringer is known and within reach, this should be the first party to be addressed. Contributory infringers in the upstream distribution chain may be treated somewhat differently if it can be reasonably established that they deliver component parts that are material to the IP infringement. Still, the assessment of this fact is realistically dependent on the establishment of primary infringement. Threats for any other purpose should be *ex-ante* unjustifiable and actionable for injunctions and damages; 3) Threats to non-infringers serve no other purpose than to discredit and mislead, and they should be actionable based on an *ex-ante* rule for injunctions and damages. When addressed to private individuals, punitive damages are even justified should (constructive) knowledge of the incorrect nature of the threat be established.

Until now, coherent rules on pre-litigation behaviour for IP rightholders have not been harmonised at EU level. This leads to market distortions, especially where a Member State like Germany allows for the recovery of pre-litigation costs that acts as a perverse incentive for lawyers to send threatening letters to secondary infringers and customers. In this instance, the question as to whether the threat is factually correct is even irrelevant. The duty on the IP rightholder in these cases is to act expeditiously to settle the dispute with the primary infringer, rather than to allow the issue of infringement to remain unsettled. Threatening communication that is addressed to secondary infringers ought to be considered *a priori* unlawful in a future harmonisation effort. The onus should then be on the IP rightholder to justify his actions by proving contributory infringement, or by demonstrating that the nature of the communication was merely to uncover the location of the primary infringer. Punitive damages for knowingly making unjustified threats may very well be justified from a market regulatory perspective. These are also grounds for not shielding legal counsel from liability for unjustified threat actions.

F. CONCLUSION

In most jurisdictions, an action for unjustified threats is available on the basis that communications in commerce must be correct and not abusive. This is also the central tenet of Art. 10*bis* Paris Convention, which is implemented in Member States under *sui generis* legislation addressing unjustified threats, or acts of unfair competition in general, or common law tort for interference with business relations and reputation, or goodwill. In this sense, developments like the primary act and actor exceptions greatly reduce the efficacy of the groundless threats action as a means to address the apparent unwillingness for many rightholders to test the validity of their right in court. Ultimately, the question ought to be whether a party aggrieved by a threatening communication that relies on incorrect or untested assertions should have the means to obtain certainty in trade, in the knowledge that if threats are found to be unfounded, at a minimum the costs of litigation can be claimed, and that in addition any damages resulting from the threats can be recovered. In an open and competitive economy, information may never be 'perfect', but when it contains a threat of litigation, it better be justified.

IEEM SERIES ON INTERNATIONAL INTELLECTUAL PROPERTY LAW

1. Intellectual Property in the Digital Age – Challenges for Asia
   Christopher Heath and Anselm Kamperman Sanders (eds.)
   Published by Kluwer Law International 2001
   ISBN 90-411-9847-4

2. Intellectual Property in the Bio-Medical Age – Challenges for Asia
   Christopher Heath and Anselm Kamperman Sanders (eds.)
   Published by Kluwer Law International 2003
   ISBN 90-411-9926-8

3. New Frontiers of Intellectual Property Law
   Christopher Heath and Anselm Kamperman Sanders (eds.)
   Published by Hart Publishing 2005
   ISBN 1-84113-538-0

4. Intellectual Property and Free Trade Agreements
   Christopher Heath and Anselm Kamperman Sanders (eds.)
   Published by Hart Publishing 2007
   ISBN 978-1-84113-801-5

5. Spares, Repairs and Intellectual Property Rights
   Christopher Heath and Anselm Kamperman Sanders (eds.)
   Published by Kluwer Law International 2009
   ISBN 978-90-411-3136-2

6. Landmark Intellectual Property Cases and Their Legacy
   Christopher Heath and Anselm Kamperman Sanders (eds.)
   Published by Kluwer Law International 2011
   ISBN 978-90-411-3343-4

7. Intellectual Property Liability of Consumers, Facilitators and Intermediaries
   Christopher Heath and Anselm Kamperman Sanders (eds.)
   Published by Kluwer Law International 2012
   ISBN 978-90-411-4126-2

8. Employees, Trade Secrets and Restrictive Covenants
   Christopher Heath and Anselm Kamperman Sanders (eds.)
   Published by Kluwer Law International 2017
   ISBN 978-90-411-8379-8

9. Intellectual Property Rights as Obstacles to Legitimate Trade?
   Christopher Heath, Anselm Kamperman Sanders and Anke Moerland (eds.)
   Published by Kluwer Law International 2018
   ISBN 978-94-035-0330-1